EDUCATION UNDER GLOBALISATION

Burial of the Constitutional Dream

EDUCATION UNDER GLOBALISATION

Burial of the Constitutional Dream

Neeraj Jain

AAKAR

EDUCATION UNDER GLOBALISATION: Burial of the Constitutional Dream
Neeraj Jain

First Published, 2015

ISBN 978-93-5002-338-9 (Pb)

Published by
AAKAR BOOKS
28 E Pocket IV, Mayur Vihar Phase I, Delhi 110 091
Phone : 011 2279 5505 Telefax : 011 2279 5641
aakarbooks@gmail.com
www.aakarbooks.com

in association with
LOKAYAT
129 B/2, Erandwane,
Pune 411 004
lokayat.india@gmail.com
www.lokayat.org.in

with the support of
ALL INDIA FORUM FOR RIGHT TO EDUCATION

Printed at
Sapra Borthers, Delhi 110 092

Dedicated to the wonderful activists of AIFRTE who came together to organise such an inspiring and exhilarating month-long All India Shiksha Sangharsh Yatra 2014. It is their efforts which motivated the writing of this book.

Disclaimer:

The views and opinions expressed in this book are those of the author and Lokayat, Pune. They do not necessarily reflect the views of the various other member organisations and individuals associated with AIFRTE.

Contents

List of Tables, Charts and Boxes

Tables

Charts

Boxes

INTRODUCTION

In 1981, Justice Bhagwati of the Supreme Court of India ruled:

(T)he right to life includes the right to live with human dignity and all that goes along with it, namely, the bare necessaries of life such as adequate nutrition, clothing and shelter over the head and facilities for reading, writing and expressing oneself in diverse forms ...[1]

In July 1992, delivering judgement in the Mohini Jain case, the Supreme Court of India further elaborated upon the above judgement with regard to the right of citizens to education and ruled that:[2]

- Right to life guaranteed under Article 21 of the Constitution of India includes the right to live with human dignity; and dignity of an individual cannot be assured unless it is accompanied by right to education.
- The Preamble to the Constitution has promised to secure to all citizens of India justice, liberty and equality. These objectives cannot be achieved and shall remain on paper unless the people of the country were educated.
- The fundamental rights guaranteed under Part III of the Constitution, including the right to freedom of speech and expression and other rights under Article 19, cannot be appreciated and fully enjoyed unless a citizen is educated.
- The Directive Principles of State Policy, which are to be "fundamental in the governance of the country", enjoin upon the State to reduce inequalities and ensure adequate livelihood for all citizens. This vision expressed in the Constitution cannot be realised without education.

In making these judgements, the highest court of the land was actually only reiterating what has been the wisdom regarding the relationship between education (and other social and economic rights) and freedom/liberty/equality for centuries.

During the Age of Enlightenment, also called the Age of Reason by Thomas Paine (generally considered to have begun in the 17th century in Europe), when Martin Luther and other religious leaders challenged the dogma and authority of the Catholic Church and an increasing interest in science and scientific methods called into question traditional ways of thinking, the spread of education played a key role in the spread of these ideas and ideals. The most prominent Enlightenment philosophers, from Locke to Rousseau, wrote treatises on the importance of education. John Locke (1632–1704), one of the most influential of the Enlightenment thinkers, stressed the importance of education for development of people's capacities to recognise and prevent oppression at the hands of authorities—intellectual, political or religious—and thereby to improve the possibilities for a humane and tolerant politics.[3]

Étienne-Gabriel Morelly (b. 1717) was probably the first Enlightenment thinker who saw education as the vehicle through which individual liberation, social harmony and political unity could be achieved.[4]

Thomas Jefferson, one of the founding fathers of the USA and the principal author of the *Declaration of Independence*, passionately believed that the young nation's survival as an independent democracy absolutely depended upon its success in educating the people.[5]

By the mid-20th century, the inter-relationship between social and economic rights (including the right to free education) and human rights had become such an integral part of the global human rights discourse that in 1950, the United Nations General Assembly declared that "the enjoyment of civic and political freedoms and of economic, social and cultural rights are interconnected and interdependent." The General Assembly requested the Commission on Human Rights—that had been set up under the aegis of the United Nations to draft an International Bill on Human Rights—"to draft two Covenants on Human Rights ... one to contain civil and political rights and the other to contain economic, social and cultural rights." The Assembly specified that the two covenants should contain as many similar provisions as possible. These covenants, known as the the International Covenant on Civil and Political Rights and International Covenant on Economic, Social and Cultural Rights, were adopted by the General Assembly in 1966.[6] The latter covenant recognises the right of everyone to free education; it sees education both as a human right and as "an indispensable means of realising other human rights."[7]

✯ ✯ ✯

Even if we leave aside such high flown objectives as realisation of freedom and liberty, education is crucially important even for something as basic as human development.

Education unlocks the inherent potential of human beings, allowing people to enjoy an enhanced quality of life. Amartya Sen, internationally renowned for his work on human development theory, explains the transformative effects of education on the individual:

> First, of course, being able to read, write, do your sums really transforms a human being. That a lot of people know. It's a very ancient thought. Secondly, the ability to get a job depends very much on whether you can follow instructions, especially in the globalising world today—whether you can produce according to specification, quality control, and so on. Thirdly, your ability to participate socially, read the newspapers, be politically active is very important. Fourthly, and this applies particularly to women, your voice is much more articulate and people listen to you if you've been to school. In family decisions, not surprisingly, the biggest impact in reducing fertility is girls' education.

And so Amartya Sen emphasises,

> nothing really is as important in the world as getting children to school, especially female children.[8]

Education does not benefit only those taking education, it benefits society as a whole. It leads to a more dynamic citizenry. A more educated population leads to faster economic growth. It makes the society more informed, and so makes people appreciate diversity, reduces ethnic, religious and social tensions, and thus leads to better social cohesion. It leads to increased age of marriage and improved health conditions. The more educated a country's people, the more they can read and enjoy serious writings, develop critical thinking, become involved in scholarly debates, and thus become more socially and politically engaged—thereby deepening democracy. In this sense, education is not only a means for development, it is development! The close relationship between education and societal development is so self-evident that even Adam Smith, the celebrated economist who laid the foundation for 'free market economics', was a vocal champion of education for all, at public expense![9]

That is why an important characteristic of all developed societies is universal, high-quality education. This does not mean that first these societies developed, and then they implemented universal education for their citizens. In Europe, the spread of the Industrial Revolution in the 19th century and the spread of education went hand in hand. In fact, by the turn of the 20th century, not only had many West European countries and the USA achieved universalisation of elementary education, many European countries even moved towards implementing a common school system at the elementary level, that is, free, compulsory, common and equitable elementary education for all children.[10]

Japan launched its industrial revolution nearly a century after Western Europe. Universalisation of basic education played a key role in Japan's development story too. Following the Meiji Restoration of 1868, the new interest groups that came to power in Japan not only initiated a radical redirection of Japan's economic development, they also took steps to build a social framework conducive to rapid industrialisation. One of the first measures taken by them was the issuance of the Fundamental Code of Education in 1872, wherein they expressed the public commitment to make sure that there must be "no community with an illiterate family, nor a family with an illiterate person". By 1910 Japan was almost fully literate, at least for the young, and by 1913, though still very much poorer than Britain or America, Japan was publishing more books than Britain and more than twice as many as the United States. This concentration on education was an important factor that contributed to Japan's

Box 0.1: Bolivarian Education in Venezuela

After his victory in the Venezuelan Presidential elections in 1998, Hugo Chavez launched the Bolivarian Revolution in the country. One of the first programmes launched by President Chavez was to tackle the country's widespread illiteracy and lack of access to schooling. Huge sums were allocated for various educational measures at all levels.

An adult education programme called Mission Robinson was launched with the target of ensuring 100% enrolment. In less than a decade, by 2005, UNESCO declared the country as a "territory free of illiteracy," with over 1.5 million people having newly learned to read and write.

The government launched a new school system, called Bolivarian schools. It has refurbished existing schools and opened new schools in all areas of the country. The students in these schools are closely connected to the life of their surrounding communities through student projects and adult education services. South American Spanish is taught as the first language in the schools, besides various tribal languages in the indigenous schools.

The government launched Missión Simoncito that tackles early education by providing free day-care and pre-school facilities for youngsters between one and six years; some 70% of all Venezuelan children attend these schools.

New public Bolivarian universities have been set up to provide higher education to children from poor families. Among the new initiatives are the opening of territorial universities (where the curriculum is focused on projects intended to contribute to the local communities), a Workers' University (where studies are conducted at the workplace and build on workers' knowledge), an experimental art university, and an Indigenous University (located in a remote area and designed by indigenous people).

Public education in Venezuela is free—from pre-school to university level, because the right to free education is guaranteed by the Venezuelan constitution: "Education is a human right, a fundamental social right. It will be free, democratic, and mandatory. Every person will have access to education, providing equal quality and equal opportunity." Free meals and transportation are also provided.

Teachers' salaries have been successively raised over the past years. Today, Venezuelan public school teachers earn 700% more than they earned in 1998.

All these measures have led to reduction in repetition and dropout rates in the country by as much as 50% in just a decade. The rate of secondary school enrolment rose from 53.6% in 2000 to 73.3% in 2011. Recently, UNESCO put Venezuela in the fifth place in the world for the percentage of people enrolled in higher education, and in second place in Latin America (behind Cuba).

[Sources: Ken Jones, "Bolivarian Education in Venezuela", July 26, 2013, http://venezuelanalysis.com; Olivia Kroth, "Venezuelan Socialist Education with President Chávez", September 26, 2012, http://venezuelanalysis.com.]

remarkable economic progress in the late 19th century.[11]

Later, in the 1950s, South Korea and other East Asian countries too followed the Japanese route when they launched their industrialisation drive. They firmly focused on general expansion of education, achieving near universal primary education within just a decade by 1960,[12] which was an important contributing factor to their rapid development because of which these economies came to known as East Asian tigers.[‡]

☆ ☆ ☆

India dreams of becoming a superpower by 2020/2030. From all that we have discussed above, it follows that an essential condition for India to truly develop (which does not mean high growth rates, but that development should percolate down to the ordinary people) is that the country should provide at least basic education to its people. Unfortunately, the harsh reality is that India's education system is in deep crisis. Despite clear-cut Constitutional provisions that the Indian State should take time-bound steps to provide free, compulsory, equitable and good quality education to all children, the Government of India has never seriously attempted to implement these directives. With the result that even today, nearly seven decades after

‡ *Of course, there were other specific historical circumstances too that were responsible for their high growth rates—discussing this is beyond the scope of this book. For more on this, see: Neeraj Jain, "Globalisation or Recolonisation?" pp. 176–77, Lokayat publication, Pune, 2006, book available on Lokayat website, http://lokayat.org.in.*

independence, more than 40% children drop out of school without completing elementary education*! The quality of education is so bad that a very large number of those who do complete basic schooling cannot even read, write or do sums expected of children in Class 2 or 3![13] UNICEF has described the state of education in India as a national emergency.[14]

Over the last two decades, ever since India began globalisation and opened up its economy to foreign multinationals in 1991, the crisis gripping the education system has only become worse. Kowtowing to the dictates of the World Bank (WB) and the International Monetary Fund (IMF)—international financial institutions that are essentially in the control of the developed countries led by the USA[15]—the government is gradually privatising the education system of the country and transforming it into a tool for profiteering by the moneyed classes. The education system is gradually becoming a monopoly of the privileged sections of Indian society. The underprivileged sections—the poor, Dalits, minorities, adivasis and women—are gradually being pushed out of the system. They are once again deliberately being denied access to the education system like it was during the medieval period, the only difference being that then it was by religious diktat, now it is by hiking costs. An important aspiration of our nation's founding fathers was to build an education system that provides education of equitable quality to all children and youth, that develops their abilities to think and critically analyse, that seeks to unfold the immense creative potential inherent in all children, that aims to build a citizenry that will help build and sustain an egalitarian, just, plural and enlightened society; India's rulers have now jettisoned that dream, and the entire orientation of the education system has become to produce a slavish workforce for foreign and Indian corporate houses.

But then, isn't the government taking steps to rectify this situation? It amended the Constitution (86th Amendment) in 2002 to make education a fundamental right, and then in 2009 enacted the Right of Children to Free and Compulsory Education Act (also called the

* *Elementary education: means education up to Class VIII.*

Right to Education Act or RTE Act) to give effect to this Constitutional amendment. According to the government, the passage of this Act means that "every child has a right to full-time elementary education of satisfactory and equitable quality in a formal school which satisfies certain essential norms and standards."[16]

The sad truth is, this is mere government and media propaganda. The 86th Constitutional Amendment and the Right to Education Act, 2009 have actually got nothing to do with providing 'free' and 'compulsory' education to all our children. Their real purpose is the exact opposite of government claims; their real purpose is to undo the relevant provisions of the Constitution of India (that is, the original Constitution that was adopted by the country on January 26, 1950) directing the State to provide free and compulsory education to all children in a time-bound manner.

For most young people fed on a daily diet of media propaganda that India is not only on its way to becoming an economic superpower, we are also heading towards becoming a knowledge economy, all this would be unbelievable. They have come to believe that the country is rapidly developing and educational and employment opportunities are rapidly expanding—and that if some have missed the bus, are out of school/college or without a decent job, it is because they are not capable enough, or because of their bad luck or fate.

This book is an attempt to clear the smog ...

About this Book

We, on behalf of Lokayat, have been actively campaigning to make the people aware of the various aspects of the crisis afflicting the education sector as well as its roots in the policies being followed by the country's rulers, and mobilise them to fight for transforming the education system and change the underlying economic system. We are also an active part of the 'All India Forum for Right to Education' (AIFRTE), an all-India platform of students' and teachers' organisations, eminent educationists and people's organisations. AIFRTE was launched in 2009 to fight for the fundamental right of all children to free holistic early childhood care and cost-free education of equitable quality from pre-primary to Class XII and further for equitable access to free/affordable higher education as a democratic right.

To create awareness among the people regarding the Constitutional vision of "free and compulsory education for all children", its neglect by successive governments at the Centre since independence, and now the full-scale assault on the education system to commercialise it and convert it into yet another means for profiteering by the elites, we have brought out numerous pamphlets in Marathi and English, and have also published a booklet in Marathi. AIFRTE too has brought out numerous booklets, and is also publishing a regular magazine. As a part of our awareness campaign, in 2013, we decided to bring out a comprehensive book in English that would cover a broader range of issues related to the educational policies being implemented in the country as a part of globalisation. Because of our involvement in the many activities of Lokayat, it has taken us more than a year to write this book.

Outline of this Book

We begin by taking a look at the present state of education in the country in Chapter 1. In Chapter 2, we discuss the dreams of our founding fathers and their struggle for 'education for all' during the pre-independence period. The economic policies adopted in India after independence, popularly known as the mixed economy model or the Nehruvian model, are examined in Chapter 3; in this backdrop, we then take a look at the educational policies adopted in the country during the 1950s–70s. The Nehruvian model became crisis-ridden by the 1970s. In Chapter 4, we analyse the reasons for this crisis, and the factors that pushed India's rulers to begin globalisation of the Indian economy in 1991 and adopt neoliberal economic policies.

We examine the impact of globalisation on elementary education in Chapter 5. In 2009, the Indian Parliament passed the Right to Education Act. The Government of India claims that with the passage of this Act, all children in the country now have 'a fundamental right to education'—we examine this claim in Chapter 6. In Chapter 7, we take a look at how the passage of the RTE Act has cleared the way for accelerated commercialisation of the elementary education system in the country.

Chapters 8–12 are devoted to discussing the higher education system in the country. In Chapter 8, we discuss the higher education system, or the lack of it, during the British colonial period. The higher education policies adopted by India's rulers during the Nehruvian period are critically examined in Chapter 9. In Chapters 10–12, we take a look at the impact of the neoliberal winds blowing across the country on the higher education system: the World Bank conditionalities and the sharp reduction in government spending on higher education in the 1990s (Chapter 10), the rapid growth of the private sector in higher education and the transformation of higher education into a business (Chapter 11), and the introduction of new bills in the Parliament by the government to facilitate the growth of the private sector, including foreign universities, in higher education (Chapter 12).

Most people, while agreeing that all children should be provided free, compulsory and good quality education, will nevertheless argue that there is no alternative to privatisation of education as the government school system has become sick. In the same breath, they will argue that in any case, the government does not have sufficient revenues to provide good quality education to all children. How true are these propositions? We discuss these issues in Chapters 13 and 14, respectively.

It is not just the education sector that is being privatised. Under World Bank dictates, the government is gradually scaling down its expenditures on all social services, and privatising them. The people of the country are refusing to take this assault on their lives lying down. They are beginning to organise in small groups all across the country, and fighting back. We conclude by taking a look at these inspiring developments in Chapter 15.

Additional Note About this Book

We started writing this book in mid-2013, when the UPA Government led by Manmohan Singh was in power, but by the time we finished the first draft of this book, the UPA Government had been voted out of power and the Narendra Modi-led BJP Government had taken over. This change of government at the Centre has not made any difference to the analysis made in this book, as the new government has made it more than clear that it is going to implement the very same neoliberal policies of the previous UPA Government, albeit at an accelerated speed.

Since a major part of this book was written when the UPA Government was in power, Manmohan Singh and P. Chidambaram are referred to as Prime Minister and Finance Minister (rather than as former Prime Minister and former Finance Minister). But we have made additions where necessary to show how the new BJP Government is continuing with the policies of the UPA Government, including its neoliberal educational policies.

NOTES

1. Justice H. Suresh (retd.), "Socio-Economic Rights and the Supreme Court", *www.escr-net.org.*
2. Ibid.; Saurav Shome, "Supreme Court Judgement on Mohini Jain Case: Right to Education as a Fundamental Right", http://metastudio.org.
3. Ruth W. Grant and Benjamin R. Hertzberg, "John Locke on Education", http://people.duke.edu; *Education in the Age of Enlightenment*, http://en.wikipedia.org.
4. Natasha Gill, Columbia University, USA, *Educational Philosophy in the French Enlightenment*, http://www.ashgate.com.
5. *Reading 1: Education as the Keystone to the New Democracy*, http://www.cr.nps.gov.
6. *Fact Sheet No. 2 (Rev.1), The International Bill of Human Rights*, The Office of the High Commissioner for Human Rights, Switzerland, http://web.archive.org.
7. *International Covenant on Economic, Social and Cultural Rights*, http://en.wikipedia.org; *Implementation of the International Covenant on Economic, Social and Cultural Rights*, Committee on Economic, Social and Cultural Rights, United Nations Economic and Social Council, December 8, 1999, http://daccess-dds-ny.un.org.
8. "Time for School Series – Interview: Amartya Sen", September 2, 2004, http://www.pbs.org.
9. "Amartya Sen: The Importance of Basic Education", October 28, 2003, http://www.theguardian.com.

10. "Western Europe–Educational Roots, Reform in the Twentieth Century, Contemporary Reform Trends, Future Challenges", http://education.stateuniversity.com; *History of Education*, http://en.wikipedia.org; Praveen Jha et al., *Public Provisioning for Elementary Education in India*, Sage Publications, 2008, p. 37, http://books.google.co.in.
11. "Amartya Sen: The Importance of Basic Education", op. cit., Harry Magdoff, *Imperialism: From Colonial Age to the Present*, Monthly Review Press, New York, Reprinted by Aakar Books, Delhi, p. 53.
12. "Amartya Sen: The Importance of Basic Education", ibid.; Praveen Jha et al., "Public Provisioning for Elementary Education in India", op. cit.
13. See Chapter 1 for details.
14. "Out of School Children and Dropout a National Emergency: UNICEF", *The Hindu*, April 13, 2013, http://www.thehindu.com.
15. See for example: David Harvey, *A Brief History of Neoliberalism*, Oxford University Press, 2005, p. 29; Harry Magdoff, *The Age of Imperialism*, Monthly Review Press, 1968, Reprinted by Aakar Books, Delhi, p. 142.
16. *Right to Education (RTE)*, Department of School Education and Literacy, http://mhrd.gov.in.

1

INDIA: STILL IN THE DARK AGES

The struggle for education for all in modern India is more than one and a half centuries old. Among the pioneers who laid the foundations of this struggle were Jyotiba and Savitribai Phule, who gave the call for education for all, including women and the backward classes, and Dr. Bhimrao Ambedkar who coined the epic slogan 'Educate, Organise, Agitate'. India's freedom struggle kindled new hopes among the people. It nurtured the dream of equal opportunity for all, and as a precondition for that, equitable education for all. The reflection of this dream can be seen in the educational provisions of the Constitution of India.

The Constitutional vision as regards education for the people of India becomes clear from reading Article 45* in conjunction with other related provisions of the Constitution. The Indian State is directed to "provide within a period of ten years from the commencement of the Constitution (that is, by 1960), free and compulsory education for all children until they complete the age of fourteen years". Another important implication of these provisions is that children below the age of six must be provided early childhood care and support for nutrition and healthcare. The State is also enjoined to take special care to promote the educational interests of the Scheduled Castes and Scheduled Tribes.

When these provisions were being drafted by the Constituent Assembly, a member contended that the commitment made in the draft article (later to be known as Article 45) to provide "free and

* *We are here referring to the original Article 45 before it was amended in 2010.*

compulsory education" to children up to 14 years should be limited to only 11 years of age as India would not have the necessary resources. This was vehemently opposed by Dr. Ambedkar. He stated that children in this age group in independent India should be in schools, and not in factories and farms.[1] In arguing thus, Dr. Ambedkar was in fact voicing the hopes of the common people.

Although not enforceable as a fundamental right, it is obvious from the language of the Constitution that the country's founding fathers laid great emphasis on providing free and compulsory education to all children, and that too, urgently, "within a period of ten years from the commencement of the Constitution!" This is the only Constitutional provision with a time frame. Yet, more than five decades since the original time frame ended in 1960, this dream still remains to be realised.

Today's Situation

The Government of India claims that 'significant strides' and 'considerable progress' has been made in the spread of elementary education, and that there is now near-total universalisation of school enrolment at the primary level, in almost all the states of India. It cites the Gross Enrolment Ratio (GER)* as proof: GER at the primary level has gone up from 96.3% in 2001–02 to 114.6% in 2007–08, that for upper primary from 60.2% to 77.5%, and for the total elementary cycle (I–VIII) from 82.4% to 100.5%.[2] According to the Twelfth Five Year Plan of the Government of India, there are today only about 8.1 million out-of-school children in the country (that is, around 4% of the total children in the country).[3]

However, official figures on enrolment are much inflated. In many instances, enrolment figures are fudged for a variety of reasons,

---

* *GER: The number of children enrolled in a level (primary or secondary), regardless of age, divided by the population of the age group that officially corresponds to the same level. The GER exceeding 100 is a technical aberration, as it includes children enrolled in the primary stage who are outside the age group of 6–11 years. So, basically, it should be interpreted as meaning that the government is claiming almost universal enrolment.*

including the pressure to report universal enrolment, the opportunity to get additional allocations of food and other materials that can be siphoned out, and sometimes even the need to retain a teacher's post.[4] Thus for instance, the Public Report on Basic Education in India (PROBE) survey* of 2006 on the state of primary schooling in the country found that while almost 95% of children in the age group 6–12 years were enrolled in school, children's attendance as noted in the school registers was far below enrolment: only around 66% of children enrolled in the primary classes were marked present. And actual attendance was even lower, as observed by the field investigators.[5]

Apart from fudging of enrolment figures, another trick being resorted to by the government to inflate the number of children in school is by narrowing the definition of 'out-of-school children' to only 'non-enrolled children' (that is, those children who have never enrolled in a school), thus excluding the huge category of so-called 'drop-outs' (that is, children who have enrolled and then dropped out of school) from its figures of 'out-of-school' children. As per the requirements of Article 45 (original version), the State has failed to provide elementary education to these children too. The drop-out rates are very high. For the country as a whole, the drop-out rate in 2009–10 was 27% at the primary level (Class I–V), 41% at the elementary level (Class I–VIII), and 49% at the secondary level (Class I–X).[6] The Twelfth Plan too admits that even after three years of the passage of the Right to Education Act which is supposed to guarantee free and compulsory education to all children in the age group 6–14, the drop-out rate at the elementary level is still as high as 42.39%.[7]

The drop-out rates are even higher for scheduled caste (SC) and scheduled tribe (ST) students. For scheduled castes, the drop-out rates were 30% at the primary level, 52% at the elementary level and 68% at the secondary level (all figures for 2007–08); while for scheduled tribes, the figures were an even more dismal 40%, 63% and 79%, respectively (all figures for 2005–06).[8] Even after the completion of the Eleventh Five Year Plan, that had been hailed as an 'education plan', the drop-out rates for SC and ST children have not significantly

* *PROBE: A landmark study on the state of primary education in India.*

declined, and are 51.25% and 57.58%, respectively, at the elementary stage.[9]

Taking the total number of children in the country in the age-group 6–14 as 20 crores,[10] this means that more than 9 crore children in the country have either never enrolled in school or drop out of school without completing even basic schooling!

Single Teacher, Single Classroom Schools

These dismal figures represent just one aspect of the terrible state of education in the country. Seven decades after independence, the conditions in a majority of the schools are so bad that it is a 'national shame'. Official DISE* data for 2011 reveals that more than 50% of the 8.4 lakh primary schools in the country are single, or at best, two teacher schools. And a staggering 70% schools have three or less than three teachers. Implying that a single teacher is teaching two or three different classes at the same time, in an overwhelming majority of the primary schools in the country![11]

The same DISE survey of 2011–12 found that even in 2011, 12% or more than 1 lakh primary schools in the country were single classroom schools (or were functioning in the open, without any classrooms), and a whopping 64% of the primary schools (5.3 lakh schools) functioned with three classrooms or less. What must be the quality of education being imparted to students in schools where a single teacher is teaching two or more than two different classes in a single room![12]

Worse, of the roughly 11 lakh elementary schools in the country (in 2010), 87,000 are what the government calls non-formal education centres under the Education Guarantee Scheme (EGS).[13] These are schools only in name—running with hardly any government funding, in a premise provided by the local community, staffed by a local unemployed youth who is paid a stipend by the village. The only

---

* *DISE, or District Information System for Education, is a comprehensive school information system developed and maintained by the National University of Educational Planning and Administration, Delhi. It provides regular information on all aspects of elementary education in the country.*

purpose of these 'schools' is to inflate school enrolment statistics, nothing more.

Ill-Trained Teachers

Not only is there an acute shortage of teachers, in the rush to achieve enrolment targets without spending much, states are appointing para-teachers or contractual teachers en masse. As per the DISE survey of 2011–12, there were more than 8 lakh contractual teachers in all schools (12.16% of all teachers), of which nearly 4.4 lakh teachers were in primary schools.[14] Para-teachers are being appointed by various state governments in a very arbitrary way; there is no parity between states on their qualification norms, training requirements, pay scale, and other service requirements. According to DISE data, more than 45% of para-teachers are not even professionally trained.[15]

More shockingly, DISE also reports that in 2011–12, as many as 20.4% of the regular teachers in all schools, a whopping 12 lakh teachers, were not professionally trained![16] An even bigger problem is, many of our so-called 'trained' teachers are also not adequately trained. In an alarming indictment of our teacher training system, over 99% aspirants failed to clear the Central Teacher Eligibility Test (CTET) in 2012. The CTET was introduced in 2011 by the Human Resource Development Ministry to improve the quality of teachers in schools. All B. Ed. graduates need to clear this test to work as a teacher. In 2012, 7.96 lakh appeared for the test, of whom only 4,849 managed to clear the exam.[17]

Not Even Drinking Water, Toilets

The DISE survey of 2010–11 found that around 1 lakh elementary schools in the country did not even have drinking water facilities; and in an additional 1.9 lakh schools, the drinking water facilities were not functional; in all, a whopping 21% of all elementary schools did not have functional drinking water facilities![18]

Around 2 lakh, or 16% of all elementary schools, did not have toilet facilities even on paper in 2010–11, while in many schools, the toilet facilities existed only in name; in all, a huge 40% of the schools did not have usable toilet facilities. The survey found that only 60% of the elementary schools had separate toilet facilities for girls; obviously, the proportion of schools having functional separate toilets for girls would be much less than this![19] The Twelfth Five Year Plan document too admits to this: "the retention of girls in school remains difficult given that over 63% of rural schools have no usable toilet facilities for them."[20]

As of 2011:

- nearly 60% elementary schools were not electrified;
- 49% schools did not have libraries;
- 47% schools did not have playgrounds;
- almost 40% schools did not have furniture for students;
- 36% schools operated from makeshift/temporary (kuccha/tent) buildings,
- and nearly 45% schools did not even have a boundary wall for the school![21]

Given this state of our schools and teachers, is it any wonder that the all-India Annual Status of Education (ASER) survey of 2012 by the Delhi-based NGO, Pratham, found that 53% of Class 5 students were unable to read Class 2-level text while 47% of Class 5 children could not solve simple two–digit subtraction problems with borrowing. More than 75% of children enrolled in Class 5 could not do division problems. Not only that, ASER data show that over the years, learning levels are declining![22]

What this really means is that even though only 60% of students enrolling in Class I complete Class VIII, and 50% complete Class X, both of which are shamefully low figures, in reality, the percentage of our children who can be considered to have truly completed basic schooling is much lower than this.

Elite Schools for a Few

While this is the state of education for the overwhelming majority of children in our country, on the other hand, for a small percentage of children from the middle classes, the government does makes the necessary investment on school infrastructure and teacher salaries to provide them education in good quality government schools—the

Navodaya Vidyalayas and Kendriya Vidyalayas. Additionally, in recent years, as commercialisation of school education has accelerated, five-star private schools—equipped with hi-tech equipment, fully air-conditioned classrooms, low student–teacher ratio of around 15:1, all kinds of extracurricular facilities like auditoriums, gyms, swimming pools and studios, and so on—have also been opening across the country to cater to the children of the very rich. The fees of these elite schools ranges from anywhere between Rs 5 and 15 lakh.

Higher Education Beyond Reach

As it is, only 16% of the students enrolling in Class I cross the Class XII barrier to become eligible for higher education. This percentage is much lower for the historically deprived sections: just around 10–11% of 'other backward caste' (OBC) students, 8% of scheduled caste (SC) students, 6% of scheduled tribe (ST) students and 9% of Muslim students (out of those admitted to Class I) complete higher secondary education (that is, Class XII).[23] (The actual percentage would be even lower, as not all children enrol in Class I.) This means that more than 92% of Dalit children and 94% of tribal children never reach the threshold of higher education.

Of this low percentage of students crossing Class XII, only a very small section enters higher education, as college fees are going through the roof because of rampant privatisation of this sector under the neoliberal policy regime. While at the primary and secondary level, there still exist a large number of government schools which charge low or no fees, higher education, especially professional courses like engineering, medicine and management, has virtually become inaccessible for children from poor and lower middle class families. Fees for these professional courses has zoomed to as much as Rs 1 to 3 lakh per year, apart from other expenses like lodging and boarding expenses, which can also go up to as much as Re 1 lakh per year and more. For a certain number of seats, called 'management quota' seats, colleges are allowed to charge as much fees as they want; a management quota MBBS seat today costs as much as Rs 25–35 lakh, and a postgraduate degree in medicine (MD/MS) a whopping Rs 1–1.5 crore.

Consequently, it is not surprising that the Gross Enrolment Ratio (GER) for higher education* was a mere 15% in 2011–12.[24] Even this figure is much inflated! That is because the government includes in this statistic enrolment in all kinds of diploma courses popping up all over the country, in which students are enrolling in large numbers in the hope of getting some or the other job.

It is not just that the private colleges springing up across the country like mushrooms are charging extortionate fees, in many of these colleges the quality of education too is simply abysmal. Therefore, it is not surprising that only 25% of technical graduates and 10–15% of other graduates are considered employable by industries, according to a National Association of Software & Services Companies (NASSCOM) report.[25] Another survey by the industry body Assocham found that barring graduates from IIMs, only 10% of graduates from B-schools were employable.[26]

New BJP Government: Educational Crisis Worsening

Now, a new BJP Government is in power at the Centre. The people were thoroughly fed up with the economic policies of the previous UPA Government that had led to rising inflation, worsening unemployment, huge increase in poverty and destitution, and most importantly, with the numerous corruption scandals that were regularly hitting the headlines. Taking advantage of the people's anger with this worsening economic crisis, the BJP launched a slick propaganda campaign funded by the country's leading corporate houses, promising the people 'better days' (achhe din). Not realising the implications of enthroning fascist forces in power at the Centre, the people voted the BJP-led NDA Government to power in the elections to the 16th Lok Sabha held in April–May last year.

However, since coming to power, the BJP has expectedly been implementing the very same policies of the previous UPA Government, only at a much faster pace. In the field of education, it is in fact

---

* *GER for higher education is the total enrolment in higher education (both degree and diploma programmes) as a percentage of the population in the age group of 18–22 years.*

implementing a very regressive agenda. Not only is it implementing policies that are accelerating the educational polarisation in the country, what is even more disturbing is, the BJP is blatantly promoting saffronisation of the education system. Text books written by Dinanath Batra, an RSS ideologue, which according to historian Romila Thapar contain "not history, but fantasy", have been introduced into the state curriculum in Gujarat; more recently, the newly elected BJP Government in Haryana has appointed Batra as its advisor on education.[27] The process of filling important research, educational and cultural institutions and committees with people associated with the Hindutva agenda has begun. The government pressurised the Indian Council of Historical Research (ICHR) director Prof. Parvin Sinclair to resign and replaced her by Y. Sudarshan Rao, who has openly eulogised the caste system.[28] Baldev Sharma, former editor of the RSS mouthpiece, *Panchjanya*, has been appointed the Chairman of the National Book Trust.[29] There are plans to introduce the Gita in government schools.[30] This naked promotion of a communal agenda in such a sensitive field as education grossly violates two most fundamental principles of the Indian Constitution, secularism and democracy.

☆ ☆ ☆

Such is the present state of the dream that our freedom struggle had nurtured—of providing free and compulsory education to all our children, initially up to the age of 14 years, and as the country became more prosperous, up to higher education level.

Why has the state of education in the country come to such a pass? To understand the reasons for this, it is important to take a look at the evolution of the education system in the country since independence.

NOTES

1. Anil Sadgopal, "Right to Education vs. Right to Education Act", *Social Scientist*, September–December 2010, http://www.scribd.com.
2. *Mid-term Appraisal, Eleventh Five Year Plan, 2007–12*, Planning Commission, Government of India, 2011, p. 121, available on internet

at: http://planningcommission.nic.in.

3. *Twelfth Five Year Plan: 2012–17, Vol. III: Social Sectors*, Planning Commission, Government of India, p. 53, available on internet at: http://planningcommission.nic.in.
4. Muchkund Dubey, "Right of Children to Free and Compulsory Education Bill, 2009: The Story of a Missed Opportunity", *Mainstream*, Vol. XLVII, No. 40, September 19, 2009, http://www.mainstream weekly.net; A.K. Shiva Kumar, Preet Rustagi, *Elementary Education in India: Progress, Setbacks, and Challenges*, September 2010, http://www.oxfamindia.org.
5. A.K. Shiva Kumar, Preet Rustagi, ibid.
6. Ministry of Human Resource Development, Government of India and Rajya Sabha Unstarred Question No. 867, dated 30.11.2012, taken from: Nithiya Amirtham S. and Saidalavi Kundupuzhakkal, *Gender Issues and Dropout Rates in India: Major Barrier in Providing Education for All*, http://www.confab journals.com.
7. *Twelfth Five Year Plan: 2012–17, Vol. III: Social Sectors*, op. cit., p. 53.
8. GOI, Ministry of Human Resource Development, *Selected Educational Statistics, 2007–08*, taken from: "Section 10: Scheduled Castes & Scheduled Tribes", http://www.nird.org.in.
9 *Twelfth Five Year Plan: 2012–17, Vol. III: Social Sectors*, op. cit., p. 53.
10 Twelfth Five Year Plan estimates this figure to be 192 million: *Twelfth Five Year Plan: 2012–17, Vol. III: Social Sectors*, ibid., p. 52.
11. Calculated from: *Elementary Education in Urban India: Analytical Reports, 2011-12*, and *Elementary Education in Rural India: Analytical Reports, 2011-12*, NUEPA, http://www.dise.in; data collected up to September 30, 2011.
12. Calculated from ibid.
13. *Mid-term Appraisal, Eleventh Five Year Plan, 2007–12*, op. cit., p. 121.
14. *Elementary Education in India: Progress Towards UEE: Analytical Tables 2011-12*, http://www.dise.in.
15. *Flash Statistics, Elementary Education in India—Progress Towards UEE: DISE 2012–13*, NUEPA, New Delhi, available on internet at: http://dise.in.
16. Calculated from data given in ibid.
17. Manash Pratim Gohain, "99% Fail Test for School Teachers", *TNN*, January 2, 2013, http://articles.timesofindia.indiatimes.com.
18. DISE survey, NUEPA, New Delhi, taken from: "An overview of status of drinking water and sanitation in schools in India", http://www.dise.in.
19. Ibid.; "30 million Indian school children have no access to toilets",

April 25, 2012, http://indiatoday.intoday.in.

20. *Twelfth Five Year Plan: 2012–17, Vol. III: Social Sectors*, op. cit., p. 54.
21. Calculated from: *Elementary Education in Urban India: Analytical Reports, 2011-12*, and *Elementary Education in Rural India: Analytical Reports, 2011-12*, NUEPA, http://www.dise.in; *Elementary Education in India: Progress Towards UEE: Analytical Tables 2011-12*, http://www.dise.in.
22. *Annual Status of Education Report 2012: Major Findings*, http://www.aser centre.org.
23. Estimates made by Prof. Anil Sadgopal, one of the most renowned educationists of India; taken from: Lokesh Malti Prakash, "Education in the Neo-Liberal Limbo", November 2, 2012, http://khwabesahar.wordpress.com.
24. *Annual Status of Higher Education of States and UTs in India, 2012, Summary Report*, Planning Commission, Government of India, http://eduvisors.com.
25. "85 Per Cent Graduates in India Not Employable", August 29, 2011, http://www.rediff.com.
26. "Only 10% Graduates Employable: Survey", January 31, 2013, http://www.business-standard.com.
27. "Dinanath Batra", *Wikipedia*, http://en.wikipedia.org, accessed on April 4, 2015; "Dinanath Batra Books to Edify Gujarat School Students", July 25, 2014, http://www.outlookindia.com.
28. T.K. Rajalakshmi, "Twisted Texts", *Frontline*, December 26, 2014, http://www.frontline.in; Praful Bidwai, "How the Sangh Parivar Is Taking Over Education and Culture Institutions", December 25, 2014, http://scroll.in.
29. "Baldev Sharma Appointed as Chairman of National Book Trust", March 2, 2015, http://www.thehindu.com.
30. "Haryana to Introduce Bhagvad Gita in Schools This Year", March 15, 2015, http://indiatoday.intoday.in.

2

THE STRUGGLE FOR 'EDUCATION FOR ALL' DURING THE PRE-INDEPENDENCE PERIOD

A Shudra is unfit to receive education. The upper varnas should not impart education or give advice to a Shudra. It is not necessary that the Shudra should know the laws and codes and hence need not be taught. Violators will go to as amrita hell (IV, 78 to 81). One must never read the Vedas in the presence of the Shudras (IV, 99). He who instructs Shudra pupils and he whose teacher is a Shudra shall become disqualified from being invited to a shradha (III, 156).

–Manusmriti

India's Indigenous Education System

We have only limited information about the indigenous education system in India during the mid-18th century, before the British began colonising India.

Indian society during this period was a feudal society, ruled by kings and the priestly class. The rulers were not concerned about educating the people, and they confined themselves to financially supporting scholars and institutions of higher learning. There existed a very limited formal system of education, as the structure of society was such that it was not much needed. The small priestly class needed a formal education system for religious instruction; the small class of officials, moneylenders, merchants and well-to-do landlords also found it necessary to acquire some elementary education. These classes organised a limited formal education system for themselves, supported by donations from the wealthy, and probably by the kings too.

The majority of the population did not go to formal educational institutions. This of course does not mean that they did not acquire any education. Indian society, by the 17th century, had achieved "an unprecedented level of industrial and commercial prosperity, reflected in general urbanisational growth. There was an intensification, expansion and multiplication of crafts, and of both internal and international trade."[1] It is estimated that in 1750, India accounted for almost a quarter of the world manufacturing output.[2] A British Royal Industrial Commission of 1916–18 recalled that Indian industrial development was "not inferior to that of the more advanced European nations" when "merchant adventurers from the West" arrived in India; other British studies indicate that it may even be "that the industries of India were far more advanced than those of the West up to the advent of the industrial revolution."[3] Obviously, to support such an extensive and developed manufacturing system, the craftsmen must have been highly skilled. To quote Irfan Habib, one of India's greatest historians, "medieval India had developed an exceptional level of manual skill."[4] For people to acquire such high levels of skills and knowledge about their vocation, there obviously must have existed a fairly well-developed traditional system of imparting vocational education.

Returning to our main topic of discussion, the indigenous formal education system in India in the mid-18th century comprised two types of institutions: the elementary schools, and the schools of learning which roughly correspond to the colleges of today.

(i) The schools of learning were staffed by learned teachers of repute; instruction to students was provided free; the teachers were renumerated either by land grants made by rulers or by allowances made by the wealthy; the schools generally did not have special buildings of their own, and in most cases classes were held in temples and mosques and not infrequently in the house of some wealthy patron or the teacher himself; students entered the school at an early age and often studied for 12 years or more.

(ii) While the schools of learning gave mostly religious instruction, and their chief objective was to produce maulvis

> and pandits, the indigenous elementary schools were the main agency for mass education. It appears that indigenous schools abounded in every part of the country, and some humble means of education was available even in very small villages. However, we have no quantitative data on their reach, and the level of literacy in pre-colonial times.

Instruction in these schools too was free. The teachers in these schools were not very well educated and their remuneration was much lower than that of the teachers in the schools of learning. It appears that unlike schools of learning, the pupils in these schools included a small number of girls and children of many communities, although the children from the upper castes formed the large majority. There is little information available about the content of education imparted in these schools. Apparently, education in these schools "served the practical needs of daily life". Thus, the well-known sociologist Hetukar Jha writes that the network of indigenous schools in early 19th century Bihar was "an institutionalised part of rural life .... The children of the peasantry belonging to different castes and communities were equipped with enough competence in such schools for carrying on their occupational obligations." Similarly, commenting on the pathshalas or indigenous schools of early 19th century Bengal, the noted educationist Kazi Shahidullah has written that they were "secular educational institutions imparting practical instruction in accordance with the requirements of the local community."[5]

While some of the higher castes had a high percentage of literacy in so far as the male population was concerned, the biggest limitation of the formal indigenous education system was its exclusion of lower castes and women (with a few individual exceptions) from acquiring education. This prohibition had been in existence for nearly 2000 years.

The caste system in India began emerging around the middle of the first millennium BCE. Before this time, during the Rgvedic period (1500–1000 BC), society was characterised by an absence of sharp class divisions among its members. It was a predominantly pastoral, near egalitarian society; while agriculture was practised, it was not yet the basis of the economy. It is during the Later Vedic period (1000–500 BC) that pastoralism gradually gave way to agriculture and semi-nomadism to large-scale settlements. By the 5th century BC, there was a huge expansion of the economy, agriculture had considerably developed, and for the first time, there was a substantial agrarian surplus over and above the subsistence needs of the toilers. Conditions thus arose for the emergence of class divisions in society; and along with that, the caste system evolved to justify and reinforce this stratification. Historians consider the period from the rise of Buddhism (about 500 BC) to the Gupta Age (4th–5th centuries AD) to be the period of the formation of the Indian caste system and its supporting ideology.[6] With the gradual entrenchment of the caste system, the upper classes/castes reserved education only for the higher castes. Manu (between around 200 BC to 200 AD), the most prominent ideologue of the Brahminical system, explicitly prohibited the Shudras from taking education, and this prohibition remained in force for the next two millennia.

While on the one hand it is true that the level of technology in India around the 15th century was not lagging behind other parts of Eurasia, on the other hand, it is also true that this development would have been much more but for the caste system. The caste system definitely inhibited the development of science and technology. The development of science requires experimentation and then development of scientific theories from the results. However, since the upper castes were prohibited from engaging in any kind of labour, this prevented them from engaging in any practical experiments; it also prevented them from taking an interest in the technology used by the common people and exploring and developing upon the scientific principles involved therein. While the lower castes could not contribute to the development of science since they were prohibited from acquiring education. The labouring, that is, the lower castes, were unable to make improvements in the technology involved in their own particular caste craft too, since the caste system prevented them from acquiring knowledge about other crafts—technology often develops by integrating the scientific principles inherent in different crafts. The Mughal empire did not produce a single worthwhile text on crafts or agriculture, however many volumes of poetry or histories it might have to its credit. One of the reasons for the advance of the industrial revolution in Western Europe was the gradual merger of theoretical science and craft technology there in the 16th and 17th centuries.[7]

Caste purity can only be ensured by subjugating and controlling the sexuality of women. That is why along with caste hierarchy, gender hierarchy was also an essential organising principle of the Brahminical social order of ancient and medieval India.[8] And so, as the caste system intensified, the position of women in society also deteriorated, and they too came to be excluded from education along with the Shudras.

Despite this serious drawback, J.P. Naik, who has been included by UNESCO in its honour roll of the world's 100 greatest educationists, writes that with suitable improvement and extension, the indigenous system of education could have been developed into a national system of education, "it certainly had these potentialities". In support of his opinion, he cites several British educationists who studied the Indian indigenous education system during the late 18th–early 19th centuries and expressed a similar view.[9] However, other experts, such as the eminent historian Sabyasachi Bhattacharya, caution that because of the limited information available about the pre-colonial education system, "it is advisable to be cautious against idealisation of the indigenous schooling for the masses in pre-colonial or early colonial times."[10]

Colonial Intervention

The British had come to India to colonise it; their sole interest was in maximising their plunder. The caste system eminently suited them as it helped them consolidate their rule over the land. (In fact, the depth and scope of caste discrimination got exacerbated and magnified under their rule.)[11] Therefore, they made no attempt to change the indigenous education system in India in such a way as to ameliorate the condition of the lower castes and women. Keeping Indians entrapped in a feudal mindset eminently suited them, and so they made little or no effort to educate Indians in the values of the Enlightenment, such as scientific reasoning, rationalism, secularism, humanism and democracy.

As the British went about systematically plundering and raping India, destroying its vibrant industry and agriculture and turning its cities into ruins, simultaneously, the indigenous education system also gradually decayed.[12]

While making no attempt to stop this decay of indigenous education, the British also introduced changes in the education system whose sole objective was to further consolidate their control over India —the impact of these changes was so far-reaching that we continue to suffer from their consequences even today!

Macaulayan System of Education

In 1835, William Bentinck, then Governor General of India, promulgated the first education policy for colonial India, known as the English Education Act. As its name suggests, the aim of the Act was to establish the hegemonic influence of English as the medium of colonial 'instruction' (not education). The purpose of this was made clear by Thomas Babington Macaulay, a member of the council of advisors to the Governor General, in his Minutes of 1833, on the basis of which the Act was drafted:

> to "form a class who may be interpreters between us and the millions whom we govern—a class of persons Indian in blood and colour, but English in tastes, in opinions, in morals and in intellect ..."[13]

The British were so successful in creating a class of people entrapped in a colonial mindset that more than six decades after the victory of the anti-colonial freedom struggle, the upper classes of independent India continue to be steeped in the same mindset.

On the basis of this Act, the British expanded the education system only so much so as to produce just the adequate number and categories of educated people to run their exploitative colonial administrative and judicial system. It was again the upper castes who took advantage of their social position to monopolise the new opportunities in the civil service, legal profession, media, teaching and so on.

Box 2.1: Mahatma Phule's Memorandum to the Hunter Commission

Mahatma Phule's memorandum to the Hunter Commission actually questioned the very foundations of Macaulayan education. The Memorandum demanded that the mother tongue be the medium of education in school education. Phule stated: "The system (of primary education) is imperfect in so far as it does not prove practical and useful to the future career of the pupils." He went on to express concern that almost all the teachers employed in primary schools were Brahmins not used to productive manual labour, and "the boys who learn under them generally imbibe inactive habits and try to obtain (government) service." He proposed that primary school teachers should be those "who will not feel ashamed to hold the handle of a plough or the carpenter's adze when required, and who will be able to mix themselves readily with the lower orders of society." Further, "knowledge of agriculture and a few lessons on moral duties and sanitation" along with practical experience and "some useful arts" should be included in the curriculum. Regarding higher education, Phule argued in favour of providing equal access to all and ensuring that its curriculum is relevant to the aspirations and needs of the young people.

[*Source: "Memorial to Hunter Comission by Jotirao Phule", http://www.scribd.com.*]

Demand for Education for All

By the mid-19th century, a middle class had started taking birth in India. Not all were 'English in opinions and intellect', many were concerned with the plight of their fellow countrymen, and began the social reform movements of the 19th century as well as laid the foundations of India's struggle for freedom. One of the early demands raised by them was that of education for all.

The demand for free and compulsory primary education was probably first raised in Bengal by the renowned Bengali professor and journalist Lal Behari Dey in 1869 at a meeting of the Bethune Society of Calcutta.[14] In September 1882, the nationalist economist Dadabhai Naoroji demanded of the Indian Education Commission—also referred to as the Hunter Commission—that four years of compulsory education (which would ensure effective literacy) should be provided to all children.[15]

Mahatma Jyotirao Phule, in a detailed memorandum to the Hunter Commission in October 1882, pointed out that the British Government's funding of education tended to benefit "Brahmins and the higher classes only" while leaving "the masses wallowing in ignorance and poverty." He drew attention to the fact that this was happening despite it being "an admitted fact that the greater portion of the revenues of the Indian Empire are derived from the ryot's labour—from the sweat of his brow. The higher and richer classes contribute little or nothing to the State exchequer." Phule went on to demand that "primary education of the masses should be made compulsory up to a certain age, say at least 12 years." He urged the Commission to open separate schools for Mahars, Mangs and other lower classes as these children were practically excluded from all schools due to caste prejudices, and also sanction measures for the spread of female primary literacy.[16]

During the late 19th century and the first half of the 20th century, several social reformers and educators like Syed Ahmad Khan, Ishwar Chandra Vidyasagar, Begums of Bhopal viz. Sikandar Begum, Shah Jehan Begum and Sultan Jehan Begum, Madan Mohan Malviya, Lala Lajpat Rai, Karmaveer Bhaurao Patil and many others promoted education by opening schools and colleges, often with public support. A few rulers of princely states like Baroda, Bhopal, Gondal, Kolhapur, Vijayanagaram and Travancore also either supported or set up school systems to universalise free primary education.

In 1910, Gopal Krishna Gokhale moved a resolution in the Imperial Legislative Council seeking provision of 'Free and Compulsory Primary Education' in India, and the following year, he brought in a private member's bill on the subject. Both his efforts failed.[17]

Mahatma Gandhi too was (in his own words) "a firm believer in the principle of free and compulsory primary education for India."[18] The All India Conference on Education held in Wardha on October 22–23, 1937, passed a resolution approving Gandhi's proposal that free and compulsory education in the mother tongue be provided nationwide to all children for seven years, from the age of 7 to 14. A year later, the Haripura session of the Indian National Congress too gave its approval to this resolution.[19]

Demand for 'Education for All' as a Fundamental Right

The demand for State-funded free primary/elementary education for all children as a fundamental right was raised by the leaders of India's freedom struggle from its very early days. This demand was probably first raised in the Constitution of India Bill of 1895, popularly known as the 'Swaraj Bill' which was inspired by Lokmanya Tilak. It was included in the seven fundamental rights listed in the non-official Commonwealth of India Bill of 1925 (drafted by Annie Besant and introduced in the British House of Commons by the Labour Party MP George Lansbury).[20] It was also one of the nineteen fundamental rights listed in the Nehru Report of 1928. The Nehru Report was an outline of a draft Constitution of India and was prepared by a committee (headed by Motilal Nehru) set up by the All-Parties Conference that was convened at the initiative of the Indian National Congress in May 1928. It declared that the first concern of Indians was "to secure the fundamental rights that had been denied to them", and stated that these fundamental rights should be "guaranteed in a manner which will not permit their withdrawal under any circumstances."[21]

In 1931, the Congress at its session held at Karachi adopted the historic *Resolution on Fundamental Rights and Economic and Social Change*, which was a declaration of rights and also included an economic programme with an explicit socialist orientation. The Karachi resolution in its Article I (xi) pledged: "The State shall provide for free and compulsory primary education."[22]

Beginnings of Dalit and Women's Education

The British were not interested in spreading the ideas of enlightenment and ameliorating the condition of Dalits and women in India. They were more interested in consolidating their control over the country to maximise their plunder, and the caste system eminently suited them for this.

Therefore, even though they passed the Caste Disabilities Removal Act in 1850, one of whose implications was that Dalits could now access education, the British attitude regarding education of Dalits was to compromise with upper caste opposition to the education of Dalits. Thus, on the one hand the declared government policy was that "no boy be refused admission to a government college or school merely on the ground of caste"; and on the other, it was also emphasised that "this principle be applied with due caution ..." Generally, the British policy was to either open special schools for Dalit children, or if the school was a common school, the Dalit children were seated separately, invariably in the verandah, and were not touched either by the teachers or by other students. Official reports of the late 19th century and early 20th century are replete with accounts of opposition by upper caste Hindus to Dalit education, which sometimes even led to closure of some of these 'special' schools set up exclusively for Dalit children, or forced Dalit children to drop out of school.[23]

With the British not willing to antagonise the dominant castes, it was actually the persistent efforts of the Dalit intellectuals and other social reformers—who boldly persevered in their efforts despite severe opposition by the upper castes—that played a crucial role in the spread of education among the Dalits. In Western India, the pioneers in this were undoubtedly Mahatma Jyotirao Phule (1827–90) and his wife, Savitribai Phule (1831–97). They started what was probably the first school for girls in the country in Pune in 1848 and then opened more schools for girls and Dalit children in the early 1850s.[24] The Phules were followed by several other social reformers who made considerable contributions to the cause of education for Dalits, such as Vithal Ramji Shinde (1873–1944) and 'Karmaveer' Bhaurao Patil (1887–1959). Enlightened rulers like Sayajirao Gaikwad (1863–1939), the Maharaja of Baroda state, and Chhatrapati Shahu (1874–1922), the Maharaja of Kolhapur, also did much for the spread of Dalit education.[25] The greatest reformer of the early 20th century who played a stellar role in the spread of education among Dalits was of course Dr. B.R. Ambedkar. He exhorted the Dalit youth to acquire education for their social and economic advancement, for which he established the Bahiskrit Hitkarini Sabha in 1924, the Depressed Classes Education Society in 1928, and the People's Education Society in 1945.

There were similar reform movements in many other regions of India, that questioned oppressive medieval orthodox customs and superstitions, mobilised people to fight these irrational practices, and advocated education as a means of modernisation of society. For instance, in Kerala, one of the pioneering Dalit activists was Ayyankali (1863–1941), who formed an organisation for Dalits named 'Sadhujana Paripalana Sangham' (Association for the Welfare of the Poor) and fought for the right of Dalit children and girls to study in school, among other reforms. Ayyankali was supported in his efforts by his great contemporary Sree Narayana Guru and other social reformers of Kerala. Another prominent Dalit activist of Kerala who did much for the upliftment and education of the Dalits was Poykayil Appachan (1878–1939).[26] Similarly, in Tamil Nadu, during the late 19th century, a whole galaxy of Dalit intellectuals, Iyothee Thaas being one of the most outstanding amongst them, laid the foundations for the socio-cultural awakening that led to the spectacular rise of the Dravidian movement in the second decade of the 20th century. They were vehement critics of casteism, Brahminism and the social evils rampant in Hindu society.[27]

Towards a National System of Education

By the early 20th century, the Indian freedom struggle had started voicing the demand for a national system of education. In 1906, the Indian National Congress adopted a resolution that said that the time had arrived

> for the people all over the country earnestly to take up the question of national education for boys and girls, and organise a system of education, literary, scientific and technical, suited to the requirements of the country, on national lines, and under national control, and directed towards the realisation of the national destiny.[28]

Gandhi's Criticism of Macaulayan Education

Probably the most elaborate conceptualisation of an alternate vision of education can be seen in the writings of Mahatma Gandhi.

He based his alternate perspective on a complete repudiation of Macaulay's education policy. Macaulay, in his minutes of 1835, had based his advocacy of English as the medium of education by denigrating not just Indian languages, but India's vast intellectual and literary heritage. He had written:[29]

> (T)he dialects commonly spoken among the natives of this part of India contain neither literary nor scientific information, and are moreover so poor and rude that, until they are enriched from some other quarter, it will not be easy to translate any valuable work into them ... the intellectual improvement of those classes of the people who have the means of pursuing higher studies can at present be affected only by means of some language not vernacular amongst them ...

and further:

> (A) single shelf of a good European library was worth the whole native literature of India and Arabia.

In his very first definitive writing, *Hind Swaraj* (1908), Gandhi severely criticised the Macaulayan education policy:

> To give millions a knowledge of English is to enslave them. The foundation that Macaulay laid of education has enslaved us.... Is it not a painful thing that, if I want to go to a court of justice, I must employ the English language as a medium, that when I become a barrister, I may not speak my mother tongue and that someone else should have to translate to me from my own language? Is not this absolutely absurd? Is it not a sign of slavery?[30]

In an article published in the weekly *Young India* in 1921, he wrote:

> The foreign medium has caused brain fag, put undue strain upon the nerves our children, made them crammers and imitators, unfitted them for original work and thought, and disabled them for filtrating their learning to the family or the masses.... The foreign medium has prevented the growth of our vernaculars.[31]

Speaking at the Wardha Educational Conference in 1938, he stated:

> The present system of education is not only wasteful but positively harmful. It does not meet the requirements of the country in any shape or form. English has been made the medium of education in all the highest branches of learning, and it has created a permanent bar between the highly educated few and the uneducated many.[32]

Gandhi did not restrict his critique of Macaulayan education to just English education. Addresing students in Madras soon after his return to India, he assailed the very aim of colonial education:

> Is the goal of the education that you are receiving that of mere employment whether in the government departments or other departments? If that be the goal of your education, if that is the goal that you have set before yourselves, I feel and I fear that the vision which the poet (Rabindranath Tagore) pictured for himself is far from being realised.[33]

In an article in *Young India*, he wrote:

> I have never been able to make a fetish of literary training. My experience has proved to my satisfaction that literary training by itself adds not an inch to one's moral height and that character-building is independent of literary training. I am firmly of opinion that the government schools have unmanned us, rendered us helpless and godless.... They have made us what we were intended to become, clerks and interpreters.[34]

and further:

> The vast majority of people that sent their children to the English schools were agriculturists ... There is no doubt that the young people when they came back knew not a thing about agriculture, were indeed deeply contemptuous of the calling of their fathers ... The fact that the tragedy of this destructive breach was limited by the need of government for only a specified number of clerks and deputies, should not really mask the reality of the transaction.... The system must be scrapped ...[35]

Deepening his critique of colonial education, Gandhi asserted:

> The curriculum and pedagogic ideas which form the fabric of modern education were imported from Oxford and Cambridge, Edinburgh and London. But they are essentially foreign, and till they are repudiated, there never can be national education.[36]

Gandhi's Alternate Vision

While critiquing Macaulayan education, Gandhi simultaneously outlined an alternate vision of "national education".

Education in Mother Tongue

One of the most important elements of Gandhi's pedagogy* was education in the vernaculars, which today has come to be well-established worldwide. Gandhi wrote:

> [T]he vernacular medium alone can stimulate originality in thought in largest number of persons.[37]

and therefore:

> We have to make them (that is, Indian languages) true representatives of our culture, our civilisation, of the true genius of our nation.[38]

But while advocating education in the mother tongue and development of the vernaculars, Gandhi was in no way insular or parochial. He emphasised:

> India has to flourish in her own climate and scenery and her own literature ... We and our children must build on our own heritage. If we borrow another, we impoverish our own. We can never grow on foreign victuals. I want the nation to have the treasures contained in that language, and for that matter in the other languages of the world, through its own vernaculars. I do not need to know Bengali in order to know the beauties of Rabindranath's matchless productions. I get them through good

---

* *Pedagogy does not just mean method of learning. It means the art and science of education. Its aim ranges from acquisition of skills to full development of the individual.*

translations.... Why need I learn English to get at the best of what Shakespeare and Milton thought and wrote?[39]

I do not want my house to be walled in all sides and my windows to be stuffed. I want the cultures of all lands to be blown about my house as freely as possible. But I refuse to be blown off my feet by any ... I would have our young men and women with literary tastes to learn as much of English and other world languages as they like, and then expect them to give the benefits of their learning to India and to the world like a Bose, a Roy or the Poet himself. But I would not have a single Indian to forget, neglect or be ashamed of his mother tongue, or to feel that he or she cannot think or express the best thoughts in his or her own vernacular.[40]

Aims of Education

For Gandhi, education did not mean "mere literacy".[41] For him, education meant the moral and spiritual upliftment of the people. As he explained in an interview to Carlton Washburne, education should aim at trying to

> develop courage, strength, virtue, the ability to forget oneself in working towards great goals. That is more important than literacy, academic learning is only a means towards this greater end.[42]

Gandhi emphasised that such a goal of education can only be achieved if education is viewed in a holistic manner, that is, it needed to embody the integrated development of the mind, body and soul. As he explained:

> Man is neither mere intellect, nor the gross animal body, nor the heart or soul alone. A proper and harmonious combination of all the three is required for the making of the whole man and constitutes the true economics of education.[43]

Based on this understanding, he defined the purpose of education to be:

> I would develop in the child his hands, his brain and his soul. The hands have almost atrophied. The soul has been altogether ignored.[44]

and further:

> By education I mean an all round drawing out of the best in child and man — body, mind and spirit.[45]

Nai Talim

Gandhi presented his vision of an alternate system of education that he called *Nai Talim* at the All India Educational Conference held in Wardha on October 22–23, 1937. The conference was attended by several well-known educationists and also the Ministers of Education of the seven elected provincial governments headed by the Congress Party.

At this conference, Gandhi outlined his plan to free India from Macaulayan education and establish in its place what he called *Buniyaadi Shiksha*, or Basic Education. Gandhi's basic proposition was simple: *place productive work at the centre of school curriculum, from which would organically emerge knowledge, values and skills.* Gandhi explained that he was not advocating the teaching of some handicraft side-by-side with so-called liberal education, but imparting the whole science and art of a craft through practical training and thereby imparting whole education. He explained his concept through the example of takli-spinning, and stated that through this, a student will not only garner knowledge of various varieties of cotton, but also of different soil-types, of the ruin of native industries under colonialism, of the history of British rule in India, and of basic arithmetic.[46]

Gandhi had himself often admitted that he had very little knowledge of educational theory. However, through common sense and experience, he had arrived at an educational pedagogy that is today accepted as a sound pedagogy for the harmonious development of 'head, heart and hand' or 'body, mind and spirit' — the concept of viewing productive work as a pedagogic medium.[47]

Gandhi's choice of occupations to be brought at the centre of the curriculum included:[48]

- Spinning
- Weaving
- Farming
- Animal husbandry and dairying
- Building and cleaning latrines
- Pottery
- Leather tanning
- Shoemaking

- Manual Agro-processing
- Forestry
- Horticulture
- Tailoring
- Ironsmithy and metal work
- Carpentry

In his pathbreaking pedagogical scheme, Gandhi intuitively had come to the same understanding as had been articulated by Dewey, the great American sociologist, three decades earlier. All these productive tasks have a strong knowledge-cum-skill content, including scientific, and each of them also has its own specific socio-cultural history. Education centred around these tasks therefore provided an excellent base for acquiring knowledge, formation of values, and building skills.[49]

But there was an even more revolutionary content to the Gandhian alternative educational model. Gandhi's education scheme incorporated Ambedkar's powerful critique of traditional caste-based Hindu society!

Even a casual look at the above list makes it clear that all these productive-manual occupations are undertaken by the lower castes/classes, and have historically carried the stigma of being inferior to the essentially non-productive and non-manual occupations of the upper castes/classes. By placing these manual occupations at the centre of school learning, Gandhi was according them a dignity they had never been given in Indian history.

Not only that, the Gandhian educational scheme also mounted a powerful challenge to the prevailing dichotomy between work and knowledge that has prevailed in India ever since the caste system deepened its hold on Indian society and that had continued under the British educational system. This dichotomy is rooted in the Brahminical concept that those who work with their hands and produce wealth are denied access to formal education while those who have access to formal education not only denigrate productive manual work but also lack the necessary skills for the same and often have a parasitic relationship with the society. The Gandhian proposal of Nai Talim struck at the very roots of this Brahminical-cum-colonial paradigm by placing productive manual work at the centre of the school curriculum itself.

As Krishna Kumar, one of India's best-known educationists, writes:

> Gandhi's scheme ... implied a violation of India's old concepts of learning.... 'Basic education' involved direct conflict with the indigenous tradition because it introduced into the school curriculum a form of knowledge on which low caste groups had monopoly. This kind of knowledge was not just given the status of a compulsory subject in the 'basic' plan; it was announced to be the core curriculum. In a school following this curriculum, a low-caste child would feel far more at home than an upper-caste child. Both in terms of worldview and functional skills, the curriculum of a 'basic' school favoured the child belonging to the lowest stratum of society. From this point of view, Gandhi's proposal intended to make the education system stand on its head.[50]

The Wardha Education Conference passed the following resolutions:[51]

(*i*) That free and compulsory education be provided on a nation-wide scale.
(*ii*) That the medium of instruction be the mother-tongue.
(*iii*) That the process of education should centre around some form of manual and productive work suitable for the local condition.

The Wardha Conference appointed a committee under the chairmanship of Dr. Zakir Husain to prepare a scheme of basic education on the lines of the above resolutions. The committee submitted its report in December 1937, approving Gandhiji's concept of *Nai Talim*.

The Haripura session of the Indian National Congress held in 1938, while accepting the above report, resolved to build up a national system of education which will, among others, aim at providing education "through the medium of some productive trade or handicraft and, to the extent possible, all other activities be built around this central craft, the latter being chosen in accordance with the conditions in which the child is placed."[52]

Reaction

That, however, is only one side of the educational discourse in India during the early 20th century. These proposals for universalisation of primary education faced strong resistance from India's traditional elites, the 'native' princes and the zamindars, the collaborators of the British in their rule over India, as well as many prominent Brahminical intellectuals. When Gokhale moved his Bill for compulsory primary education in the Central Assembly, these 'native' eminencies put forth the argument that conditions in the country were not ripe for such a Bill and that haste should be avoided. The Maharaja of Darbhanga went so far as to collect 11,000 signatures from princes and landlords on a memorandum expressing concern about what would happen to their farm operations if all children were required to attend school! Gokhale's proposal was soundly defeated.

Even the Western educated Indian middle classes were apathetic to the idea of State-funded compulsory primary education for the masses, due to their class/caste prejudices. Sizeable sections of them were in fact hostile towards it, an important reason being that they felt that State-funded compulsory primary education would mean a corresponding reduction in government funding for higher education. In the words of educationist Joseph Bara, the Indian middle class "had firmly entrenched itself into the bureaucracy and the social system in general and it could not compromise with any educational measure that it feared could destabilise their established social position."[53]

At the Wardha Education Conference, Mahatma Gandhi had to use all the moral powers at his command to persuade the Ministers of Education of the seven provinces where Congress had won the recently held elections to give priority to Basic Education (Nai Talim) of seven years and allocate adequate funds for this purpose. The Ministers continued to parrot the British argument that there was no money.[54] A definitive indicator that a majority of the Congress leadership was really not interested in fulfilling the promise to ensure free and compulsory education for all children once the country won independence.

Education in the Constitution

Note that during India's freedom struggle, the leaders of the movement made no distinction between fundamental rights (or civil and political rights) and social and economic rights. [Fundamental rights are those rights that are broadly included in the Right to Liberty (Right of Equality, Right of Freedom, Right to Freedom of Religion, etc.). The social and economic rights, included in the Directive Principles of the Indian Constitution, are those rights that guarantee all citizens the basic necessities of life; Amartya Sen defines them as basic entitlements.] They were seen as indivisible, and had developed as a common demand during the independence struggle.[55]

The distinction between these two sets of rights was only made during the drafting of fundamental rights by the Constituent Assembly. The Constituent Assembly in January 1947 voted to create an Advisory Committee that would report to the Constituent Assembly on the list of fundamental rights, minorities, etc. The Advisory Committee set up number of sub-committees for this purpose, one of which was the Fundamental Rights Sub-Committee chaired by Acharya Kripalani; among the members of the Rights Sub-Committee were B.R. Ambedkar, Minoo Masani, K.T. Shah and K.M. Munshi, to name a few. The Rights Sub-Committee during its deliberations decided to split fundamental rights and social-economic rights. The latter were included in the Directive Principles of Social Policy, as they were then called. The Sub-Committee drafted a preamble explaining that these were for general guidance of the government and were not cognizable in any court. Ambedkar, Munshi and Shah were not very happy with making the Directive Principles non-justiciable; they in fact would have preferred an even more rigorous social programme than that laid out in the Directive Principles, and a justiciable one at that. However, in the end, they went along with the majority view in the belief that half a loaf was better than none.[56]

The Rights Sub-Committee included the right to "free and compulsory education" for all children up to 14 years of age among the list of justiciable fundamental rights. The recommendation was considered by the Advisory Committee of the Constituent Assembly at its meeting on April 21–22, 1947. The Chairman of the Advisory Committee, Sardar Vallabhbhai Patel, directed the Advisory Committee to "restrict [ourselves] to the rights which are actually considered necessary ... and not go into detailed description of theoretical rights which are not enforceable at all." As if taking the cue from this caution, a member wondered, "Is this a justiciable right? Suppose the government has no money?" Another wanted the "deletion of this clause." Eventually a compromise was worked out. The provision was shifted to the list of Non-Justiciable Fundamental Rights (later to be termed as Directive Principles of State Policy, i.e. Part IV of the Constitution).[57] Yet another indicator of what was going to happen to the 'fundamental right' of all children to free and compulsory education after independence.

K.T. Shah was the only member of the Advisory Committee who gave a dissenting note. His note read:

> [O]nce an unambiguous declaration of such a right is made (justiciable), those responsible for it would have to find ways and means to give effect to it. If they had no such responsibility placed upon them, they might be inclined to avail themselves of every excuse to justify their own inactivity in the matter, indifference, or worse.[58]

His words have proven to be prophetic! This is precisely what has happened, as we shall see in the next chapters.

NOTES

1. Chris Harman, *A People's History of the World*, Orient Longman, New Delhi, 2005, p. 226.
2. David Clingingsmith, Jeffrey G. Williamson, *India's Deindustrialization in the 18th and 19th Centuries*, Harvard University, 2005, http://www.tcd.ie.
3. Noam Chomsky, *Year 501: The Conquest Continues*, South End Press, Boston, 1993, p. 13.
4. Irfan Habib, *A People's History of India, Vol. 20: Technology in Medieval India, c. 650–1750*, Tulika Books, New Delhi, p. 121.
5. J.P. Naik, Syed Nurullah, *A Student's History of Education in India, 1800–*

1973, Macmillan, Delhi, 1974, pp. 23–32; available on the internet at http://www.arvindguptatoys.com; Sabyasachi Bhattacharya (ed.), *The Contested Terrain: Perspectives on Education in India*, Orient Longman, Hyderabad, 1998, pp. 10–11.

6. See for instance: Irfan Habib, *Essays in Indian History*, Tulika Books, New Delhi, pp. 164–170; Uma Chakravarti, *Everyday Lives, Everday Histories: Beyond the Kings and Brahmanas of Ancient India*, Tulika Books, New Delhi, pp. 76–78.
7. For more on this, see: Irfan Habib, *A People's History of India, Vol. 20: Technology in Medieval India, c. 650–1750*, op. cit., pp. 120–27.
8. See, for example: Uma Chakravarti, *Everyday Lives, Everday Histories: Beyond the Kings and Brahmanas of Ancient India*, op. cit., pp. 144–45.
9. J.P. Naik, Syed Nurullah, *A Student's History of Education in India, 1800–1973*, op. cit., pp. 27–31.
10. Sabyasachi Bhattacharya (ed.), *The Contested Terrain: Perspectives on Education in India*, op. cit., p. 11.
11. This was also the opinion of Dr. Ambedkar. See for instance: Sasha Riser-Kositsky, "The Political Intensification of Caste: India Under the Raj", *Penn History Review*, University of Pennsylvania, Fall 2009, http://repository.upenn.edu.
12. J.P. Naik, Syed Nurullah, *A Student's History of Education in India, 1800–1973*, op. cit., p. 31.
13. See: *English Education Act 1835*, Wikipedia, http://en.wikipedia.org.
14. Poromesh Acharya, "Law and Politics of Primary Education in Bengal", in Sabyasachi Bhattacharya (ed.), *The Contested Terrain: Perspectives on Education in India*, op. cit., p. 229.
15. Satya Pal Ruhela, *India's Struggle to Universalize Elementary Education*, http://books.google.co.in; "A Consultation Paper on: Literacy in the Context of the Constitution of India", National Commission to Review the Working of the Constitution, September 26, 2001, http://lawmin.nic.in.
16. *Memorial to Hunter Comission by Jotirao Phule*, http://www.scribd.com.
17. Jayakumar Anagol, *Compulsory Primary Education: Challenges And Opportunities*, Centre for Multi-Disciplinary Development Research, Dharwad, p. 7, http://cmdr.ac.in; Ram Nath Sharma, *Problems of Education in India*, p. 108, http://books.google.co.in.
18. Jayakumar Anagol, ibid., p. 8.
19. *Sadler Commission Report 1917, Wardha Scheme of Education 1937*, http://mohitpuri.pbworks.com; Makrand Paranjape, *The Relevance of Mahatma Gandhi's Educational Philosophy for the 21st Century*, http://makarand.com.

20. G. Austin, *The Indian Constitution: Cornerstone of a Nation*, Oxford University Press, New Delhi, 1972, pp. 66–68; "Annie Besant – Indian National Congress", http://www.inc.in.
21. Bipan Chandra, Aditya Mukherjee, Mridula Mukherjee, *India After Independence*, Penguin Books, India, 2000, p. 35; G. Austin, ibid., p. 69; "Nehru Report 1928 excerpts", https://sites.google.com.
22. Harkishan Singh Surjeet, "Struggle to Consolidate the Republic's Gains", *People's Democracy*, January 29, 2006, http://archives.peoples democracy.in.
23. Geeta Nambissan, "Equity in Education? – Schooling of Dalit Children in India", *Economic and Political Weekly*, April 20–27, 1996, www.teindia.nic.in; Madhu Prasad, "Commoditising Higher Education: The Assault of Neoliberal Barbarism" in Ravi Kumar (ed.), *Education, State and Market: Anatomy of Neoliberal Impact*, Aakar Books, Delhi, 2014, p. 89.
24. Hari Narke, "Dnyanajyoti Savitribai Phule – I", September 6, 2012, http://roundtableindia.co.in.
25. For more on their contributions, see: Sabyasachi Bhattacharya (ed.), *Education and the Disprivileged: Nineteenth and Twentieth Century India*, Orient Blackswan, http://books.google.co.in.
26. Sanil Neelakandan and Smita Patil, "Complexities of Inclusion and Exclusion: Dalit Students and Higher Education in India", 2012, http://www104.griffith.edu.au; *Ayyankali*, Wikipedia, accessed on March 28, 2014, http://en.wikipedia.org; *Poykayil Johannan*, Wikipedia, accessed on March 28, 2014, http://en.wikipedia.org.
27. A. Loyola, *Iyothee Thass Pandithar (1845–1914)*, http://loyolatony.blogspot.in; *Iyothee Thass – A Writer, Journalist, Social Reformer and Buddhist Scholar*, http://mulnivasiorganiser.bamcef.org; K. Velmangai and L. Selvamuthu Kumarasami, *Iyothee Thass and Depressed Class Intellectuals' Print and Press Media in Liberation Struggle in Tamil Nadu*, January 2013, www.isrj.net.
28. J.P. Naik, *The Education Commission and After*, APH Publishing Corporation, New Delhi, 1997, pp. 2–3, available on internet at www.arvindguptatoys.com.
29. "Minute by the Hon'ble T.B. Macaulay, dated February 2, 1835", http://www.columbia.edu.
30. M.K. Gandhi, *Hind Swaraj or Indian Home Rule*, pp. 84–85, http://www.mkgandhi.org/ebks.
31. Anil Sadgopal, "Countering Neoliberal Conception of Knowledge, Building Emancipatory Discourse: A Historical Overview of Phule–

Ambedkar's Critique and Gandhian Nai Talim", in Ravi Kumar (ed.), *Education, State and Market: Anatomy of Neoliberal Impact*, Aakar Books, 2014, pp. 248–49; Mohit Chakrabarti, *The Gandhian Dimensions of Education*, p. 123, http://books.google.co.in.

32. Ravi S. Samuel, *A Comprehensive Study of Education*, pp. 231–32, http://books.google.co.in; also: Anil Sadgopal, ibid., p. 248.
33. Speech at Y.M.C.A., Madras, April 27, 1915 – cited in: "Gandhi on Education", National Council for Teacher Education, www.ncte-india.org; Anil Sadgopal, ibid., p. 242.
34. *Young India*, June 1, 1921, cited in: M.K. Gandhi, "Literary Education", http://www.mkgandhi.org; Anil Sadgopal, ibid., pp. 242–43.
35. *Young India*, March 20, 1924, cited in: M.K. Gandhi, "New Education to be Rooted in the Culture and Life of the People", http://www.mkgandhi.org; Anil Sadgopal, ibid., p. 243.
36. Anil Sadgopal, ibid., p. 242.
37. *Young India*, April 21, 1920; cited in: Mohit Chakrabarti, *The Gandhian Dimensions of Education*, p. 122, http://books.google.co.in.
38. Anil Sadgopal, "Countering Neoliberal Conception of Knowledge, Building Emancipatory Discourse: A Historical Overview of Phule–Ambedkar's Critique and Gandhian Nai Talim", op. cit., p. 248.
39. *Harijan*, July 9, 1936, p. 176, cited in: Mohit Chakrabarti, *The Gandhian Dimensions of Education*, op. cit., p. 125.
40. Nirmal Kumar Bose, *My Days with Gandhi*, p. 54, http://books.google.co.in.
41. *Indian Opinion*, May 18, 1907, cited in: "Gandhi on Education", National Council for Teacher Education, www.ncte-india.org.
42. Carlton Wasburne, "Remakers of Mankind", 1932, pp. 104-05, cited in: Mohit Chakrabarti, *The Gandhian Dimensions of Education*, op. cit., p. 114.
43. Anil Sadgopal, "Countering Neoliberal Conception of Knowledge, Building Emancipatory Discourse: A Historical Overview of Phule–Ambedkar's Critique and Gandhian Nai Talim", op. cit., p. 247.
44. Ibid., p. 244.
45. *Harijan*, July 31, 1937, p. 197, cited in: Mohit Chakrabarti, *The Gandhian Dimensions of Education*, op. cit., p. 97.
46. *Position Paper : National Focus Group On Work And Education*, NCERT, 2007, pp. 3–4, http://www.ncert.nic.in; Makrand Paranjape, "The Relevance of Mahatma Gandhi's Educational Philosophy for the 21st Century", http://makarand.com.
47. Anil Sadgopal, "Countering Neoliberal Conception of Knowledge,

Building Emancipatory Discourse: A Historical Overview of Phule–Ambedkar's Critique and Gandhian Nai Talim", op. cit., pp. 247–48.

48. Ibid., p. 252.
49. Ibid.
50. Krishna Kumar, *Political Agenda of Education*, pp. 179–180, http://www.arvindguptatoys.com.
51. *Introduction to Wardha Scheme of Basic Education-1937*, http://www.kkhsou.in.
52. *Position Paper: National Focus Group On Work And Education*, op. cit.
53. Poromesh Acharya, "Law and Politics of Primary Education in Bengal", pp. 229–49; and Joseph Bara, "Colonialism and Educational Fragmentation in India", pp. 150–61; both essays in: Sabyasachi Bhattacharya (ed.), *The Contested Terrain: Perspectives on Education in India*, op. cit.
54. Anil Sadgopal, "Right to Education vs. Right to Education Act", *Social Scientist*, September–December 2010, http://www.scribd.com.
55. For more on this, see: G. Austin, *The Indian Constitution: Cornerstone of a Nation*, Chapter 3, op. cit.; also: Jayna Kothari, *Social Rights and the Constitution*, Eastern Book Company, http://www.ebc-india.com.
56. G. Austin, ibid., pp. 95–101.
57. Anil Sadgopal, "Right to Education vs. Right to Education Act", op. cit.; "How was the Original Article 45 of the Constitution Arrived At?", http://righttoeducation.in; M.S. Thirumalai, B. Mallikarjun, "The Evolution of Language Policy in the Constituent Assembly of India", Language in India, March 3, 2006, www.languageinindia.com.
58. S.N. Chaudhary (ed.), *Human Rights and Poverty in India: Theoretical Issues and Empirical Evidences*, Vol. IV, p. 180, http://books.google.co.in.

3

EDUCATION POLICIES DURING THE NEHRU ERA

Where the mind is without fear and the head is held high;
Where knowledge is free;
Where the world has not been broken up into fragments by narrow domestic walls;
Where words come out from the depth of truth;
Where tireless striving stretches its arms towards perfection;
Where the clear stream of reason has not lost its way into the dreary desert sand of dead habit;
Where the mind is led forward by thee into ever-widening thought and action –
Into that heaven of freedom, my Father, let my country awake.

– ***Rabindranath Tagore***

Mixed Economy Model, 1947–80

Most people think Nehru was a socialist and his 'mixed economy model' was meant to develop socialism in India. The reality is quite the opposite. The development model implemented in India under Nehru's leadership was essentially a model of capitalist development. Its most essential features—the public sector and the private sector, the Industrial Policy Resolutions of 1948 and 1956, and restrictions on foreign capital inflows—closely followed the economic plan proposed by the "Post-War Economic Development Committee" set up by the Indian capitalists in 1942. The committee comprised of eight leading Indian industrialists, including Purshottamdas Thakurdas, J.R.D. Tata, G.D. Birla and Sri Ram. Its proposal, titled

A Plan of Economic Development of India, popularly came to be known as the Bombay Plan or the Tata–Birla Plan.[1]

After winning independence, the Indian capitalist class was keen to duplicate the industrial revolution of the developed capitalist countries at an accelerated speed. That meant high priority be given to development of core and heavy industries. As the Bombay Plan put it: "In carrying out the stages of development, we shall have to pay special attention to basic industries.... On these industries will depend the development not only of all other industries but of the whole economic life of the country." During the colonial period, the indigenous capitalists had been dependent on foreign plant and machinery to set up their industries; post-independence, independent industrial development of India was only possible if this dependence was broken. The Bombay Plan was very clear on this. It stated: "Till these industries are developed, we shall naturally be at the mercy of foreign countries. To shorten this period of dependence it is necessary to give priority to basic industries over other industries and thus to speed up development."[2]

However, indigenous development of heavy and core industries required massive long-term investments, often with low profits and that too accruing after a time lag. In 1947, the Indian capitalists did not have the capital needed to set up these industries, nor did they have such long-term staying power. The only other solution was investment by the State. The Indian capitalists observed: "In executing [such] a comprehensive plan of economic development, especially in a country where the beginnings of such development have yet to be laid, the State should exercise ... a considerable measure of intervention and control." Explaining this further, J.R.D. Tata stated that "State control of industries and even ownership of some industries" was not to be considered from a "narrow capitalist point of view", rather, it was to be supported as it was "essential for the achievement of a rapid rise in general standard of living." Better results, said the Bombay Plan, would be yielded by a combination of State and private enterprise, each doing what is "appropriate" for that sector, rather than by having only free enterprise.[3]

Thakurdas–Tata–Birla recommended to Nehru that large scale

projects in energy, transportation, steel, oil, telecom and other infrastructural areas be set up in the public sector, using the hard-earned savings of the people and by burdening them with indirect taxes. The Indian capitalist class invested its limited capital in consumer goods industries where there were quick profits to be made. Even here, a major part of the financing was done by the public sector financial institutions, while the running of the industry and siphoning off of the profits was left in the hands of the Indian capitalists. Till the late 1970s, the total assets of many of India's biggest industrialists—including luminaries like Tatas, Birlas, Mafatlals and Singhanias—in the total assets of the companies they controlled was less than one percent![4]

The Indian State transferred huge sums to the capitalist classes through other mechanisms too—such as lucrative contracts and procurement policies, a variety of subsidies, and tolerance of fairly widespread and growing tax evasion.

The Indian State intervened in the economy in many other ways to help the growth of domestic capitalism—rationing scarce resources and directing them to planned uses, putting in place a regulatory regime to reduce industrial concentration and promote a more dispersed industrial sector, adopting special measures to promote the growth of small-scale industry, and so on. It also actively intervened to limit the penetration and influence of foreign capital. For instance, foreign multinational corporations were not allowed to enter strategic sectors of the economy. Even in the areas where they could invest, restrictions were imposed on the quantum of investment and conditions were imposed on profit repatriation.

Nehruvian Model and Education

The first few decades after independence saw rapid growth in the education system. By 1988–89, the education system in India employed 4.2 million teachers and enrolled 154 million students in 7,76,000 institutions. The primary education system was the largest sector in the education system, accounting for nearly 62% of the total students and teachers and 70% of the educational institutions (Table 3.1).[5]

Table 3.1: Growth of Education in India[6]

	Primary	*Upper Primary*	*Secondary*	*Higher Secondary*
Enrolment (in millions)				
1950–51	19.1	3.1	1.2	0.42
1988–89	95.7	30.9	18.4	9.21
Increase (%)	401%	897%	1433%	2093%
Institutions (in thousands)				
1950–51	209.7	13.6	7.3	0.84
1988–89	548.1	144.1	73.3	10.48
Increase (%)	161%	960%	904%	1148%
Teachers (in millions)				
1950–51	0.54	0.09	0.13	0.024
1988–89	1.60	1.03	1.24	0.307*
Increase (%)	196%	1044%	854%	1179%

* *Refers to the year 1982–83*

In absolute terms the expansion of the education system appears to be huge. However, that is because it began from a very low base, due to the utter neglect of the education system during the colonial period. In reality, these figures hide a complete betrayal of the dreams of the freedom struggle by the leaders of post-independent India: (i) to build a national system of education replacing Macaulayan education; and (ii) to provide free and compulsory education to all children.

(i) Betrayal of Promise to Build a National System of Education

The noted educationist J.P. Naik writes that because of the long and intense debate regarding educational policy that took place during the pre-independence period, it was expected of post-independent India's leadership that it would take concrete steps to prepare a blueprint for a national system of education. Gandhi had proposed one such scheme of 'Basic Education' (Nai Talim) in 1937. As we have seen in the previous chapter, there was considerable resistance within the Congress to Gandhi's proposal of Nai Talim; if the Congress passed a resolution at its Haripura session endorsing its basic elements, it was basically out of reverence to Gandhi's stature. And therefore, soon after Gandhi's death, it was thrown into the wastepaper basket. Be that as it may, no attempt was made by the Congress leadership to build any other national system of education. On the contrary, instead of viewing the entire spectrum of education in a holistic manner, the Nehru Government continued to view education in a fragmentary manner just like the British had done. It first appointed a Commission for university education in 1948, and then another for secondary education in 1952.

Kothari Commission

The first Commission to examine comprehensively almost all aspects of the education system was only set up in 1964 by a government resolution dated July 14, 1964, a month after Nehru's death. The Commission did commendable work and its report, submitted in 1966, is considered to be a landmark in the history of Indian education. In the words of the renowned educationist J.P. Naik, member-secretary of the Commission and who played an important part in drafting the voluminous report, the Commission aimed to create a democratic, secular and egalitarian society, which would be based on science and spiritual values and wherein the evils of poverty, ignorance and ill-health would be eliminated through humane use of scientific and technical knowledge.[7] It emphasised the critical role of education in social and economic development, and observed that education "determines the level of prosperity, welfare and security of the people."[8]

The Kothari Commission's recommendations were of a far-reaching nature, and had the Indian government implemented them in a holistic manner, they would have had a major transformative impact on Indian society. The government however examined its recommendations in a piecemeal manner.[9] While accepting some of its recommendations, such as the suggestion to set up what is known as the 10+2+3 structural pattern of education, it trashed its most important recommendations. We take a look at two of these important recommendations of the Kothari Commission that have remained unimplemented till date—no Central government has had the political will to implement them. (A third important recommendation that has also never been implemented is discussed in the next section of this chapter.)

(a) Setting up a Common School System

The Indian Constitution forbids an education system that reinforces inequality and socio-economic stratification. The Kothari Commission made a strong plea for implementation of this fundamental feature of the Indian Constitution, and recommended the setting up of a 'common school system' to provide equitable education to all children regardless of the economic status of their parents.

The Commission stated: "History shows numerous instances where small social groups and elites have used education as a prerogative of their rule and as a tool for maintaining their hegemony and perpetuating values upon which it has rested." It observed that the education system in India is also tending to reinforce the traditional hierarchy that has existed for centuries in Indian society: at present, the education system in India "is tending to increase social segregation and to perpetuate and widen class distinctions. At the primary stage, the free schools to which the masses send their children are maintained by the government and local authorities are generally of poor quality. Some of the private schools are definitely better; but since many of them charge high fees, they are availed of only by the middle and the higher classes. At the secondary stage, a large proportion of the good schools are private but many of them also charge high fees which are normally beyond the means of any but the top ten percent of the people, though some of the middle class parents make great sacrifices to send their children to them. There is thus segregation in education itself—the minority of private, fee-charging, better schools meeting the needs of the upper classes and the vast bulk of free, publicly maintained, but poor schools being utilised by the rest. What is worse, this segregation is increasing and tending to widen the gulf between the classes and the masses."

The Commission unequivocally maintained: "In a democracy, the individual is an end in himself and the primary purpose of education is to provide him with the widest opportunity to develop his potentialities to the full." It went on to state: "In a situation of the type we have in India, it is the responsibility of the educational system to bring the different social classes and groups together and thus promote the emergence of an egalitarian and integrated society."

Based on these observations, the Commission came up with the profound recommendation:

> If these evils are to be eliminated and the educational system is to become a powerful instrument of national development in general, and social and national integration in particular, we must move towards the goal of a common school system of public education
>
> - which will be open to all children, irrespective of caste, creed, community, religion, economic conditions or social status;
> - where access to good education will depend not on wealth or class but on talent;
> - which will maintain adequate standards in all schools ...
> - in which no tuition fee will be charged.[10]

On April 5, 1967, the Government of India constituted a committee of Members of Parliament to consider the report of the Commission and prepare the draft of a statement on the National Policy on Education. One of the salient recommendations of the Committee was:[11]

> The unhealthy social segregation that now takes place between the schools for the rich and those for the poor should be ended; and the primary schools should be made the common schools of the nation by making it obligatory on all children, irrespective of cast, creed, community, religion, economic condition or social status,to attend the primary school in their neighbourhood.

However, the government made no effort to implement this recommendation of the Kothari Commission and that was subsequently endorsed by *Report of the Committee of Members of Parliament on Education.* Had it done so, it would have been an important blow to India's hierarchical society, and laid the foundations for a truly egalitarian society.

(b) Education in Indian Languages

The centrepiece of the Macaulayan education policy was denigration of Indian vernaculars and promoting education in the English language. Macaulay himself had admitted that this would lead to the formation of a class of clerks and interpreters who would help the British rule over India. And so, from the very beginning, the leaders of India's freedom struggle voiced the demand that education in the English language be replaced with education in Indian languages. Even though the Congress leadership may have differed on other aspects of an alternate national policy of education vis a vis the British colonial education policy, on this issue, there was a broad consensus. Gandhi had unequivocally stated:

> Among the many evils of foreign rule, this blighting imposition of a foreign medium upon the youth of the country will be counted by history as one of the greatest. It has sapped the energy of the nation, it has shortened the lives of the pupils. It has estranged them from the masses; it has made education unnecessarily expensive. If this process is still persisted in, it bids fair to rob the nation of its soul. The sooner, therefore, educated India shakes itself free from the hypnotic spell of the foreign medium, the better it would be for them and the people.[12]

Let us discuss the significance of this demand voiced during India's freedom struggle in greater detail, as today, there is a complete backpedalling on this issue in the country.

Language at the Primary Level

So far as education at the primary level is concerned, there is complete unanimity among educational experts that children should receive basic education in their mother tongue. Educational psychologists have pointed out the close link between mother tongue and emotional and cognitive development in children. When learning is disseminated in the mother tongue language, it is easier for the learners to grasp the concepts and build their own intellectual skills. Their creativity and critical thinking abilities are enhanced and it becomes easier for them to express themselves effectively.[13] To quote from a report by a UNESCO committee of experts way back in 1953:

> It is axiomatic that the best medium for teaching a child is his mother tongue. Psychologically, it is the system of meaningful signs that in his mind works automatically for expression and understanding. Sociologically, it is a means of identification among the members of the community to which he belongs. Educationally, he learns more quickly through it than through an unfamiliar linguistic medium.

Explaining why in the early stages children should be imparted education in the mother tongue, D.P. Pattanayak, the renowned linguist and educationist explains:[14]

> For a child, learning a language is not easy, as it is a difficult process to isolate meaningful units from flowing language. To master the complexity of moving from letter to syllable to word to sentence and context, the child takes about four years. In learning language and social meaning of the different words and sentences, a child needs a collaborator. Scholars who have studied children from birth have established that the mother is the first collaborator in communication for the child, as the child comprehends her from birth. She is the first 'other'. Then gradually, this 'other' extends to family, extended family, kin group, village community, and so on.

Even if children need to be taught a second language other than their mother tongue, today, it is acknowledged that when children are taught throughout primary school in their mother tongue, and then gradually transition to learning a second language in secondary school, they learn the second language quickly. This has also been accepted in a UNICEF report:

> (T)here is ample research showing that students are quicker to learn to read and acquire other academic skills when first taught in their mother tongue. They also learn a second language more

Box 3.1: Importance of Education in Mother Tongue

Prof. D.P. Pattanayak
Reputed Indian Linguist and Educationist

Piaget [Jean Piaget, the renowned Swiss developmental psychologist and philosopher known for his epistemological studies with children], following the growing-up of children, reached the conclusion that the child learns what he or she is prepared to learn. In terms of language use, this means that the language in which the child is prepared to learn, the language through which he or she apprehends meaning, must be the medium of his or her primary education. The language which the child knows well, in which he or she can form sentences and express meanings, and that is his or her own, is the best medium of education. In later stages, if a child's peers speak English or Hindi, then he or she will learn English or Hindi. Once the mother tongue is established for the child, he or she may learn English or Hindi as a subject and prepare to move over to using those languages as a medium. But English as the medium of primary education is harmful for the child; there is no doubt about it. The language that brings joy to the child is good for learning, reading and writing. ...

To move from the known to the unknown, from the recognised to the unrecognised, is the mark of a living education. The growing child seeks momentary mental shelter in the known environment and among known characters. The small child ready to bloom, ready to learn, wants to grow up accumulating and assimilating newer experiences. But where there is nobody to answer a question, where there is a word but no meaning, where there are people without identity, where there is a message but nobody to share it, how frightening it is to grow up in such a situation. ...

Those who ignore this and plead for primary education in English are responsible for stealing the children's childhood from them.

[Source: Adama Ouane (ed.), "Towards a Multilingual Culture of Education", pp. 27–28, *UNESCO Institute for Education, 2003, www.unesco.org.]*

quickly than those initially taught to read in an unfamiliar language.[15]

On the contrary, if children are forced to start learning the second language too quickly, it is a recipe for 'pedagogic disaster'. As a UNESCO report points out, "their self-confidence as learners and their interest in what they are learning may decline, leading to lack of motivation, school failure, and early school leaving."[16] It kills the creativity of the child and stunts his/her mental growth (See Box 3.1).

And so the Kothari Commission unequivocally recommended that children be taught only in their mother tongues at the lower primary stage till Class IV, and no other language including English be introduced till then.[17]

Language at Secondary and College Levels

After independence, the Official Language Commission of the Government of India, in its report of 1956, recommended the replacement of English with Indian languages not just at the primary level, but also in higher education, as a part of a policy to replace English with Indian languages in all spheres of life, including administration and the courts.[18]

The Kothari Commission too emphasised this. To quote from the report:[19]

> It is hardly necessary to emphasise that the development of the Indian languages is both urgent and essential for the development of the Indian people and as a way of bringing together the elite and the masses. It can make scientific and technical knowledge more easily accessible to the people in their own languages and thus help not only in the progress of industrialisation but also in the wider dissemination of science and the scientific outlook ...
>
> The development of the modem Indian languages is inextricably linked with the importance given to them in the educational system, specially at the university stage. The medium selected should enable students to acquire knowledge with facility, to express themselves with clarity and to think with precision and vigour. From this point of view, the claims of the mother tongue are preeminent ...
>
> Learning through a foreign medium compels the students to concentrate on cramming instead of mastering the subject matter.

Box 3.2: Why English Needs to be Displaced by Indian Languages

(T)here is a fundamental difference between the system of governance under which we lived until 1947 and the system which we have forged for ourselves in the Indian Constitution since then... The British Government had a different relationship with the masses of India ... since they did not draw their power from the people of the country or depend for its exercise on majorities in parliamentary legislatures, (they) could afford to conduct the administration in a language that was not understood ... by the vast masses of the country." In constrast, "Our Constitution has enfranchised the entire adult male and female population of the country .... The Indian citizen of today has potentially a greater stake and through his elected representatives the final voice in the affairs of the government of the country .... Is it conceivable against this background that we should continue to carry on the country's administration in all its higher levels in a language which is not understood by 99% of the country's population? Does it not constitute inherently a grave danger to the smooth and peaceful working out of democratic processes ... that the functioning of all superior administrative personnel and of law courts and of everybody of importance and authority in public life, should be in a language outside the comprehension of practically the entire population affected?

["Report of the Official Language Commission", pp. 31-42, Government of India, 1956.]

> Moreover, as a matter of sound educational policy, the medium of education in school and higher education should generally be the same. As we have rightly adopted the regional languages as the media of education at the school stage, it follows that we should adopt them increasingly at the higher stage also.

The Commission quoted Rabindranath Tagore from a speech he had delivered thirty years ago:[20].

> In no country in the world, except India, is to be seen this divorce of the language of education from the language of the pupil. A full hundred years have not elapsed since Japan took its initiation

into Western culture. At the outset she had to take recourse to textbooks written in foreign languages, but from the very first, her objective had been to arrive at the stage of ranging freely over the subjects of study in the language of the country. It was because Japan had recognised the need of such studies, not as an ornament for a select section of her citizens, but for giving power and culture to all of them, that she deemed it to be of prime importance to make them universally available to her people. And in this effort of Japan to gain proficiency in the Western arts and sciences, which was to give her the means of self-defence against the predatory cupidity of foreign powers, to qualify her to take an honoured place in the comity of nations, no trouble or expense was spared. Least of all was there the miserly folly of keeping such learning out of easy reach, within the confines of a foreign language.

And so the Commission recommended that urgent steps be taken so that this changeover from English to Indian languages can take place in at the most ten years, as the problem will only become more complex and difficult with the passage of time.[21]

Betrayal on the Language Issue

In post-independent India, in the initial years, some effort was made to promote education in the many languages of India. However, English continued to remain the most important medium of instruction in education, for several reasons. The Indian State had continued with the British administrative and judicial system after independence, and its language continued to be English. English continued to be the dominant medium of instruction in higher education. Most importantly, the Indian elites and middle classes, who had been trained in the British education system, were comfortable with English; moreover, being generally from the upper classes and castes, they had little concern for the Indian masses (we have pointed out in the previous chapter that the Indian middle classes were apathetic to providing compulsory and primary education to all children in the country); and so they made no serious effort to replace English with Indian languages even in schools.

Box 3.3: Why Can't We Teach Science and Do Research in Indian Languages?

Supporters of English argue that English is a leading international language, and science teaching and scientific-technological development can only be done in the English language. Indian languages are not developed enough for this.

Today, the world population is 700 crores. All the leading countries of the world in science, technology, literature, philosophy and other branches of knowledge impart education to their children and carry out all their scientific research, government work and economic transactions and business in their native languages. These countries include Russia (4% of the world population), Japan (2%), Germany (2%), France (3%), other West European countries (6%) and China (20%). All these countries do all their work in their native language, and not English. Spain and a number of Latin American countries who together constitute 8% of the global population do all their work in the Spanish language. In contrast, English is the mother language of only England, Canada, United States, Australia and New Zealand, who together constitute just 6% of the global population.

Compare this to the proportion of people speaking Indian languages in the global population. People who speak Hindi and Hindi dialects together constitute 7% of the global population. The share of Indian languages in the global population is a huge 17%. If countries with just 2–4% of the global population can teach science and do scientific research in their native languages, then why can't India with 17% of the world population teach its children science and do scientific research in Indian languages?

Russian, Italian, Spanish, Arabic, Turkish and other languages developed because their respective countries promoted their use in schools and colleges, research, trade, administration, technology and other areas, which led to the gradual development of these languages. As science, technology, the arts, law and other fields developed, common people/artisans/literateurs coined words to explain different new concepts, and thus the vocabulary of these languages gradually got enriched. In India, because the language of science and technology and higher education has remained English since the advent of the British, the growth of Indian languages has remained stunted, which is why it is difficult to teach science in Indian languages today.

[Source: Sulabha Brahme, "Engrezi Madyamacha Ved", Shankar Brahme Samaj Vigyan Granthalaya, 129 B/2, Erandwane, Pune.]

As the Indian society got more and more polarised due to the economic model implemented in post-independent India, a language segregation took place in the country. English became the common language of the elites all over the country. Gradually, it also came to be that knowledge of English became essential for getting a good job. Not just the upper classes, even the lower classes began aspiring to send their children to English-medium schools. Over time, English-medium schools—even at the primary level—began sprouting up all across the country. This has hobbled the creativity and learning abilities of children, forcing them to learn by rote instead of learning being a joyful experience.

What is far more worse, as children from poor families are unable to cope with English education, this has been an important contributing factor to the very high school drop-out rate in the country.

(ii) Betrayal of Constitutional Promise of 'Education for All'

Article 45 of the Constitution of India directs the Indian State to provide within ten years of the commencement of the Constitution "free and compulsory education to all children" up to the age of 14 years. This has been interpreted to include: (a) elementary education of eight years (Class I–VIII) for the 6–14 age group children; and (b) early childhood care, nutrition, health and pre-primary education (kindergarten, nursery) for children below six years of age.[22]

Post-independence history stands witness to the neglect and disdain with which this critical provision has been treated by the State. In the late 1980s, that is, more than four decades after independence, of the estimated 153 million Indian children between the ages of 6 and 14 years, as many as 28 million had never gone to school.[23] And of those enrolling in Class I, a majority dropped out before completing Class VIII. The drop-out rate at the primary level (Class I–V) in 1987–88 was 46.97%, and 62.29% at the elementary level (Class I–VIII).[24] Even for those children in school, the quality of education being imparted left much to be desired. The government itself admitted that in 1986, as many as 60% of the primary schools—a whopping 3.2 lakh schools—had at the most two teachers (27.47% had only one teacher and 32.38% two teachers), and 37.8% of the primary schools had only two instructional rooms![25]

So far as providing early childhood care, nutrition, health and pre-primary education for children below six years of age is concerned, official data as to the state of delivery of these services is very scant. But that this too was severely neglected by independent India's leadership and the neglect has continued till today is obvious from the fact that malnutrition in children under five years of age in India continues to be amongst the highest in the world. According to UNICEF, nearly half—48%—of children under the age of five are too short for their age (stunted), an indicator of chronic malnourishment; and 70% children in the age 6–59 months are anaemic.[26] In the case of Scheduled Castes (SCs) and Scheduled Tribes (STs), the situation is far worse—despite Article 46 of the Constitution directing the State to "promote with special care the educational and economic interests ... of the Scheduled Castes and the Scheduled Tribes ..."[27]

What explains this distressing situation in the field of elementary education, four decades after independence? That too, when the founding fathers of the nation had directed the State to provide free and compulsory to all children, and that too, urgently, within a period of ten years—the only constitutional provision with a time frame!

Reason One: Low Investment in Education

The most important reason for India's failure to universalise elementary education was inadequate public investment in education. Why did India's ruling classes not make sufficient investment in education, especially elementary education? The answer lies in the basic orientation of the 'mixed economy model'. Its primary aim was to promote broad-based development of indigenous industry along capitalist lines. With the Indian State having only limited resources in the immediate post-independence period, and since it was more interested in using these scarce resources to help the indigenous capitalist classes to grow, it made only minimal investment to provide essential services like education and health to the people. During the entire period of Nehru's prime ministership, the proportion of GNP spent on education remained at below 2%. (This issue is discussed in greater detail later in this chapter; see also Chart 3.1.)

Kothari Commission: Increase Expenditure on Education to 6% of GDP

The Kothari Commission, which rightly emphasised the close relationship between educational expenditure and development, observed:

> [T]he proportion of national income devoted to education in India is small in comparison with that in educationally advanced countries of the world. The absolute amount per capita spent by us on education is about one-hundredth of that spent by a highly industrialised country like the USA. This reflects the close interaction and interlocking between the level of education and the level of industrialisation.

After a detailed review of the trends in expenditure on education in the past and based on certain reasonable assumptions regarding economic growth and population growth over the next 20-year period, and after making detailed comparisons with other countries, the Commission came up with the recommendation that "if education is to develop adequately", the proportion of GDP* allocated to education must rise from 2.9% in 1965–66 to 6.0% in 1985–86.[28]

The Kothari Commission's recommendation of allocating 6% of the national income to education has been endorsed later by several other international organisations. The International Commission on Education for the 21st Century (Delors Commission), in its report submitted to the UNESCO in 1996 has argued: "Increasing public spending on education, in place of expenditure under other budget

* *Note: The Kothari Commission has actually mentioned GNP and not GDP. For India in the 1960s-70s, GNP and GDP were very similar, as the country was a closed economy and there was not much foreign investment. Today, with the economy opened up to foreign investment, GDP is usually used for measuring national income, and GNP is losing its meaning, and so in this booklet, we are using GDP as a measure of national income in preference to GNP. For more on GDP and GNP, see: "Gross Domestic Product", Springer, www.springer.com.*

heads, should be regarded as a necessity everywhere, and especially in developing countries, since it is a vital investment for the future. As a rule of thumb, not less than 6 percent of GNP should be devoted to education." UNESCO and UNDP have also favoured it, as a desirable level for developing countries.[29]

Chart 3.1: India: Share of Public Expenditure on Education as Percentage of GDP[30]

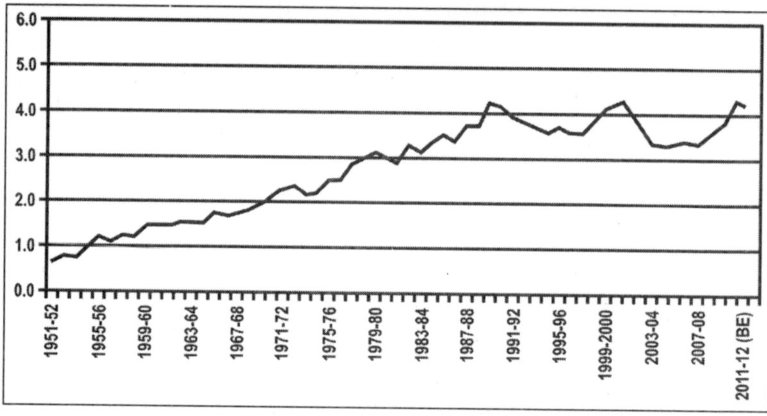

Of the several recommendations made by the Commission, this is one that was accepted by the Government of India in its National Policy on Education of 1968: "To increase the investment in education so as to reach a level of expenditure of 6 percent of the national income as early as possible."[31] However, it made no serious effort to implement it. The expenditure on education increased very slowly, and only reached 3.5% of the GDP by 1985–86 and actually decreased to 3.4% the next year (Chart 3.1). In subsequent years, the government repeatedly reiterated the promise to devote 6% of national income to education, in every Five Year Plan, in every policy statement, economic survey(s), reports of the Ministry of Education/Human Resource Development, reports of several committees/commissions on education, and even in the Independence Day speeches of the Prime Minister from the ramparts of the Red Fort. But in practice, the rate of increase has virtually flattened. After crossing 4% in 1989–90, it again slid down to 3.6% by 1997–98. It again rose to above 4% at the beginning of the present century (2000–01), only to fall back in the following years. The Eleventh Five Year Plan (2007–12) was proclaimed as an 'Education Plan'. But even during this Plan period, expenditure on education only gradually inched up, rising from a dismal 3.4% of the GDP in 2007–08 to reach only 4.2% of the GDP in 2010–11, and then fell to 4.17% of GDP in 2011–12 (Chart 3.1).[32]

Table 3.2: Expenditure on Education in Five Year Plans[33]
(Rs in million)

	At Constant Prices (1970–71)	*% of Total Plan Outlay*
I Plan (1951–56)	304	7.86
II Plan (1956–61)	526	5.83
III Plan (1961–66)	966	6.87
IV Plan 1966–74)	764	5.17
V Plan (1974–79)	585	3.27
VI Plan (1980–85)	1088	2.70
VII Plan (1985–90)*	2540	3.70

* *Likely expenditure.*

Chart 3.2: Expenditure on Education in Five Year Plans[34]
(% of Plan Outlay)

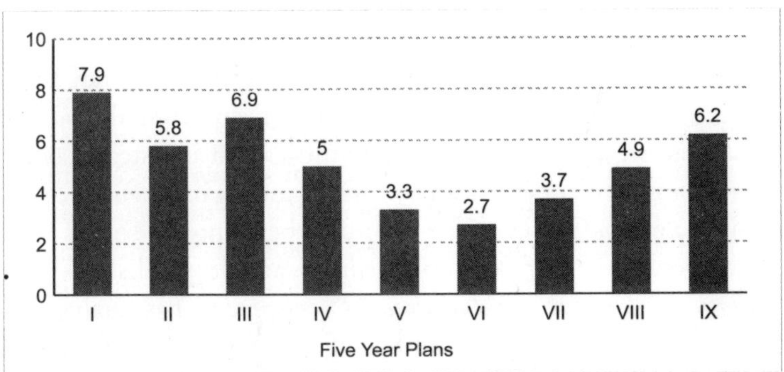

Plan allocation denotes current priorities and the government's commitment to new initiatives. The Kothari Commission had strongly recommended that "the efforts to increase allocations to education should be intensified." The utter disdain with which the Government of India took the recommendations of the Kothari Commission is obvious from the fact that Plan allocations to education (in real terms) actually went down after the Kothari Commission submitted its report, that is, during the Fourth and Fifth Plan periods (see column 2, Table 3.2)!

One can observe from the third column in Table 3.2 (depicted graphically in Chart 3.2) that the relative importance given to education in the Five Year Plans has also declined during the post-Commission period. In the first three Five Year Plans, on average about 6% of the total Five Year Plan expenditure was spent on education. After that, in the Fourth Five Year Plan (1969–1974), the very first Plan after the report was submitted, it declined to 5%! It went down further to 3.3% in the Fifth Five Year Plan and then to 2.7% in the Sixth Five Year Plan.[35] It was only after the second National Policy of Education was approved by the Parliament in 1986 that there was some rise in Plan allocations to education. But even then, the allocation to education at the end of the Ninth Plan (1998–2002) was much below the allocation in the First and Third Plans. It was only in the Tenth Plan that the allocation to education went up above the allocation in the First Plan, to nearly 10%.[36]

Lack of Resources or Question of Priorities?

The reason for the low allocations to education was not lack of resources, it was more a question of priorities. Even within the capitalist frame, there are several third world countries that invested heavily in universalising elementary education after winning independence from colonial rule. J.B.G. Tilak, one of India's best-known experts in the field of economics of education, in an article published in the *International Journal of Educational Development*, has analysed the education expenditure of a number of countries. He comes to the conclusion that the percentage of national income a nation allocates to education is not determined by the level of economic development, but by other factors, the most important being political will.[37] (See also Chapter 4 for more on this.)

This is also borne out by developments in the field of education in the states of Kerala and Tamil Nadu. In these states, during the chief ministerships of E.M.S. Namboodripad and K. Kamaraj, a series of progressive measures were adopted to strengthen the government school system and universalise elementary education. Implying that had the central leadership so wished, it could have done so too.

Reason Two: More Priority to Higher Education

At the time of independence, there existed a certain amount of primary education in the country. However, there were very few higher educational institutions due to the complete neglect of higher education by the British. As pointed out earlier, the basic orientation of the Nehru model was to develop indigenous industry along capitalist lines. Big public and private sector industry badly needed engineers–scientists–technicians. And so, within the limited expenditure on education made by the Central government, more attention was given to higher education and to a lesser extent secondary education, while elementary education was neglected, completely ignoring the provisions of Article 45.

Table 3.3: Intra-Sectoral Allocation of Plan Outlays for Education in Five Year Plans[38] (%)

Education Level	*Expenditure Outlay*							
	I 51–56	*II 56–61*	*III 61–66*	*Ann. 66–69*	*IV 69–74*	*V 74–79*	*VI 80–85*	*VII 85–90*
Elementary*	56	35	34	24	30	35	36	29
Secondary	13	19	18	16	18	17	16	16
University	9	18	15	24	25	22	19	12
Technical	13	18	21	25	13	12	11	11
Other°	9	10	12	11	14	14	18	33
Total	100	100	100	100	100	100	100	100

* *Includes pre-school education*

° *Includes teacher education, vocational and adult education, social education, cultural programmes, etc.*

This is obvious from an analysis of intra-sectoral allocation of resources during the successive Plan periods. In the First Plan, 56%

of the total Plan resources to education were allocated to elementary education, while low priority was given to higher and technical education. In the subsequent Plans, the allocation to elementary education came down drastically, to around 30%. It in fact declined to as low as 17% in 1966–67 (Annual Plan). On the other hand, allocation to university education doubled and even nearly trebled, reaching a high of 25% by the Fourth Plan.[39]

J.B.G. Tilak and N.V. Varghese have argued that had the pattern of intra-sectoral allocation of resources in the education sector adopted in the First Five Year Plan continued, the universalisation of elementary education would in all probability have been accomplished by the 1990s![40]

Towards a 'New Path of Development'

Provision of equitable, good quality elementary education to all children is an essential prerequisite for sustainable human development and sustained development of any nation. Independent India's leaders, despite all their rhetoric of socialism, did not think it important enough to make adequate investments in education, improve the quality of all government schools, and implement the recommendation of the Kothari Commission to "move towards the goal of a common school system of public education ... where access to good education will depend not on wealth or class but on talent." It is not that the country did not have the necessary resources, it was a question of priorities.

As early as the 1960s, the Kothari Commission had observed that there is segregation in the education system in the country. The upper classes were sending their children to private, fee-charging, better quality schools, while the vast bulk of free, publicly maintained, but poor schools were being utilised by the masses.

Nevertheless, even till the late 1980s, the proportion of private schools in the total school system of the country was very small. According to J.B.G. Tilak, till the late 1980s, the share of private recognised unaided schools in the total number of schools in the country was only 2.5% at the primary level and 8.4% at the upper primary level. The majority of the middle classes continued to send their children to the government school system.

Table 3.4: Share of Private Unaided Schools in Total Number of Schools, 1986–87[41]

Primary	Upper Primary	Secondary	Higher Secondary
2.5 %	8.4%	12.7%	6%

The Nehruvian mixed economy model was essentially a model of capitalist development. Due to the inherent logic of capitalism, the Nehruvian model led to a gradual deepening of polarisation in society, with a small section acquiring immense wealth.

By the 1980s, this autonomous capitalist development model was in crisis. The stage was set for the country's ruling classes to embark on a new path of capitalist development. Not only has the new model sharply worsened the gap between rich and poor in society, it has taken the segregation in the education system to obscene levels...

NOTES

1. Aditya Mukherjee, *Imperialism, Nationalism and the Making of the Indian Capitalist Class*, Sage Publications, New Delhi, pp. 49–50, 358.
2. Ibid., pp. 397–98, 401.
3. Ibid., pp. 396–98.
4. Study by: Corporate Study Group of the Indian Institute of Public Administration, New Delhi, published in *The Telegraph*, June 23, 1983, cited in *Aspects of India's Economy*, Mumbai, No. 24, pp. 86–87, published by Research Unit for Political Economy, Prabhadevi, Mumbai-25; same facts also cited in: Yechury S., "Why this New Economic Policy?" *The Marxist*, January–June, 1992.
5. N.V. Varghese and Jandhyala B.G. Tilak, *The Financing of Education in India*, International Institute for Educational Planning, UNESCO, Paris, 1991, available on internet at: http://unesdoc.unesco.org.
6. Ibid.
7. "The Bigger Picture", *TNN*, September 14, 2009, http://articles.timesof india.indiatimes.com.
8. J.B.G. Tilak, "The Kothari Commission and Financing of Education", *Economic and Political Weekly*, March 10, 2007, http://www.rteforum india.org.
9. J.P. Naik, quoted in: J.B.G. Tilak, ibid.
10. *Report of the Education Commission, 1964–66: Vol. I – General Problems*,

National Council of Educational Research and Training, 1970, pp. 6–7, 14–15, http://www.teindia.nic.in.

11. *National Policy on Education Committee of Members of Parliament*, http://www.teindia.nic.in.
12. *Young India*, July 5, 1928, cited in: *The Selected Works of Mahatma Gandhi: The Voice of Truth–Medium of Education*, http://www.mkgandhi.org.
13. Syyeda Farhat Batool, "English as 'Mother' Tongue", March 22, 2014, http://www.pakistantoday.com.pk.
14. Summarised from: D.P. Pattanayak, "Mother Tongues: The Problem of Definition and the Educational Challenge", in Adama Ouane (ed.), *Towards a Multilingual Culture of Education*, UNESCO Institute for Education, 2003, pp. 27–28, www.unesco.org.
15. *The State of the World's Children*, UNICEF, 1999, New York, p. 41, http://www.unicef.org.
16. *Enhancing Learning of Children from Diverse Language Backgrounds: Mother Tongue-Based Bilingual or Multilingual Education in the Early Years*, UNESCO, 2011, p. 6, http://unesdoc.unesco.org.
17. *Report of the Education Commission, 1964–66: Vol. 2 – School Education*, National Council of Educational Research and Training, 1970, pp. 358–59, 363–65, http://www.dise.in.
18. *Report of the Official Language Commission*, Government of India, 1956, pp. 31–42.
19. *Report of the Education Commission, 1964–66: Vol. I – General Problems*, op. cit., p. 19.
20. Ibid., pp. 19–20.
21. Ibid., p. 21.
22. See *Report of the Committee for Review of NPE–1986 (1990)*, Government of India, Sections 5.1.1 to 5.1.6 and 6.1.1 to 6.1.3 , along with the related recommendations; cited in Anil Sadgopal, "India's Education Policy: A Historical Betrayal", *Combat Law*, May–August 2009, p. 16, http://combatlaw.org.
23. "Structure, Organisation and Progress of Education in India", in *Development of Education in India 1995-96 with Special Reference to Teacher Education*, http://www.teindia.nic.in.
24. "Elementary and Adult Education: The Present Scenario", in *Report of National Development Council Committee on Literacy,* Planning Commission, 1993, http://www.teindia.nic.in.
25. Ibid.
26. *UNICEF India—Nutrition*, http://www.unicef.org; Pratul Sharma,

"Child Growth Stats Show Half of India's Children are Chronically Malnourished", October 7, 2012, http://www.dailymail.co.uk.

27. Anil Sadgopal, "India's Education Policy: A Historical Betrayal", op. cit., p. 16.
28. J.B.G. Tilak, "The Kothari Commission and Financing of Education"; op. cit.; J.B.G. Tilak, "On Allocating 6 Percent of GDP to Education", *Economic and Political Weekly*, February 18, 2006, http://www.nuepa.org; *Report of the Education Commission, 1964–66: Vol. 4: Planning, Administration, Finance*, National Council of Educational Research and Training, 1970, pp. 923, 938, 961, http://www.teindia.nic.in.
29. J.B.G. Tilak, "The Kothari Commission and Financing of Education", ibid.
30. Ibid.; Chart given in this article modified to include figures for 2000–01 onwards, taken from: *Analysis of Budgeted Expenditure on Education 2009–10 to 2011–12*, MHRD, 2013, http://mhrd.gov.in.
31. J.B.G. Tilak, "The Kothari Commission and Financing of Education", ibid.
32. Ibid.; *Analysis of Budgeted Expenditure on Education 2009–10 to 2011–12*, MHRD, 2013, http://mhrd.gov.in.
33. N.V. Varghese and Jandhyala B.G. Tilak, *The Financing of Education in India*, op. cit., p. 26.
34. J.B.G. Tilak, "The Kothari Commission and Financing of Education", op. cit.
35. Note that there is a sudden jump in the allocation of resources to education between the Sixth and Seventh Plans. The Sixth Plan expenditure on education was nearly double that of the Fifth Plan and the Seventh Plan expenditure was more than twice the Sixth Plan expenditure. This sudden spurt in expenditure on education was not as a result of any prioritising of education. It was because during the Sixth Plan, the government went in for a massive loan from the International Monetary Fund, in order to support a programme of investment, growth and structural adjustment. The total investment in the economy was raised to extraordinary levels, being around 150% of the GDP in the base year of the respective plans; and so, as a part of this trend, there took place a spurt in expenditure on education too. However, even with such an increase, its share in the total plan outlay continued to remain low. In fact, the relative share of education in the total plan outlay was lowest during the Sixth Plan period. (*Reference:* N.V. Varghese and Jandhyala B.G. Tilak, *The Financing of Education in India*, op. cit., p. 26; Vijay Joshi, I.M.D. Little, *India: Macroeconomics*

and Political Economy, 1964–1991, World Bank, 1994, http://books.google.co.in.)

36. J.B.G. Tilak, "The Kothari Commission and Financing of Education", op. cit.; J.B.G. Tilak, "Inadequate Funding for Elementary Education", *Combat Law*, May–August 2009, p. 42, http://combatlaw.org.
37. J.B.G. Tilak, "The Kothari Commission and Financing of Education", ibid.; J.B.G. Tilak, "Political Economy of Investment in Education in South Asia", *International Journal of Educational Development*, available on internet at: http://www.researchgate.net.
38. N.V. Varghese and Jandhyala B.G. Tilak, *The Financing of Education in India*, op. cit., p. 28.
39. Ibid., p. 28.
40. Cited in: Ibid., p. 30.
41. Ibid., p. 7.

4

WHY GLOBALISATION?

"Globalisation" is just another name for US domination.
*– **Henry Kissinger**, Former US Secretary of State,*
Lecture at Trinity College, Dublin, October 12, 1999

Nehru Model in Crisis

The basic orientation of the mixed economy model or the Nehruvian model implemented in India after independence was to promote indigenous capitalist development. For this, the basic strategy adopted was: (i) using State resources to help the development of domestic infant private industry; and (ii) restricting the entry of foreign capital, in order to protect the nascent domestic industry, which did not have the economies of scale of the older industries of the developed capitalist countries. It is important to note that in adopting this strategy, the Nehruvian model of economic development—that is much maligned today—was only duplicating the strategy adopted by the developed capitalist countries in the 18th and 19th centuries.[1] Not just India, but many other third world countries* that became free from colonial rule in the years after the Second World War attempted to follow a similar path of autonomous capitalist development.

However, there are inherent limitations to capitalist development in a third world country like India. Duplicating the industrial revolutions of the West was simply not possible for these ex-colonial

---

* *Third World: This term is used to define the 'developing' (actually underdeveloped) countries of Asia, Africa and Latin America, most of whom were colonies or neo-colonies of the developed countries in the 19th–early 20th centuries.*

countries. The developed capitalist countries had got the huge amount of capital needed to finance their industrial revolutions by colonising, looting and plundering the countries of Asia, Africa and Latin America. And when their industrial revolutions took off, these same colonies also provided them with the huge quantities of raw materials as well as the markets needed for their industrial revolutions to continue without interruption.[2]

On the other hand, when these colonies became free from colonial rule and attempted to carry out their industrial revolutions duplicating the Western capitalist model, they had no region to plunder to finance their industrial revolutions. On top of it, their own economies were totally devastated due to centuries of colonial plunder. Not just devastated, but crippled too, owing to the policies of the colonial rulers.[3] And therefore, within just two decades of independence, by the 1970s, the autonomous capitalist development models of most third world countries became crisis-ridden—one consequence of which was that their foreign debt rose to astronomical levels.

Even within these limitations, the limited capitalist development possible in India was throttled due to the failure of independent India's new rulers to empower the people by investing in education, health, nutrition and gender equality, which would have unleashed the inherent potential of the people. One important reason for the rapid development of the East Asian countries during the 1960s–70s (apart from the aid provided to these countries by the USA for geopolitical reasons) was that their governments invested heavily to provide education, health and other welfare benefits to their people.[4]

Why did India not make the necessary investments in educating its people? Prabhat Patnaik, the renowned economist and political commentator, while delivering the First Foundation Day lecture of the National University of Educational Planning and Administration in New Delhi on August 11, 2007, made the perceptive observation that:

> (T)he proportion of GDP that the white-supremacist South African State spent on the education of the black majority even

during the apartheid period, notwithstanding the massive drain on its exchequer that the maintenance of the highly oppressive police, military, and intelligence apparatus entailed at the time, was higher than what the Indian State has ever done on education as a whole throughout its entire post-independence history. The matter in short is one of priorities.[5]

Patnaik's argument is further substantiated by Charts 4.1 and 4.2. In Chart 4.1, we have compared India's public expenditure on education as a percentage of GDP with other developing countries. For India, this has fluctuated between 3.5 and 4% of GDP over the last 3 decades, and was even lower before that. Even by the standards of developing countries, that is an embarrassingly low ratio. It is below the equivalent ratio for countries like Kenya, Malawi and Ethiopia, and is substantially below the weighted average of all the countries in the world.

Chart 4.2 gives India's public expenditure per student as a proportion of per capita GDP at the primary level. As the chart shows, this is amongst the lowest in the world. For most countries, this ratio is between 10% and 20%, and is above 20% for the developed countries and several developing countries. For India, it is a dismal 6.9%.

Chart 4.1: Government Education Spending as % of GDP, 2002[6]

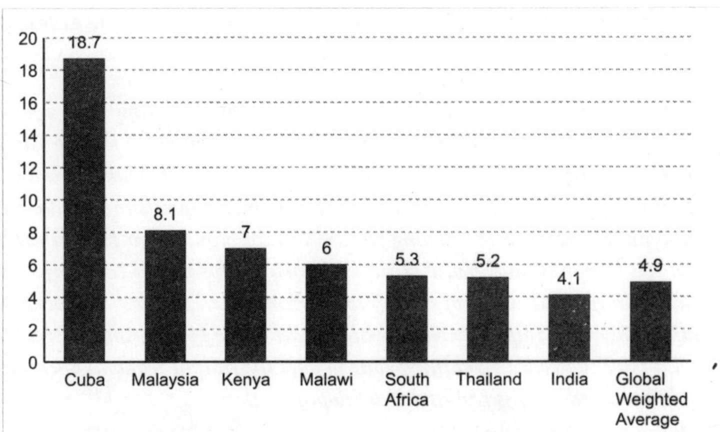

Chart 4.2: Expenditure Per Student, Primary, 2009–11[7]
(% of Per Capita GDP)

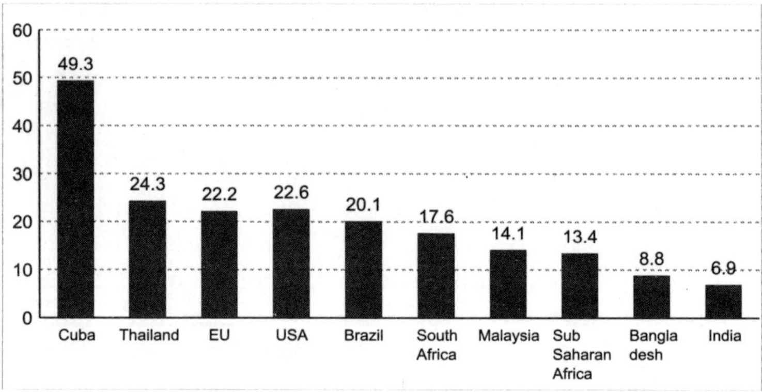

Despite Nehru's socialist rhetoric, the truth is that the Congress leadership made no serious attempt to eliminate medieval backwardness—religious backwardness, casteism, patriarchy continued to hobble the creative power of the masses. Little land reform was done, and the large mass of peasantry continued to wallow in desperate poverty. This seriously limited the growth of the market in the countryside. With focus on growth of large industries, industrial growth was also not sufficiently employment-generating to create a significant increase in demand.

By the mid-1960s, the Nehru model was in crisis.* The economy

* *Note that our critique of the Nehruvian model is much different from the present ruling BJP's criticism of Nehru. We are not critiquing Nehru for his anti-imperialism and imposition of restrictions on entry of foreign capital into the country. The BJP, while talking of 'swadeshi' and 'Make in India', is actually an even more ardent advocate of free market capitalism, privatisation of the public sector, and opening up the Indian economy to foreign capital than the Congress, and hence criticises Nehru for his mixed economy model and non-alignment (and of course, secularism). Had the post-independence Indian leadership implemented this BJP model in the 1950s, American capital would have succeeded in gaining control over the Indian economy then itself, the limited indigenous industrial development that has taken place in India would never have taken place, and all the gains of the freedom struggle would*

had started stagnating, and both industry and agriculture were in a serious crisis. While during the first fifteen years after independence (1951–65), manufacturing output grew at a healthy average annual rate of 7.1%, the subsequent 15 years (1965–80) saw this rate fall to only 3.8%.[8]

1980s: Partial Liberalisation

The Nehru model had led to a gradual growth of capitalist classes both in the cities and countryside. With the domestic market saturating and economic growth slowing down, the capitalist classes started pressing the government for a relaxation in import controls on raw materials and machinery, in the hope that this would lead to a boost in exports.[9]

In the early 1980s, the Indian government, under the Prime Ministership of Indira Gandhi, decided to change the orientation of India's economic model, reduce the importance of economic planning and promote private sector-led development, while putting brakes on growth of public sector industries and reducing social sector expenditures. To promote private sector-led industrialisation, it decided to liberalise imports of machinery and other technology. That required foreign exchange, and so it decided to approach the IMF for a huge dollar loan of SDR 5 billion (roughly $6 billion). Indira Gandhi knew that taking any such loan would require the acceptance of an economic reform package. Anticipating that there would be huge domestic opposition to these conditionalities, the government in its negotiations with the IMF offered to voluntarily implement economic reforms and partially liberalise the economy as a part of the Sixth Five Year Plan (1980–85) and government budget, without signing a formal agreement with the IMF on such an economic reform programme.

The reforms that the Indian government agreed to undertake included:

---

have been negated. That is why, as discussed briefly in Chapter 3, India's leading capitalists themselves were supportive of the Nehruvian model—that these same capitalists (that is, their sons and grandsons) today support globalisation and privatisation is another matter.

- reducing government expenditures through reducing subsidies given to the people;
- reducing the financing of the budget deficit through creation of fresh money, and shift to financing the budget deficit by market borrowings (which leads to higher interest payments);
- changing the orientation of India's industrial policy and shifting from an import-substitution development model to an export-oriented development model by gradually removing restrictions and reducing tariffs on a large percentage of imports and taking vigorous steps to promote exports (this was given the high sounding name—'making domestic production competitive with the world').

The IMF agreed to grant this loan, the largest ever given by the IMF to a third world country at that time, as it wanted to increase its lending to the underdeveloped countries (or 'developing countries'—as they are called in international official jargon). India was a leading member of the Non-Aligned Movement, which had officially opposed IMF conditionalities, and so its acceptance of an IMF loan would greatly increase IMF's acceptability amongst the underdeveloped countries. The loan was granted in November 1981.[10]

The economic reforms led to a revival of manufacturing growth in the 1980s, to an average annual rate of 5.7% in the first half of the 1980s and 8.8% per annum during the second half of the decade. An important reason for this was a substantial liberalisation of imports, especially of capital goods and components required for manufacturing a number of commodities catering to luxury consumption, especially of electronics and automobiles. The import liberalisation was not tied to a larger export effort; its main immediate thrust was towards producing more goods—especially luxury goods— for the domestic market. Despite the development of the Bombay High oilfield, which led to a reduction in oil imports, the huge increase in non-oil imports led to a rising trade deficit. This in turn led to a large increase in the current account deficit.[11]

To finance the growing trade and current account deficit, the government resorted to external commercial borrowings. Debt

Box 4.1: Some Economics

International trade only takes place in the currencies of the developed countries, like the dollar, euro or yen. When a third world country like India imports goods from abroad, it cannot make the payment for these imports in its domestic currency, it needs to make the payment in any of these internationally accepted currencies, say for instance, dollars. India therefore needs to earn dollars to pay for imports, which it does by exporting goods. The difference between export earnings and import payments is called trade deficit.

servicing of the borrowings led to a further rise in current account deficit, and eventually necessitated further borrowings. As fresh debt was contracted even to pay off old debt, the loan terms became stiffer, the maturity period shorter, and this led to a rapid escalation of the country's external debt. The debt in dollar terms nearly quadrupled during the 1980s, from around $20 billion in 1980 to nearly $82 billion in 1990.[12]

Entrapped in Debt

And so, by the late 1980s, the Indian economy was caught in an external debt trap: we were borrowing from abroad to pay even the service charges on our previous debt.

The developed capitalist countries, who not very long ago were the imperial masters of the entire third world, were looking for just such an opportunity. They had been forced to retreat and grant independence to India and other third world countries after a tidal wave of powerful independence struggles had swept across these countries in the years after the end of the Second World War. By the early 1970s, the post-war boom in the economies of the developed countries had come to an end, and stagnation had returned to afflict their economies once again, that is, their economies began to slow down once again.* Therefore, they desperately wanted to bring the

---

* *The giant monopoly corporations dominating the economies of the advanced capitalist countries have an enormous capacity to expand production, as well as earn super-profits. And so the capitalist system in these countries has come*

Box 4.2: Some More Economics

A third world country like India can pay its trade deficit by earning dollars through other ways, like foreign exchange earnings from foreign tourists visiting India, or remittances from Indian workers abroad who send in dollars to their families. The net deficit of the government in its day-to-day external transactions (including trade, services like tourism and software, remittances and investment income—this includes earnings by Indian industry abroad, profit outflows, debt payments, etc.) is called current account deficit. One way in which India can pay its current account deficit is by taking a dollar loan from abroad. But it will have to pay an interest on this loan. This interest payment is also in dollars. Therefore, debt servicing leads to yet more debt.

former colonial world back under their hegemony and ensnare it once again in the imperialist network, so that they could once again control its raw material resources and exploit its markets.[13] Since it was no longer possible to outright colonise the third world countries as before, they now began looking for alternate ways to do so.

With the Indian economy caught in an external debt trap, the Western imperialist powers sensed that the time was opportune to force the Government of India to submit to a restructuring of the Indian economy and open it up to foreign capital flows and imports. The World Bank, an international financial institution that is decisively

---

to be gripped by a problem of where to get the profitable investment opportunities to invest the growing pool of accumulated capital. The result has been a slow down in the rate of growth, along with rising unemployment and falling rates of utilisation of productive capacity. This crisis, which is different from the temporary crisis of recession faced by these economies in the 19th century, is defined as stagnation. While during the small-scale capitalism of the 19th century, rapid growth was the norm, and economic crisis the exception, now, in the monopoly capitalism of the 20th–21st century, "stagnation is the norm, good times the exception". (Discussing this issue in greater detail is beyond the scope of this essay. For more on stagnation, see: Paul M. Sweezy, "Why Stagnation?" Monthly Review, June 2012, http://monthlyreview.org.)

controlled by the US and West European countries, submitted a memorandum to the Indian government in November 1990 'suggesting' economic reforms like opening up the economy to foreign investment, liberalising trade, privatisation of the public sector, reforming the financial sector, and so on. Simultaneously, the Western creditors put on hold fresh loans to the Indian government, demanding that it first implement these policy changes.[14]

With foreign loans drying up, the foreign exchange reserves of the country plummeted to just $1.2 billion by the end of December 1990.[15] By early 1991, the Indian government was entrapped in a situation wherein, if it wanted to avoid external account bankruptcy, it had no option but to accept the demands of its international creditors.

1991: Globalisation Begins ...

The Nehruvian model of capitalist development had sharply polarised Indian society. Society was split into two camps. In one camp were the capitalists, big farmers, big traders, politicians, bureaucrats, smugglers, dealers, distributors, blackmarketeers, mafia, etc.—the parasites. They comprised less than 5% of the population. In the other camp were the working people, the students and youth, the pro-people intellectuals—the ordinary folk. These were 95% of the population. It is the first camp which controls political power in the country. Most mainstream political parties serve only its interests.

By the 1970s, the path of relatively autonomous capitalist development chosen by the Indian ruling classes was beset with a severe structural crisis. They experimented with partial liberalisation in the 1980s. While it pushed the Indian economy deeper into an external account crisis, it led to increased growth. The capitalist classes now came to the conclusion that in order to expand their profit accumulation, they must abandon their dream of independent capitalist development and open up the economy to foreign investment and imports. And so they decided to accept the World Bank and International Monetary Fund conditionalities, dismantle the

Nehruvian model, and remove the constraints placed on inflows of foreign capital and goods.

Elections to the Indian Parliament were held in May 1991. In July 1991, the minority Congress Government of Narasimha Rao–Manmohan Singh came to power at the Centre. It immediately went in for a 'Structural Adjustment Loan' from the WB–IMF, in return for which it signed an agreement pledging a thoroughgoing restructuring of the Indian economy. The main elements of this *Structural Adjustment Package* (SAP) accepted by the Government of India were:[16]

1. Removal of all curbs on imports and exports;
2. Removal of all restrictions on foreign investment in industry, financial sector and agriculture;
3. Opening up the stock markets to foreign speculative capital flows;
4. No government interference in the operation of 'free markets': ending of all subsidies to the poor including food, health and education subsidies; privatisation of the public sector, including essential services like drinking water, health, education, etc.; removal of all government controls on profiteering, even in areas like foodgrains.

It is this 'restructuring' of the Indian economy at the behest of the country's foreign creditors that has been given the high sounding name, *Globalisation*. This has been accompanied by the propagation of an economic doctrine popularly known as *neoliberalism* that claims that human well-being can best be advanced by free markets and the institution of frameworks by the State guaranteeing private property rights, free markets and free trade.[17]

The capitalist classes, their lackey intellectuals and their propaganda machinery, that is, the media, have been fully supportive of these policies. Globalisation is the consensus policy of the entire Indian ruling class. And so, ever since 1991, while governments have kept changing at the Centre, globalisation of the Indian economy has continued unabated.

NOTES

1. See for instance, Serge Halimi, "Protectionism: We've Been Here Before", *Le Monde Diplomatique*, March 2009, http://www.mondediplo.com; Keith Rankin, *Friedrich List Propagated the Myth of Adam Smith as a Cosmopolitan Thinker*, Economics Department, University of Auckland, August 4, 1996, http://keithrankin.co.nz.
2. There are numerous studies on this. See for instance, Eduardo Galeano, *Open Veins of Latin America*, Monthly Review Press, New York, 1973.
3. For instance, an excellent study of the impact of colonialism on Africa can be found in Walter Rodney, *How Europe Underdeveloped Africa*, London and Tanzanian Publishing House, Dar-Es-Salaam, 1973 (available on internet).
4. Joseph Stiglitz in *Research Observer*, World Bank, August 1996—quoted by Noam Chomsky in *Profit Over People*, Madhyam Books, Delhi, 1999, p. 32; see also: *India and its Contradictions: A Dialogue with Amartya Sen, Gurcharan Das, Meghnad Desai*, July 28, 2013, http://www.ndtv.com.
5. "First Foundary Day Lecture - National University of Educational Planning and Administration", www.nuepa.org.
6. Jayati Ghosh, "Public Spending on Education in India", June 29, 2011, http://www.macroscan.com; "Education Spending (% of GDP)", http://www.nationmaster.com.
7. "Expenditure per student, primary (% of GDP per capita)", http://www.indexmundi.com; "Expenditure per student – primary (% of GDP per capita) in India", http://www.tradingeconomics.com.
8. C.P. Chandrasekhar, "From Dirgisme to Neoliberalism: Aspects of the Political Economy of the Transition in India", *Development and Society*, Vol. 39, No. 1, June 2010, pp. 29–59; http://isdpr.org.
9. Arvind Panagariya, *India in the 1980s and 1990s: A Triumph of Reforms*, November 6, 2003, http://www.imf.org; Atul Kohli, "Politics of Economic Growth in India, 1980–2005; Part I: The 1980s", *Economic and Political Weekly*, April 1, 2006, p. 1255, http://www.princeton.edu.
10. Praveen K. Chaudhry, Vijay L. Kelkar and Vikash Yadav, "The Evolution of 'Homegrown Conditionality' in India: IMF Relations", *The Journal of Development Studies*, Vol. 40, No. 6, August 2004, http://people.hws.edu; Atul Kohli, ibid.; Arvind Panagariya, ibid.
11. C.P. Chandrasekhar and Jayati Ghosh, *The Market that Failed: A Decade of Neo-liberal Economic Reforms in India*, Leftword Books, New Delhi, 2006, available on internet at http://cscs.res.in.

12. Ibid.; Arvind Panagariya, *India in the 1980s and 1990s: A Triumph of Reforms*, op. cit.
13. For more on this, see: Neeraj Jain, *Globalisation or Recolonisation*, Chapter 1, published by Lokayat, Pune, 2006, available on the internet at lokayat.org.in.
14. Dalip S. Swamy, *The World Bank and Globalisation of Indian Economy*, Public Interest Research Group, Delhi, 1994, pp. 5, 15, 19.
15. Ibid., p. 17.
16. There are several articles available on the internet outlining these conditionalities. See for example: *Structural Adjustment in India*, World Bank, 2012, http://lnweb90.worldbank.org; Montek S. Ahluwalia, *Structural Adjustment and Reform in Developing Countries*, April 1994, www.planningcommission.nic.in; Ashwini Deshpande and Prabirjit Sarkar, "Structural Adjustment in India—A Critical Assessment", *Economic and Political Weekly*, December 9, 1995, http://www.epw.in; David Harvey, *A Brief History of Neoliberalism*, Oxford University Press, 2005, pp. 7–8, 29, 64–66.
17. For more on this, see: David Harvey, ibid.

5

IMPACT OF GLOBALISATION ON ELEMENTARY EDUCATION

Teach the ignorant as much as you can; society is culpable in not providing a free education for all and it must answer for the night which it produces. If the soul is left in darkness, sins will be committed. The guilty one is not he who commits the sin, but he who causes the darkness.

– ***Victor Hugo,*** *Les Misérables*

Articles 14 and 15(1) of Part III (Fundamental Rights) of the Indian Constitution guarantee 'equality before the law' and prohibit the State from discriminating 'against any citizen on grounds only of religion, race, caste, sex, place of birth or any of them.' Reading Article 45 of the Indian Constitution in conjunction with these two Articles makes it clear that the State is duty bound to build a system of education that provides education of equitable quality to all children without any discrimination whatsoever. Till the 1970s, while not doing anything to implement this directive of the Constitution as regards providing equitable education to all the children of the country, the Government of India had not formally declared that it was abandoning this goal.

The neoliberal winds from Washington that had started blowing across India in the 1980s affected the Indian education system too. The first indication that the government was now formally moving towards a new orientation in its educational policies came in 1985, when it changed the name of the Ministry of Education to Ministry of Human Resource Development (MHRD). This implied a change in the very purpose of education, from one of developing conscious citizens to build a democratic, socialist, secular, egalitarian and just society as envisaged in the Constitution, to one of supplying 'human resource', that is, skilled but slavish workforce, for corporations.[1]

National Policy on Education 1986[2]

In 1986, the government formulated a new National Policy on Education (NPE-1986). While providing lip-service to the principle of 'universal elementary education', it de-linked this from the principle of equitable education for all children, and formally announced that the education system in the country was henceforth going to be multi-track and discriminatory. The NPE-1986 declared that for the out-of-school children in the 6–14 age-group—who comprised almost half of the children in this age-group—a stream of non-formal education (NFE) of inferior quality shall be instituted. That is, the government now formally declared that it was abandoning the Constitution mandated goal of sending these children to regular schools. Simultaneously, it also proposed to set up an elite layer of schools, the Navodaya Vidyalayas, one per district, whose quality would be far above the regular government schools. Ironically, this violated a commitment made in the NPE-1986 itself: "Effective measures will be taken in the direction of the Common School System recommended in the 1968 policy."[3]

That the NFE was not meant to be a minor stream is obvious from a perspective document released by the Government of India as a prelude to NPE-1986, titled *Challenge of Education: A Policy Perspective*. This document states that it was expected to be a bigger stream than the 'formal' stream: "It is expected that of the additional 64 million children coming up for elementary education, nearly 39 million will be educated entirely through this system."[4]

What was the real reason for introducing NFE? This is revealed in a paragraph hidden in this perspective document. It says that any substantial progress towards universalisation of elementary education "will not only require significant increase in educational expenditure on elementary education but will also have a multiplier effect on the total education budget through increased enrolments in the secondary and higher education. Hence, policy deliberations vis-a-vis universalisation of elementary education need to be matched with hard financial decisions ..." The document goes on to say: "Alternatively, other educational approaches, such as non-formal/ distance education, and vocationalisation have to be worked out ..."[5]

Therefore, when NPE-1986 insisted that "NFE can result in provision of education comparable in quality with formal schooling,"[6] it is obvious that this was mere camouflage. The real reason was *budget constraints*. The policy makers were obviously aware that NFE meant providing inferior quality education, but they were taking this decision because it would lead to significant savings in government educational expenditure. In any case, NFE was meant for the children of the marginalised sections, not children of the middle classes and elites, and teaching them some literacy–numeracy was more than enough.

The NPE-1986 marked a watershed as it was the first policy-level acknowledgement since independence that henceforth elementary school education of comparable quality will *not* be available to all children of India in the 6–14 age group. Till then, in principle, there was only one officially acknowledged, planned and financially supported stream in Indian education (i.e. government, local body and government-aided schools of comparable quality), the relatively minor streams of private unaided schools (erroneously called public schools) and Kendriya Vidyalayas (or Central Schools) notwithstanding.

Another decision of far-reaching impact taken in NPE-1986 concerned the appointment of NFE 'instructors' in place of regular, qualified, trained and well-paid teachers. The level of qualifications, teacher training, salary and other service conditions of these instructors would obviously be of a much lower order than those of the regular teachers of the formal school system. Yet, NPE-1986 expected these under-qualified, ill-trained and under-paid 'instructors' (without any stability in service) to be, for some magical reason, "talented and dedicated young men and women."[7] One of their important tasks was supposed to be attracting the 'out-of-school' children, particularly the girls and the working children, to the NFE centres, and then ensuring that education becomes "a joyful, inventive and satisfying learning activity" for them![8] All this was supposed to be achieved by the 'miraculous' instructors by holding the NFE classes for merely 2–3 hours per day, in contrast to the formal school held for 4–5 hours per day (the policy stated that NFE's "total duration is generally shorter than in formal education"[9]). The expectations from the NFE instructors do not end here. Since no provision for even thatched huts (let alone buildings) or teaching aids is made for NFE, the instructor is expected to use her/his 'genius' to arrange for all these from the community! But what if the instructor fails to organise this? The policy prefers to remain silent on this.

As we have discussed earlier, the notion of education of *comparable* quality for all children, irrespective of their class, creed, caste, gender, linguistic or cultural background or physical/mental disability, was clearly implied in the Constitution. NPE-1986 thus marked the beginning of the free-market or neoliberal agenda in school education wherein violation of the Constitution became a practice, with the Parliament looking the other way!

Jomtien Declaration

By the late 1980s, the Indian ruling classes had more or less made up their mind to take a second foreign loan from the WB–IMF and accept a second round of conditionalities. In March 1990, the Indian government indicated its willingness to reduce its expenditure on education and privatise the education sector, thereby transforming education into a means for profiteering, by signing the Jomtien Declaration, euphemistically called the *World Declaration on Education For All*, at an international conference on education organised by the World Bank in association with three UN agencies, the UNDP, UNESCO and UNICEF, in Jomtien, Thailand. The Indian government signed this document without even consulting the Parliament on its major Constitutional implications!

The Jomtien Declaration outlined the policy framework that would determine the Indian government's educational policies subsequent to its signing the WB–IMF dictated 'Structural Adjustment Programme' in 1991. Some of the important features of this Declaration were:

(i) There is no reference to providing FREE and EQUITABLE education to all children.
(ii) Instead of education being a vehicle to build a conscious citizenship, it defines education merely as "basic learning needs", thus reducing education to acquiring literacy–numeracy and life skills, to thus create a workforce for corporate houses.
(iii) Instead of calling upon the State to prioritise funding of education to ensure education to all children by mobilising its internal resources, it supports external assistance even for primary education, and partnership with NGOs, religious bodies and corporate houses. Thus, it opens the door to privatisation of education, making it a commodity to be traded on the marketplace.[10]

SAP and Elementary Education

In mid-1991, the Government of India accepted the 'Structural Adjustment Loan' from the WB-IMF. The conditionalities of this loan implied that the government was committing itself to reducing its expenditures on essential services, including education. It now began implementing World Bank-dictated education reforms, as elucidated in the Jomtien Declaration, and World Bank-sponsored projects and schemes, in right earnest. The basic agenda of these reforms and schemes was straightforward:

(i) Starve the vast government education system, from schools to universities, of funds; consequently, their quality would gradually deteriorate.
(ii) With decline in school quality, parents, including even poor parents, would gradually begin to withdraw their children from the government education system.
(iii) This would create the demand for private schools, and fee-charging private schools would mushroom all over the country—low-fee-charging inferior quality schools for poor children, and high-fee-charging elite schools for the rich.
(iv) Meanwhile, the declining enrolment in government schools would give an alibi to the government to close down

> government schools; the school campuses could then be converted into commercial ventures such as the fee-charging elite private schools or shopping malls.[11]

That this was the undeclared objective of the World Bank dictated reforms becomes obvious from an overview of the transformation that has taken place in the elementary education sector since the reforms began in 1991.

The Assault : DPEP–SSA

The assault on the huge government school education system began with the launch of the World Bank-sponsored District Primary Education Programme (DPEP) in 1993-94. Beginning with 42 districts in seven states in Phase I, the DPEP had steadily spread its coverage to almost half of India's districts (about 280 districts) in 18 states by the time its third and the last phase was initiated in 2002–03.

Table 5.1: External Assistance to DPEP[12]

Years	*Total Expenditure on Education (in Rs crore)*	*External Assistance (in Rs crore)*	*External Assistance as % of Total Expenditure on Education*
1999–2000	74,816	683	0.91
2000–01	82,486	858	1.04
2001–02	79,866	1100	1.38

While the declared aim of this World Bank funded scheme was to revitalise the primary education system and univeralise primary education, the real objective of the DPEP was to advance the neoliberal agenda of the World Bank in this sector, as detailed in the Jomtien Declaration. The total funding provided by the World Bank was a fraction of the total government expenditure on the education system (see Table 5.1). Despite this minuscule spending, the World Bank was able to inflict serious damage on the Indian education system in just a decade. The effects included:[13]

- Reduction of the holistic goals of education to literacy–numeracy.

Box 5.1: Education Guarantee Scheme

This 'initiative' was proposed in the Union Budget 1999–2000. The scheme is meant for those areas where no school currently exists within a radius of 1 km; so these areas would generally be the areas where the poorest of the poor live. The EGS envisages the poor local community to:

a) provide the premises required for a school;
b) provide for a local part-time teacher, in other words, provide a local unemployed youth who would be willing to teach in the school; and
c) mobilise the necessary funds for paying a stipend to the 'teacher' and for maintenance of the school.

In other words, the government does not have to do anything, nor spend a single paisa to run the school! If the local community manages to successfully run the school for two years, then perhaps the government would come forward with some assistance. The then Finance Minister Yashwant Sinha, in his budget speech, declared: "This initiative will provide an opportunity to the rural poor, especially those belonging to the Scheduled Castes, Scheduled Tribes and Other Backward Classes to secure education for their children. This is the first and most important step towards their empowerment." The government proposed to open 1.8 lakh such schools over the remaining three years of the Ninth Plan, and since no funding was required, no financial allocation was made for these EGS centres in the Budget.

[Sources: Jandhyala B.G. Tilak, "National Human Development Initiative: Education in the Union Budget", EPW Special Articles, March 6–12 and 13–19, 1999, http://www.nuepa.org; "Budget Speech", Speech of Shri Yashwant Sinha, Finance Minister, Government of India, February 27, 1999, http://indiabudget.nic.in.]

- Replacement of the Constitutional commitment to provide eight years of elementary education with five years of primary education.
- Introduction of parallel layers of education (parallel to the mainstream formal schools) of relatively inferior quality such as adult literacy classes, alternative schools, education

guarantee centres, correspondence courses, etc. (See Box 5.1 for a short description of one of these NFE schemes, called Education Guarantee Scheme).

- Replacing regular teachers with under-qualified, ill-trained and under-paid teachers appointed on short-term contracts, called para-teachers.
- Introduction of the outrageous concept of multi-grade teaching wherein one teacher is actually trained to perform the 'miracle' of teaching five classes simultaneously in one classroom, thereby trashing the 1986 Education Policy norm (approved by the Parliament) of 'at least three teachers and three classrooms per primary school' (along with a verandah and separate toilets for girls and boys).
- Dilution of infrastructural, teacher-related, curricular and other norms and standards, approved under the 1986 policy, pertaining to quality of education.
- Reduction of the role of education departments of state governments by setting up parallel bodies for channelling finance and governance of DPEP.
- Reducing the responsibility of the government to provide education by allowing NGOs to enter the education sector.

In less than a decade, the DPEP 'succeeded' in its agenda of wrecking the quality of the government school system, leading to a significant loss of its public credibility.

In April 2000, the decadal follow-up of the Jomtien Conference was held in Dakar, Senegal. As was to be expected, the Dakar Framework of Action only elaborated and reinforced the fundamental premises of the Jomtien Declaration. Dutifully obeying the dictates of the World Bank, the Indian government repackaged the flaws and lacunae of DPEP and presented it to the public under a new label of Sarva Shiksha Abhiyan (SSA). By the time SSA ended in March 2010, the credibility of the government school system had hit rock bottom even as the twin problems of out-of-school children and drop-outs remained essentially unresolved.

Rapid Growth of Private Schools

The neoliberal educational reforms began having their impact almost immediately. With the deteriorating quality of government schools due to squeezing of government grants, and decline in the quality of teachers due to increasing recruitment of under-qualified and under-paid para-teachers, families began voting with their feet and exiting the government school system. Private unaided schools began sprouting up all over the country, a fact recognised by the Planning Commission too in its Eleventh Plan document.

As per official figures (Table 5.2), private unaided schools accounted for 11% of the total elementary schools in the country in 2004–05, up from around 5% in the late 1980s.[14] However, these figures underestimate the growth of private schooling in the country, because official data do not include unrecognised schools. Apart from the recognised private unaided elementary schools, many of whom have gained recognition through dubious means, a significant number of the private unaided schools that have been sprouting up all over the country are unrecognised schools.

Table 5.2: Elementary Schools by Management, 2004–05[15] ***(in lakh)***

Stages of Education	*Govt.*	*Local Bodies*	*Private Aided*	*Private Unaided*	*Total*
I–V	3.32	3.60	0.20	0.55	7.67
VI–VIII	1.18	0.80	0.18	0.59	2.75
I–VIII	4.50	4.40	0.38	1.14	10.42

A more accurate idea of the rapid growth in private schooling in the country after the beginning of neoliberal educational reforms can be obtained from household survey data. Table 5.3 shows the enrolment share of private schools in rural and urban India, according to official school returns data of 1993 and 2002, and household survey data of 1993 and 2006.

The data shows that the true size of the private education sector in India is more than three times that shown in official statistics! Thus, according to official statistics, enrolment share of private schools at

Table 5.3: Enrolment Share of Private Unaided Schools, 1993–2006[16]

School Level	*Official Data 1993*	*Household Survey Data 1993*	*Official Data 2002*	*Household Survey Data 2006*
All-India Rural				
Primary	2.8	10.1	5.8	19.5
Middle	6.5	7.9	11.1	20.4
Secondary	6.8	10.1	14.3	22.8
All-India Urban				
Primary	25.7	26.2	28.9	NA
Middle	18.8	15.4	39.1	NA
Secondary	11.5	11.2	32.4	NA

primary level in rural areas was 2.8% in 1993, and had slowly increased to 5.8% in 2006. But household survey data indicate that 10.1% of school-going rural children were attending private schools in 1993, and this number had doubled to 19.5% by 2006. For rural middle schools, while official statistics show that the number of students attending private schools increased from 6.5% in 1993 to 11.1% in 2006, household survey data show that this number had crossed 20% in 2006.

And for urban India, even official statistics admit that private schools accounted for between 30% and 40% of the total student enrolment at the elementary and secondary levels. Again, since official data does not include unrecognised schools, this implies that around 40–50% of urban children could be going to private schools.

Rate of Increase in Private Schooling

There is an even more telling statistic that brings out even more eloquently how the onset of neoliberalism immediately led to a sharp acceleration in commercialisation of education in India. That is the share of private schooling in the total *increase in school enrolment* over the period 1993–2002. Table 5.4 presents the data, based on official surveys. It shows the relative growth of private schooling in India, as compared to the growth of government and aided schooling.

Table 5.4: Share of Recognised Private Unaided Schools in Total Enrolment Increase, 1993–2002[17]

Area	*School Level*	*1993–2002*
Rural	Primary	24.4
	Middle	23.2
	Secondary	30.9
Urban	Primary	95.7
	Middle	71.7
	Secondary	46.7

The figures are simply astounding! The table shows that in urban India, over the nine year period 1993–2002, nearly all the increase (96%) in primary school enrolment took place in private schools! Government and aided primary schools together absorbed only 4.3% of the total increase in primary school enrolment. The rate of expansion of private primary schooling in rural India was slower, at 24%.

It bears emphasising that both these statistics are likely to be an underestimate since they do not take into account enrolment growth in the numerous unrecognised private schools that are excluded from the official statistics.

The conclusion is inescapable: globalisation and neoliberal reforms have led to a massive growth in private primary schooling in urban India.

Way back in the 1960s, commenting on what was then a small stream of elite 'public schools' (a nomenclature used for private schools in India), the Kothari Commission had stated:

> (The) so-called Public Schools ... system was transplanted in India by British administrators and we have clung to it so long because it happened to be in tune with the traditional hierarchical structure of our society. Whatever its past history may be, such a system has no valid place in the new democratic and socialistic society we desire to create.[18]

With our policy makers now deciding to abandon the Constitutional vision of building an egalitarian and democratic society, the small stream of private schools started becoming a flood by the late 1990s.

★ ★ ★

Thus, within a span of just 10 years, by the turn of the century, the World Bank had accomplished its mandate of creating conditions for rapid growth of private school education in India.

With the government school system in shambles, and even the poor seeking to somehow admit their students to private schools to the extent possible, the ground was laid for the next phase of 'educational reforms'. The first decade of the 21st century has seen a 'privatisation storm' sweeping across the school education sector in the country. But first we must take a look at yet another 'story' related to the elementary education sector that has been unfolding in the country over the last two decades, which began when a five-judge bench of the Supreme Court of India gave an unprecedented ruling upholding the spirit of the Constitution of India.

NOTES

1. *Chennai Declaration: All India Conference for Abolishing Commercialisation of Education and Building a Common School System*, June 30–July 1, 2012, http://www.samacheerkalvi.in.
2. This section is based on the following references: Ibid.; Anil Sadgopal, "Right to Education vs. Right to Education Act", *Social Scientist*, September–December 2010, p. 22, available on the internet at http://www.scribd.com; Anil Sadgopal, "Dilution, Distortion and Diversion: A Post-Jomtien Reflection on Education Policy", published in Ravi Kumar (ed.), *The Crisis of Elementary Education in India*, Sage Publications, New Delhi, 2006, pp. 92–136, available on the internet at xa.yimg.com.
3. *National Policy on Education 1986 (as modified in 1992)*, p. 5, downloaded from India Development Gateway, http://www.indg.in.
4. Anil Sadgopal, "Dilution, Distortion and Diversion: A Post-Jomtien Reflection on Education Policy", op. cit., pp. 92–136.
5. Ibid.
6. *National Policy on Education 1986: Programme of Action 1992*, p. 22, downloaded from www.teindia.nic.in.

7. *National Policy on Education 1986 (as modified in 1992)*, op. cit., p. 14.
8. *National Policy on Education 1986: Programme of Action 1992*, op. cit., p. 19.
9. Cited in: Anil Sadgopal, "Dilution, Distortion and Diversion: A Post-Jomtien Reflection on Education Policy", op. cit., pp. 92–136.
10. Summarised from: Ibid.; Anil Sadgopal, "Right to Education vs. Right to Education Act", op. cit., pp. 29–32; Anil Sadgopal, "India's Education Policy: A Historical Betrayal", *Combat Law*, May–August 2009, pp. 20–21, http://combatlaw.org.
11. Anil Sadgopal, "India's Education Policy: A Historical Betrayal", ibid., p. 21.
12. Ibid.
13. Ibid., pp. 21–24; Anil Sadgopal, "Dilution, Distortion and Diversion: A Post-Jomtien Reflection on Education Policy", op. cit.
14. According to data provided by Tilak and Varghese (see Chapter 3, endnote 41), private schools accounted for 2.5% of the total primary schools and 8.4% of the total upper primary schools in the country in the late 1980s.
15. *Eleventh Five Year Plan, Vol. II: Social Sector*, Planning Commission, Government of India, p. 8, http://planningcommission.nic.in.
16. All data taken from: Geeta Gandhi Kingdon, University of Oxford, "The Progress of School Education in India", Global Poverty Research Group, http://management.ind.in. The household survey data for 2006 are taken by Kingdon from ASER, which merged aided and unaided private schools into a single category 'private'. But private aided schools are very few, especially at the primary level.
17. Geeta Gandhi Kingdon, ibid.; statistics based on All India Education Surveys for various years (NCERT, 1982; 1992; 1998; 2006).
18. *Report of the Education Commission, 1964–66: Vol. I – General Problems*, National Council of Educational Research and Training, 1970, pp. 15–16, http://www.teindia.nic.in.

6

THE RIGHT TO EDUCATION ACT

[The] general education of all children without exception at the expense of the State—an education which is equal for all and continues until the individual is capable of emerging as an independent member of society ... would be only an act of justice ... for clearly, every man has the right to the fullest development of his abilities and society wrongs individuals twice over when it makes ignorance a necessary consequence of poverty.

– ***Frederick Engels*** *(February 8, 1845)*

In December 2002, the Indian Parliament passed the Constitution (Eighty-Sixth) Amendment Act making "Right to Education a fundamental right"; and then on April 1, 2010, the government brought into force the Right of Children to Free and Compulsory Education Act, 2009 (more popularly known as the Right to Education Act or RTE Act) 'to give effect' to this Constitutional amendment.

On the face of it, this Constitutional Amendment and its accompaniment, the RTE Act, go against the conditionalities of the Structural Adjustment Programme imposed on India by the World Bank. As we have discussed in the previous chapter, ever since globalisation began in 1991, the overall orientation of the Indian government has been of gradually withdrawing from its responsibility of providing free and compulsory education to all children. Then what explains its enactment of the Right to Education Act to address the "issues of school drop out, out-of-school children, quality of education and availability of trained teachers?"[1] Has the government, all of a sudden, developed a spine?

Behind this apparent U-turn is a long story, going back to 1993.

Historic Unnikrishnan Judgement

A historic judgement by the Supreme Court of India in 1993 radically transformed the status of Article 45. In its Unnikrishnan judgement (1993), the Supreme Court ruled that:

> The Directive Principles form the fundamental feature and the social conscience of the Constitution which enjoins upon the State to implement these directive principles.

The Court observed:

> (T)he provisions of Part III (fundamental rights) and Part IV (directive principles) are supplementary and complementary to each other ...

and that:

> (F)undamental rights are but a means to achieve the goal indicated in Part IV.

After making this path-breaking interpretation of the relation between Fundamental Rights and Directive Principles enshrined in the Constitution, the Court then went on to say that Article 45 in Part IV of the Constitution should therefore to be read in "harmonious construction" with Article 21 (Right to Life) in Part III of the Constitution, and concluded:

> The right to education flows directly from right to life. The right to life under Article 21 and the dignity of an individual cannot be assured unless it is accompanied by the right to education.

Referring to the 10-year time-frame given in Article 45 for providing education to all children up to the age of fourteen years, the Supreme Court observed:

> It is noteworthy that among the several articles in Part IV, only Article 45 speaks of a time-limit; no other article does. Has it no significance? Is it a mere pious wish, even after 44 years of the Constitution? ... Does not the passage of 44 years—more than four times the period stipulated in Article 45—convert the obligation created by the article into an enforceable right?[2]

And so the Supreme Court declared that Article 45 has acquired the status of a fundamental right.

Need to Amend Article 45: Free Education Till 18 Years

Any pro-people government would have welcomed the Unnikrishnan judgement. In fact, it would have gone beyond it, and amended Article 45 to expand its scope to 'all children until they complete the age of 18 years' (that is, providing them free and compulsory education up to Class XII). At the time of commencement of the Constitution, since India had just become free from 200 years of colonial plunder and so was faced with a huge paucity of resources, there might have been some validity in Article 45 being limited to "all children until they complete the age of fourteen years" (implying education up to Class VIII). Fifty years later, after so much wealth creation and development, this country was definitely in a position to guarantee its children free and compulsory education at least up to the 12th standard.

Amending Article 45 to include 'all children until they complete the age of 18 years' has also become mandatory as per international covenants like the 'Convention on the Rights of the Child' to which India became a signatory in 1992 wherein "a child means every human being below the age of 18 years."[3] In most of the advanced developing countries, like China, Mexico, Brazil, Thailand, Indonesia, etc., the task of universalising elementary education was accomplished a long time ago and the current preoccupation of the educational planners and policy-makers is for universalising quality secondary education.[4]

Providing free education up to Class XII is also essential from another perspective—without a Class XII certificate, no young person has any chance of getting any kind of a decent job; this also constitutes the minimum eligibility for pursuing even vocational courses (including para-medical, computer and IT-related courses) and courses offered by polytechnics, apart from the higher and technical education programmes. As mentioned in Chapter 1, barely 10% of OBC students, 8% of SC students and 6% of ST students (out of those admitted to Class I) cross the Class XII barrier; implying that the benefits of reservations have been limited since independence to only this small section of OBCs, SCs and STs. The exclusion of the majority of poor Muslims from higher education and public employment also needs to be understood in this context as their social status is broadly equivalent to SCs/OBCs.[5] Therefore, not providing free education to all children up to the age of 18 years makes a mockery of the fundamental right to social justice under Articles 15 (Prohibition of discrimination on grounds of religion, caste, etc.) and 16 (Equality of opportunity) of the Indian Constitution.

Subverting the Judgement: 86th Amendment

Forget providing free education to all children up to the age of 18 years, the Unnikrishnan judgement giving all children in the age-group 0–14 a Fundamental Right to Education sent jitters down the spine of the ruling elite. It was the exact opposite of the requirements of the WB-dictated Structural Adjustment Programme that they had begun implementing in earnest. It meant that the government would have to re-prioritise the Indian economy in favour of providing free and equitable education to the masses. To quote from the widely acclaimed Tapas Majumdar Committee Report (January 1999):

> UEE [Universalisation of Elementary Education] has, in consequence of the [Supreme Court's Unnikrishnan] judgement, now become a justiciable entitlement of every Indian child ... The State has to make the necessary reallocation of resources, by superseding other important claims, if necessary, in a manner that the justiciable entitlement can become a reality.[6]

The government desperately began looking for ways to extricate itself from the implications of the judgement. Bureaucrats burned the midnight oil and came up with several proposals to dilute/distort the concept of 'Fundamental Right to Education', such as the Saikia Committee Report (1997), the 83rd Constitutional Amendment Bill (August 1997) and the report of the HRD Ministry-related Parliamentary Committee (November 1997). However, public opposition to these attempts forced the government to put the entire matter in cold storage for the time being.[7]

Finally, in November 2001, the government presented the 86th

Constitutional Amendment Bill to the Lok Sabha. The ostensible purpose of making the amendment was to implement the Unnikrishnan judgement, making Right to Education a fundamental right. But why go through the trouble of amending the Constitution, when the Supreme Court had already creatively interpreted it and declared Right to Education to be a fundamental right? The real reason was: *in the name of implementing the Supreme Court judgement, actually subvert it.*

The 86th Amendment made two important changes in the Constitution:

(i) Inserted Article 21A into the Constitution (after Article 21), which read: "The State shall provide free and compulsory education to all children of the age of six to fourteen years in such manner as the State may, by law, determine."

(ii) Redrafted Article 45, replacing: "The State shall endeavour to provide, within a period of ten years from the commencement of this Constitution, for free and compulsory education for all children until they complete the age of fourteen years", with: "The State shall endeavour to provide early childhood care and education for all children until they complete the age of six years."

A closer reading of the above changes makes it clear that the Amendment had cleverly taken away the Fundamental Right to Education granted by the Supreme Court to 37 crore children. It did this by:

(a) excluding children up to six years of age (almost 17 crore children) from the provision of fundamental right to free early childhood care and pre-primary education;

(b) restricting the Fundamental Right to Education of even the 20 crore children in the 6–14 year age group by placing a conditionality in the form of the phrase "as the State may, by law, determine" (in Article 21A), thus giving the State an instrument with which to arbitrarily restrict, dilute and distort the Fundamental Right to Education given through the very same Article 21A.

Taking Away the Rights of Children of 0–6 Years

Early childhood care (which includes nutrition) and nursery and pre-school education for children up to six years of age are critical for the intellectual, emotional and physical development of the child, including curiosity, formation of character, personality, cognition, language skills, and social skills. This is recognised even by NPE-1986.[8] By denying children this fundamental right, the government is discriminating between the rich and the poor, since the former will be able to afford early childhood care and education for their children while poor children will be debilitated for the rest of their life due to this deprivation in early childhood. The Amendment would affect education of girls in the 6–14 age group too—girls of poor families are invariably required to take care of their younger siblings. The Constitution, as framed by the founding fathers of the nation, clearly directed the State to consider the entire schooling of children from age 0 to 14 years in a holistic manner. The 86th Constitutional Amendment has distorted and fragmented this vision of education!

As the State may, by law, determine ...

Inference about the real purpose of adding the conditionality "as the State may, by law, determine" can be drawn from the discussion in the previous chapter. The real purpose is to legitimise the various parallel streams of low-budget and low-quality education for poor children, started subsequently to NPE-1986 and which accelerated after the introduction of the World Bank sponsored DPEP.

That this is the real intention of the 86th Amendment is also obvious from a closer reading of the Financial Memorandum attached to the Bill which provided for an additional sum of Rs 9800 crore per year (i.e. 0.44% of GDP in 2002–03) for the next ten years for implementing the provisions under the Amendment. This commitment is much less than what had been estimated by the government's own committee, the Tapas Majumdar Committee, to provide elementary education to all out-of-school children through regular formal schools. The Tapas Majumdar Committee, in its report submitted in 1999, had estimated that an additional investment of Rs 1,37,600 crore would have to be made over a 10-year period to bring all out-of-school children into the formal school system (not parallel streams) and enable them to complete elementary education. This works out to an average investment of about Rs 14,000 crore a year, which in 1999 amounted to a mere 0.78% of the GDP. In 2002–03, the same amount worked out to an even lower proportion, that is, 0.63% of the GDP.[9]

The Tapas Majumdar Committee's calculations did not take into account the cost of providing elementary education of equitable quality; in this sense, it was an underestimate.[10] But the government was not willing to invest even this minuscule amount; the Bill was willing to provide only 70% of this! The government came to this lower estimate because while the financial estimate made by the Tapas Majumdar Committee was based on providing regular school education to all children, the government was planning to provide only cheap, low-quality parallel tracks of education to the out-of-school children.[11]

Several MPs, cutting across party lines, criticised the Bill. But then, they were just blustering; their parties were in agreement on implementing the neoliberal economic reforms. The Constitutional Amendment Bill was passed by both houses of Parliament without even a single dissenting vote! The President signed the Bill in December 2002.[12]

The Right to Education Act

Article 21A introduced into the Constitution through the 86th Constitutional Amendment stated that the State shall provide free and compulsory education to all children in the age group 6–14 "in such manner as the State may, by law, determine." Therefore, the State was now required to pass legislation to elaborate the manner in which it was going to provide "free and compulsory" education to all children in the 6–14 age group. Only after the passage of this enabling legislation could the government notify the 86th Constitutional Amendment.

The NDA Government, which had piloted the 86th Constitutional Amendment through the Parliament, had started work on such a Right to Education (RTE) Bill; the final draft was ready to be placed in

Parliament in February 2004, when general elections intervened and it was voted out of power.

The UPA Government which came to power in May 2004 set up a new committee headed by the new Minister of State for Science and Technology, Kapil Sibal, to draft a new RTE bill. It took the government nearly three and a half years to finally come up with a new draft which suited the neoliberal framework. The final Bill was passed by the Parliament on August 4, 2009. The Right of Children to Free and Compulsory Education Act or Right to Education (RTE) Act came into effect on April 10, 2010.[13]

The Ministry of Human Resource Development (MHRD) claims on its website that the Act means that "every child has a right to full-time elementary education of satisfactory and equitable quality in a formal school which satisfies certain essential norms and standards." In his address to the nation on the day the RTE Act came into effect, Prime Minister Manmohan Singh stated,

> Today, our government comes before you to redeem the pledge of giving all our children the right to elementary education. The Right of Children to Free and Compulsory Education Act, enacted by Parliament in August 2009, has come into force today. The Fundamental Right to Education, as incorporated in our Constitution under Article 21A, has also become operative from today. This demonstrates our national commitment to the education of our children and to the future of India.[14]

The Union HRD minister Kapil Sibal described the passage of the Act by Parliament as "harbinger of a new era" for children.[15] Shantha Sinha, chairperson of the National Commission on the Protection of Children's Rights, called the Act "a watershed in India's education sector."[16] The UNICEF representative in India Karin Hulshof said: "Tens of millions of children will benefit from this initiative ensuring quality education with equity."[17] The media went to town proclaiming the Act as a "historic law,"[18] with which "India had joined a group of few countries in the world" where education was a "fundamental right of every child."[19]

However, the truth about the RTE Act is that its real purpose is the exact opposite of the above claims. The MHRD website says that the RTE Act "represents the consequential legislation envisaged under Article 21-A,"[20] in other words, its agenda is to further the objective of the 86th Constitutional Amendment. And as we have discussed in detail in the previous section, the real purpose of the 86th Constitutional Amendment is to circumvent the Unnikrishnan judgement of the Supreme Court; therefore, the RTE Act is the "consequential legislation" to circumscribe this Supreme Court judgement declaring Right to Education to be a Fundamental Right.

That this is indeed so becomes clear from a closer reading of the RTE Act.

Deconstructing the RTE Act

One: Does the RTE Act guarantee free education to all children?

No, it does not! While the title of the Act incorporates the words "Free ... Education", in the text of the Act nowhere is it stated that all children will be provided completely free education. The Act clearly states [Section 3 (ii)] that 'free education' means that "no child shall be liable to pay any kind of fee or charges or expenses which may prevent him or her from pursuing and completing elementary education."

So, clearly, the word "Free" in the title of the Act is a deliberate subterfuge. What is the real purpose of this deception? Let us analyse further.

Two: How does the Act propose to provide 'compulsory' elementary education to the roughly 8 crore out-of-school children—the children who have dropped out of school without completing elementary education?[21]

There is no special provision for this in the Act! All that it says is that out-of-school children will be provided admission in a nearby school in age appropriate class and will be provided remedial coaching.

It is obvious that this provision is only going to remain on paper. Putting out-of-school children back into school will require special efforts, and the Act is silent on this. Neither does the Act set a timeline for universalisation of elementary education.

Secondly, this would also require the construction of tens of thousands of schools and recruitment of lakhs of teachers. The Bihar Common School System Commission in its report submitted in June 2007 estimated that in order to universalise elementary education in Bihar in five years (2008–13), 25,900 additional primary schools and 15,500 middle schools* will have to be built over this five-year period, and 6.5 lakh additional teachers recruited (at the primary and middle school level).[22] The corresponding numbers at the national level are going to be many times more.

However, the RTE Act makes no estimate of the additional number of schools that would have to be built and the additional number of teachers that would need to be recruited and trained in order to universalise elementary education. There are no signs that the government is at all serious about building new schools and recruiting additional teachers for these schools; on the contrary, as we shall see in the next chapter, it is closing down existing government schools in thousands.

Three: While not guaranteeing 'Free' education, what the Act does guarantee is unequal, discriminatory education!

The Act gives sanction to the multi-layer discriminating school system existing in India. It legalises [Section 2(n)] the currently operating four categories of schools in India: (a) government schools; (b) government-aided private schools; (c) special category (elite) government schools, such as the Navodaya Vidyalayas, Sainik Schools, etc.; and (d) non-aided private schools.

Within each of these four categories, there is going to be a whole range of schools—from those government and private schools that barely fulfil the infrastructural norms as required by the Schedule to the Act, to those schools (again both government and private) which will be reasonably well-endowed (e.g. teachers for fine arts, physical education and computers) and, finally, to very elite private schools with air-conditioned classrooms, swimming pools, etc.

In this context, the question arises: Can there be a 'fundamental right' to unequal, inferior education? But this is just what the Indian Parliament sanctioned, when it passed the RTE Act!

---

* *Middle school: School from Grade I to VIII*

This is precisely what neoliberalism is all about. It talks of 'freedoms'—if you have the money, you can get the best possible education, food, healthcare, housing for yourself and your family; but if you don't have the money, you have the 'freedom' to remain illiterate, starve, sleep on the footpath, die of entirely curable disease...

Four: Will the Act lead to improvement of infrastructure and other quality-related aspects of schools, especially government schools?

Some infrastructural norms have been laid down in the Schedule attached to the Act. The norms are extremely deficient. For instance, they say that for primary schools (schools from Class I to V), if the school has less than 60 children, it can make do with 2 teachers; and schools having up to 149 children need not have a head teacher. Basing himself on DISE data, the noted educationist Anil Sadgopal has estimated that even if the Act is fully implemented, almost 67% of the primary schools shall continue to be denied a separate teacher/classroom per class, and 75% of the primary schools will be without a head teacher. Even access to electricity is not guaranteed![23]

Worse, the country's ruling classes are not interested in spending any money on implementing even these pathetic norms. The Act set a deadline of three years (ending March 31, 2013) for schools to implement the norms mentioned in the Schedule. In October 2012, the Supreme Court, taking cognisance of the deplorable state of basic facilities in schools, directed all state governments to ensure that the situation was rectified in accordance with RTE norms by the end of March 2013. Eighteen state governments filed affidavits claiming they had already met the norms six months ago! Even a casual visit to government schools in any of these states will reveal the falsehood of these claims.

After completion of the March 31, 2013 deadline for meeting the infrastructural requirements stipulated by the Act, less than 10% schools were RTE–compliant.[24] *The Hindu*, in a newsreport after the deadline had passed, observed: "The Right to Education Act seems suspended in a vacuum, with the government doing virtually nothing to ensure that the norms stipulated by it were met by March 31."[25]

Five: Will the Act raise the status and quality of teachers?

The RTE Act does not prescribe any qualifications for teachers; nor does it say anything regarding their service terms and conditions. Section 23 of the RTE Act says: "Any person possessing such minimum qualification, as laid down by an academic authority, authorised by the Central government, by notification, shall be eligible for appointment as a teacher." Considering that for the past two decades, the Central and state governments have generally been appointing ill-trained, under-qualified para-teachers on contractual basis in schools means that this neoliberal policy of appointing para-teachers will continue, unless some state governments act otherwise. The budget outlays approved by the Planning Commission also provide for salaries which are in the framework of para-teachers, rather than regular teachers with pay scales.[26]

These are not unfounded fears. Many state governments have imposed a ban on recruitment of new teachers. In several states, the state governments are recruiting ad hoc or para-teachers without proper qualification and with one-fourth or less salary than regular teachers. Recently, even the Supreme Court was constrained to observe that it was "shocking" that appointment of teachers on an ad hoc basis was still being pursued three years after the implementation of the Right to Education Act.[27]

Six: Will the Act ensure that there will be no paucity of funds for elementary education?

No! There is not even a financial memorandum attached to the Act! All that the Act says in this regard is: "It is not possible to quantify the financial requirement on this account at this stage."

This is a barefaced lie. Two expert groups set up by the Government of India itself have made estimates of the additional cost that would need to be incurred for providing free, compulsory and universal school education to all children in the age group 6–14 within a time-bound framework. As mentioned earlier, the Expert Group under the chairmanship of Professor Tapas Mazumdar estimated in 1999 this additional cost to be Rs 13,700 crore per annum over the next 10 years. The Expert Group set up by a committee of the Central

Advisory Board on Education (CABE) estimated in 2004 the total additional cost for this to be approximately Rs 73,000 crore per annum over the next six years—the reason for this huge increase being the non-implementation of the Tapas Majumdar committee recommendations and the resulting cumulative gap.[28]

This, plus sections two, four and five above, clearly lead to the conclusion that the RTE Act is going to remain only on paper. Its provisions are so deliberately constructed that the deterioration of the government school system that has been taking place since the last two decades is not going to be reversed. The government schools will continue to remain underfunded and staffed with under-paid, ill-trained and under-qualified teachers, and crores of children will continue to drop out of school without completing even basic schooling.

Seven: But won't the provision of 25 percent reservation in private and special category schools for children from weaker sections and disadvantaged groups ensure better education for them?

This is supposedly the most progressive provision of the Act. It states that while government schools shall provide free and compulsory education to all children in the 6–14 age group, the aided private schools shall provide free education in proportion to the aid received by them, subject to a minimum of 25%. The special category schools and non-aided private schools shall admit in Class I, to the extent of at least 25% of the strength of that class, children belonging to the weaker sections or disadvantaged groups in the neighbourhood and provide free elementary education to them. The schools will be reimbursed the expenditure so incurred by them by the State, the maximum limit of reimbursement being the per-child expenditure in government schools.

There is a lot of hype around this provision, that finally, all the poor children in the country will get 'good quality' education—in private schools. Even assuming that private schools provide better quality education than government schools, the problem with this statement is: there are simply not enough private schools! Data collected by the HRD Ministry's DISE in 2010 tells us that in that academic year, even if all the private schools fully implemented the provision of 25% reservation for poor students, at the most 18 lakh children from weaker sections would be admitted by them in Class I under this provision. The overwhelming majority, almost 2 to 2.5 crore children, would be knocking at the doors of the deliberately neglected government school system.[29] And as we have discussed above, the government is not interested in implementing even the meagre infrastructural norms stipulated in the RTE Act in government schools.

The truth of the matter is, this is actually a very regressive provision. Why? Because private schools are essentially teaching shops, their entire orientation is to make money for their owners by charging high fees under all kinds of guises from the children of the middle and elite classes studying there. Therefore, when they are forced to admit children from poor families, the attitude will be that they are doing a 'favour' to them, and they will discriminate against these children in myriad ways. There is also no clue as to how the children admitted under this provision will meet the exorbitant and arbitrary non-fee costs of private schools. Most importantly, the attitude of both the teachers and the students from the wealthier families towards these children will be patronising. Therefore, it would not be surprising if a large number of students admitted to private schools under this reservation provision eventually drop out; and even if they do not drop out, they are almost certainly going to develop a strong inferiority complex.

Apart from this psychological aspect, another important implication of this provision of reservation in private schools is that it is a declaration by the government that it cannot run good schools. Most of our readers are going to say: "Yes, that is true, isn't it!" But the fact is, if the government wants, it can run very good schools—it is well-known that Navodaya Vidyalayas and Kendriya Vidyalayas are amongst the best schools in the country. The regular government schools are deteriorating because the government is allowing them to deteriorate, as a part of the World Bank-dictated educational reforms. Therefore, the RTE Act's provision for reservation in private schools means that the government has decided to abdicate its responsibility to improve the quality of the regular government schools and open more schools.

The Supreme Court too has upheld the provision of 25% reservation, instead of demanding of the government that it improve the quality of education in government schools and ensure equitable education to all children. It has thus sanctioned the violation of the exalted Articles 14 (Equality before law), 15 (Prohibition of discrimination), 16 (Equality of opportunity in public employment) and 21 (Right to life with dignity).

One final comment on this issue. An essential component of neoliberalism is withdrawal of government subsidies to the poor, and transfer of government funds to the private sector under various guises. The provision that private schools will be reimbursed by the government for providing free education to poor children is also a part of this policy frame; it is yet another way of transferring public funds to private hands—corporate houses, NGOs, religious bodies, etc. The UP Government recently allocated about Rs 3300 crore for this purpose.[30]

Eight: Will the Act at least lead to better regulation of the fees charged by private schools, thereby lowering cost of education?

No! The Act does not have any provision under which public authorities can regulate the fee structure of private schools. The ban in Section 13 on charging capitation fees is a smokescreen. The definition of capitation fee in Section 2(b) indeed permits private schools to charge capitation fee as long as it is included in the fee being notified at the time of admission.

In fact, the Act actually gives freedom to aided and non-aided private schools to charge as much fees as they wish from 75% of the students. Union HRD Minister Kapil Sibal told a gathering of managers of a powerful school lobby in New Delhi in February 2010 that the Act did not prevent private schools from increasing their fees or underpaying their teachers as per their convenience. When reminded about the existing laws that authorise some of the States/UTs to regulate the fee structure of private schools, Sibal assured them that in view of the concurrency of education, any provision in a State/UT law that was in conflict with a Central Act would become infructuous.[31]

★ ★ ★

From the analysis above, it is obvious that the Indian State had the following three objectives in framing the RTE Act:

1. Abdicating its Constitutional obligation to provide free and compulsory education of equitable quality to all children in the country.
2. Demolishing the government school system, except the special category schools (that is, the Kendriya Vidyalayas, Navodaya Vidyalayas, XI Plan's 6,000 model schools and similar elite schools of the state/UT governments); and
3. Increasing the pace of privatisation and commercialisation of school education.

The Act should therefore ideally be called *Commercialisation of Education Act*. It completes the process started by the 86th Constitutional Amendment to fulfil the dictates of the IMF–World Bank Structural Adjustment Programme in elementary education.

NOTES

1. *Right to Education Act*, http://india.gov.in.
2. *Unni Krishnan, J.P. and Ors. Etc. ... vs State of Andhra Pradesh and Ors. ... on February 4, 1993*, http://indiankanoon.org; also cited in: Anil Sadgopal, "Right to Education vs. Right to Education Act", *Social Scientist*, September–December 2010, http://www.scribd.com.
3. Anil Sadgopal, ibid.
4. Muchkund Dubey, "Right of Children to Free and Compulsory Education Bill, 2009: The Story of a Missed Opportunity", *Mainstream*, Vol. XLVII, No. 40, September 19, 2009, http://www.mainstreamweekly.net.
5. *Persistent Exclusion of Muslims in India*, December 2011, http://infochangeindia.org; "Contrary to Gujarat Government Claim, Latest Data Suggest Condition of Muslims in India and Gujarat is Worse than Other Communities", November 28, 2013, http://counterview.org.
6. Anil Sadgopal, "Right to Education vs. Right to Education Act", op. cit.
7. Ibid.
8. Anil Sadgopal, "Political Economy of the Ninety-third Amendment Bill", *Mainstream*, December 22, 2001, http://www.doccentre.net.

9. Ibid.; Anil Sadgopal, "Education for Too Few", *Frontline*, November 22–December 5, 2003, http://www.flonnet.com.
10. Anil Sadgopal, "Political Economy of the Ninety-third Amendment Bill", ibid.
11. Ibid.; Anil Sadgopal, "Education for Too Few", op. cit.
12. Anil Sadgopal, "Right to Education vs. Right to Education Act", op. cit.; Anil Sadgopal, "Dilution, Distortion and Diversion: A Post-Jomtien Reflection on Education Policy", published in Ravi Kumar (ed.), *The Crisis of Elementary Education in India*, Sage Publications, New Delhi, 2006, pp. 92–136, available on the internet at xa.yimg.com.
13. Anil Sadgopal, "Right to Education vs. Right to Education Act", ibid.
14. *Right to Education*, http://mhrd.gov.in/rte; *Prime Minister's Address to the Nation on The Fundamental Right of Children to Elementary Education*, Press Information Bureau, Government of India, April 1, 2010, http://pib.nic.in.
15. "Parliament Passes Landmark Right to Education Bill", PTI, August 4, 2009, http://articles.timesofindia.indiatimes.com.
16. "Right to Education a Historic Act: Shanta", March 22, 2010, http://www.newindianexpress.com.
17. "Education is Fundamental Right for Kids Aged 6–14", ET Bureau, April 2, 2010, http://articles.economictimes.indiatimes.com.
18. See for instance: *The Hindu*, April 1, 2010; *Times of India*, April 1, 2010.
19. "Education is a Fundamental Right Now", April 1, 2010, http://www.thehindu.com; "From Today, Every Child has a Right to Education", *PTI*, April 1, 2010, http://articles.timesofindia.indiatimes.com.
20. *Right to Education*, http://mhrd.gov.in/rte.
21. For details on this statistic, see Chapter 1.
22. *Report of the Common School System Commission*, Government of Bihar, Patna, June 7, 2007, pp. 182–83, 196–97, http://www.educationforallinindia.com.
23. Anil Sadgopal, "Education for Too Few", op. cit., box on pp. 6–7.
24. Madhu Prasad, "Commoditising Higher Education: The Assault of Neoliberal Barbarism", in Ravi Kumar (ed.), *Education, State and Market: Anatomy of Neoliberal Impact*, Aakar Books, Delhi, 2014, p. 95.
25. "The Passing of a Deadline", *The Hindu*, April 14, 2013, http://www.thehindu.com.
26. Anil Sadgopal, "Education for Too Few", op. cit., box on pp. 6–7.
27. "SC Slams Ad Hoc Appointment of Teachers in Primary Schools",

May 20, 2013, http://www.thehindu.com; "No Takers for D Ed Course", *TNN*, May 15, 2013, http://articles.timesofindia.indiatimes.com.

28. Muchkund Dubey, "Right of Children to Free and Compulsory Education Bill, 2009: The Story of a Missed Opportunity", op. cit.
29. Anil Sadgopal, "Neoliberal Act", *Frontline*, July 15, 2011, http://www.frontline.in.
30. Anil Sadgopal, "Education for Too Few", op. cit., box on pp. 6–7.
31. Anil Sadgopal, "Neoliberal Act", op. cit.

7

POST-RTE ACT: FULL-SCALE ASSAULT ON PUBLIC EDUCATION BEGINS

- After two decades of World Bank-sponsored District Primary Education Programme (1993–2002) and Sarva Shiksha Abhiyan (2000–2010) having enfeebled the government school system and destroyed its public credibility;
- and with the Constitution having been suitably amended and the enabling RTE Act passed to allow the government to abdicate from its responsibility of providing free and compulsory education to all children;

➡ *the government has now launched a full-scale offensive to privatise the government school system.*

PPP: Transfer of Public Resources and Funds to Private Sector

Of course, the government still needs to maintain the illusion that it is concerned with providing educational facilities to all children and that it has not completely washed its hands of the education sector. So privatisation is now being done under a new slogan, 'Public–Private–Partnership' or PPP.

PPP was initially promoted in a big way in the infrastructural sectors (electricity, railways, roads, ports, airports, irrigation, etc.). Under this, the private partner is guaranteed a minimum rate of return on its investment (the government making up for any shortfall in profits). It is given land and other resources at concessional rates. And as if this is not enough, the investment money is also often provided by the government in the form of long-term loans at concessional rates. What a partnership!

Now, the government is extending PPP to the education sector. Here, PPP means handing over school management, appointment of teachers and their supervision, curriculum, provision of educational material, etc. to the private sector, which in the education sector includes corporates, non-governmental organisations (NGOs) and religious bodies.

The chicanery of PPP in the education sector was first introduced by the Atal Bihari Vajpayee-led NDA Government. In 2002, a Working Group on Public-Private Partnership was established in the Prime Minister's Office, with representatives from select Ministries and the Planning Commission. Subsequently, a 'PPP Sub-Group on Social Sector' was established in 2003. It was tasked with exploring the feasibility of PPPs in social sector development, including elementary education. The Sub-Group dutifully did the needful. Stating that PPP had its origin in the general distrust of the bureaucracy and oppressiveness of the State, it posited PPP as a more effective and efficient way of delivering social services to citizens, claiming that it would mean greater cost-effectiveness, higher productivity and accelerated delivery. Furthermore, it claimed that PPP is not privatisation, since control remains with the government. It also uncritically accepted the argument that there is a shortage of resources and that budgetary allocations "will fall short of the requirements" to meet development targets, and additionally argued that PPP would have the added advantage of reversing years of chronic underinvestment through mobilising private capital. Given all these 'advantages' of PPP, it justified the introduction of PPPs in social services, including elementary education.[1]

The Sub-Group submitted its report in November 2004, but by then, the NDA Government had fallen and the UPA Government was in power at the Centre. However, as we have mentioned in Chapter 4, globalisation is the consensus policy of the entire Indian ruling class, and all the major political parties are in agreement over implementing neoliberal economic reforms, including privatisation of essential services. Therefore, the UPA Government had no problems in accepting the report of this Sub-Group and introducing PPP in social services, including elementary education. In fact, in September

2007, while chairing a meeting of the Planning Commission, Prime Minister Manmohan Singh announced that henceforth all new initiatives in the field of education would be taken through the PPP mode.[2] This approach of the Government of India is clearly manifest in the Eleventh Plan.

The Eleventh Five Year Plan

The Eleventh Plan (2007–12) was drawn up by the Planning Commission after the passage of the 86th Constitutional Amendment by the Parliament in 2002 and when the government was in the process of finalising the RTE Act, the "consequential legislation" to this Amendment. Therefore, an analysis of the Eleventh Plan reveals how the government plans to implement the RTE Act and provide "free and compulsory education to all children."

Eleventh Plan Objectives

The Eleventh Plan is full of rhetoric about the government's commitment to providing education to the children of the country. So much so that the Prime Minister has called it "India's educational plan."[3]

It declared that it "places the highest priority on education as a central instrument for achieving rapid and inclusive growth" and that it sought to present "a comprehensive strategy for strengthening the education sector covering all segments of the education pyramid." It promised universal enrolment in elementary education, including enrolment of the children of hard-to-reach segments, substantial improvement in quality, elimination of all gender, social and regional gaps in enrolment, elimination of the phenomenon of drop-outs altogether in primary education and a reduction in the drop-out rate by 50% in elementary education, universalisation of mid-day meals, universal coverage of information and communication technologies (ICT) at upper primary level, etc. It also announced a scheme for universalisation of secondary education—Scheme for Universal Access and Quality at the Secondary Stage (SUCCESS)—with a target of attaining an enrolment ratio of 75% by 2011-12.[4]

Not only that, the Planning Commission, in the Approach Paper to the Eleventh Plan, asserted that the role of the State needs to be expanded and public resources need to be directed to the social sectors, where expansion is sorely needed and which cannot be left solely to market forces.[5]

Eleventh Plan Financing

From all these proclamations, it appeared that the government had finally decided to implement the Kothari Commission recommendation that "if education is to develop adequately," the proportion of GDP allocated to education must rise to 6%.

Actually, even this 6% norm is very inadequate today. This goal was set more than 40 years ago, and was supposed to have been reached in 1986. However, actual government spending has always been much below this target. Given this huge backlog in funding, if the funding requirement for 'adequate development of education' is re-estimated today, it will definitely come to much more than the 6% of GDP estimated by the Kothari Commission. J.B.G. Tilak, one of India's best known educational economists, has estimated that to reach even modest goals in education development, public spending on education would need to rise to at least 8–10% of GDP.[6]

Forget 8–10%, educational spending during the Eleventh Plan did not even come near the Kothari Commission benchmark of 6% of GDP. While overall there did take place some increase in allocation to education during the Eleventh Plan, even then, the total allocation made was much below the level required. The allocation for education during the Eleventh Plan gradually rose from 3.4% of the GDP in 2007–08 to 4.2% of the GDP in 2010–11, and then declined again the next year to 4.17%.[7]

According to the Eleventh Plan document, the Sarva Shiksha Abhiyan (SSA) is the "principal programme for universalisation of elementary education,"[8] that is, it is the main scheme for the implementation of the RTE Act. Now, a genuine implementation of this Act requires huge resources, as it implies establishment of a very large number of new schools with adequate facilities, improving facilities in existing schools, a huge increase in the number of teachers, massive expansion of facilities for teacher training, etc. On top of it, the Eleventh Plan also promised conversion of all EGS centres to regular schools, improvement in quality of education in all schools to the level of Kendriya Vidyalayas, etc.[9] —all of which call for still higher levels of spending.

If the government was serious about implementing these objectives, it should have allocated at least the amount estimated by the recently constituted CABE committee for universalising elementary education—Rs 73,000 crore per annum over the next six years—for Sarva Shiksha Abhiyan in the Eleventh Plan. If not that, at the very least, it should have sanctioned the lower estimate accepted by the Ministry of Human Resource Development (MHRD) for universalisation of elementary education, of Rs 1,71,000 crore over the next five years.[10] However, the total allocation made towards SSA in the Eleventh Plan was much less than even this latter figure: it was allocated a mere Rs 71,000 crore (and the total amount spent was slightly above that, Rs 78,000 crore)[11] which is less than half the very conservative estimate of Rs 171,000 crore made by the MHRD.

Clearly, the government was never serious about implementing any of the high-sounding proclamations made in the Eleventh Plan with regard to development of the education sector.

Quality Plan ...

The Planning Commission claimed that the "Eleventh Plan would be a Quality Plan in respect of the education sector."[12]

But there was little in the Plan to suggest that it was concerned with quality of education. The Eleventh Plan noted that around 7.1 million children were out of school, and that over 50% drop out at the elementary level.[13] While admitting that this was cause for serious concern, the Plan had nothing new to offer to address this issue, the Sarva Shiksha Abhiyan continued to be the main, actually the only, scheme in the Eleventh Plan for universalising elementary education. The SSA sanctifies the most reprehensible methods of providing education, such as the education guarantee scheme and other non-formal and informal methods of education, and gives sanction to teaching through para-teachers. The Planning Commission did not question any of these aspects of the SSA; it assumed that non-formal education centres, together with the mid-day meal scheme, would solve the problem of the high rate of drop-outs.

The Planning Commission, in its Approach Paper to the Eleventh Plan, expressed concern over the poor level of learning in primary schools.[14] However, it refused to note the critical role that the teacher plays, the need for well-qualified and trained teachers and the need to do away with the large number of under-qualified, under-trained and under-paid para-teachers being recruited everywhere.

The only new strategy outlined in the Eleventh Plan to improve the dismal state of elementary education in the country was PPP ...

The Guiding Mantra of the Eleventh Plan: PPP

Going beyond financing issues, an analysis of the Eleventh Plan makes it clear that despite repeated assertions of "a greatly expanded role for the State" in social sectors, the whole thrust in the Eleventh Plan was towards a diminished role of the State in education and promotion of a strategy of privatisation of education through the PPP route. The Mid-term Appraisal of the Eleventh Plan in fact bluntly admitted that the "Eleventh Plan statement" is "that PPP in education needs to be encouraged."[15] In the words of Prachi Srivastava, Associate Professor at the University of Ottawa in the area of education and international development, "delivering education in 'PPP mode'" was the "guiding mantra" of India's eleventh development plan.[16]

PPP Storm

Ever since the launch of the Eleventh Plan, a storm of PPP has been sweeping across the education sector in the country. State governments are indulging in a mad orgy of commercialising education in their respective states.

Several state governments have entered into contracts with corporate houses to set up schools under the PPP model. Most of these contracts generally stipulate that the government will allocate land for the school at concessional rates. The school would have to admit 50% of the children from weaker sections, and their costs would be reimbursed by the state government. For the remaining seats, the school would be free to charge any amount of fees.[17]

It is not just that new schools are being set up in the private sector; state governments are privatising existing government schools too! As discussed in the previous chapters, due to the neoliberal reforms, the government school system is deteriorating and students are exiting government schools in large numbers. This declining enrolment is giving state governments the excuse to shut down government schools en masse or transfer them to the private sector. In Karnataka, the government has shut down thousands of government schools over the last few years under various pretexts; it is also drawing up plans to invite private investment into schools under the PPP mode.[18] In Uttarakhand, the state government has decided to transfer 2,200 government schools to the private sector under the PPP mode.[19] In Rajasthan, the notorious Vedanta company's Hindustan Zinc has signed an MoU with the state government to adopt 92 government schools; while the Bharti Foundation has adopted 49 government schools.[20]

In a decision which probably sets the trend for the future, in Mumbai, the Brihanmumbai Municipal Corporation (BMC) has decided to hand over all of its 1,174 schools to private organisations and companies under a 'Public Private Partnership' scheme of 'School Adoption'. These schools have 11,500 teachers and provide free education to nearly 4 lakh students in eight language mediums.[21] This decision is an unprecedented bonanza for corporate vultures, as these schools occupy prime land of the metropolis, and the value of their land alone could be thousands of crores of rupees.

Secondary Education and PPP

In the Eleventh Plan, the government acknowledged, probably for the first time, that universal education of up to eight years is not sufficient for a country that aspires to be a knowledge superpower. The Plan set out the objective of "rais(ing) the minimum level of education to Class X and accordingly universalise access to secondary education." For this, it announced a new scheme, SUCCESS, that was restructured in 2009 as the Rashtriya Madhyamik Shiksha Abhiyan (RMSA).[22] This target of universalising secondary education is of course unexceptionable, it should have been set decades ago. But like other proclamations of the Eleventh Plan, that this too is mere hype becomes obvious from the way this objective is proposed to be achieved: the Plan unabashedly promotes PPP as the main way to achieve universalisation of secondary education!

The Planning Commission admits that the share of government and local body schools and private-aided schools in secondary education has shown a declining trend, while the percentage of private-unaided secondary schools has doubled, increasing from 15% in 1993–94 to 30% in 2004–05 to 35% in 2006–07.[23] It also acknowledges that "only those who can afford to pay apparently opt for these schools."[24] Nevertheless, it stresses that the massive expansion required in secondary education calls for a huge expansion in private-unaided schools[25] and that there is considerable scope for public-private partnership in this sector.[26]

To give a fillip to PPP in secondary education, the Planning Commission proposed the setting up of 6,000 high quality 'Model Schools' across the country under the Eleventh Plan; of these, "about 2,500 schools would be set up through PPP ... These schools will be managed and run by involving corporates, philanthropic foundations, endowments, educational trusts, and reputed private providers."[27] Each school would have about 2,500 students. Of these, 1,000 will be from deprived sections; they will be given free education and their expenses would be reimbursed by the Union government (at the rate of around Rs 1,000 per student per month). For the remaining 1,500 seats, the schools can admit anyone and charge any amount of fees.

These PPP schools will be completely different from government-aided private schools. The latter are required to follow most of the government rules and regulations in terms of admissions, fees, recruitment of staff, salary structure, and so on. Therefore, even though they are managed by the private sector, there is very little scope for profit-making (though some schools do make profits due to malpractices by the managements). In contrast, while the PPP model represents a transfer of massive sums from the exchequer to the private sector—it is estimated that the Union government will have to pay Rs 10,500 crore till 2017 to the private operators of the secondary model schools—there will be no government or social control over these schools. On top of it, they are allowed to indulge in open profiteering as they are free to fix fee levels.[28]

No Regulation too!

Despite this proliferation of private recognised and unrecognised schools, the Eleventh Plan document recommended withdrawal of the State and devolution of responsibility in the areas of monitoring of schools and quality improvement to panchayats, community-based organisations (without specifying what these are and how they would be involved), and undefined 'citizens' education committees'.[29] Thus, the State is wanting to abdicate its responsibility in monitoring quality of education too!

And Now, Free Rein to Profiteering

The government is in a hurry to remove all obstacles to privatisation of elementary education. Two years after the Eleventh Plan was finalised, in its Mid-term Appraisal of the Eleventh Plan, the Planning Commission recommended that the "necessary legislative measures to facilitate private participation must be initiated... as early as possible."[30] The Mid-Year Analysis of the Budget 2010–11 tabled in Parliament in December 2010 went a step further, and argued that since the RTE Act needs huge resources, and "Government resources may themselves be insufficient and need to be supplemented", it would be advisable to allow profit-making schools to be set up.

The law as it stands today prohibits commercial for-profit organisations to provide schooling; all private-aided/unaided schools have to be non-profit organisations [set up as societies (or trusts) under the Societies Act (relevant Trust Act)]. The Supreme Court in 1993 had ruled that "commercialisation of education cannot and should not be permitted."[31] The government now wants to do away with this constraint on profiteering in the school education sector. Stating that many corporate houses are eager to set up private schools for the profits they promise, the Mid-Year Analysis recommends that it is "advisable to discontinue with the non-profit trust requirement and allow schools to be profit-making."[32]

The Emperor's nakedness is now apparent. As we have repeatedly pointed out in the previous chapters, this was from the beginning the real motive of the 86th Amendment and the RTE Act: to subvert the Unnikrishnan judgement of 1993 and allow commercialisation of school education. The 86th Amendment allows the State to determine how it wishes to provide 'free' education to children, and the RTE Act defines 'free' in such a roundabout way that it implies that schools can charge fees from those who can afford to pay—thus allowing private bodies to set up 'for profit' schools for the children of the rich as they can afford to pay high fees. The Mid-Year Analysis is only taking this to its logical end, it is calling for removal of all legal constraints on this ...

Net Result of 'Education Plan'

What is the net result of five years of implementation of "a comprehensive strategy for strengthening the education sector", the declared objective of the Eleventh Five Year Plan, as regards the elementary education sector?

Table 7.1: Number of Elementary Schools by Category[33]

	Total Number of Schools	*Government Schools*	*Private Schools*	*Unaided Schools*
2002–03	7,84,302	7,03,444 (89.7%)	29,336 (3.74%)	46,425 (5.92%)
2012–13	14,31,702	10,86,720 (75.9%)	68,149 (4.76%)	2,39,810 (16.75%)

Yet more rapid privatisation of the elementary school system! DISE data reveals that over the ten-year period 2002–03 to 2012–13, of the total number of elementary schools, the proportion of government schools has declined from 90% to 76%, while the number of recognised unaided private schools has nearly tripled, from 6% in 2002–03 to 17%. In absolute numbers, the figures are simply staggering. Over this decade, the total number of recognised private unaided schools has zoomed from 46,000 to nearly 2,40,000, by more than five times (Table 7.1)![34]

Table 7.2: Enrolment Share of Private Unaided Schools, Rural India, 2012[35]

School Level	*Household Survey Data 2012*
Primary	29.1
Middle	29.6
Secondary	33.9

Even this figure is a huge underestimate. That is because government data does not include unrecognised schools. As we have seen in Chapter 5, there has been an explosive growth in the number of unrecognised schools in the country. The extent to which private schooling has accelerated in the country during the Eleventh Plan period can be judged from household survey statistics. The provisional results from the ASER 2012 survey of households in rural areas are now available (Table 7.2). They show that in 2012, nearly one-third (29%) of school-going primary and middle school students in rural areas were going to private schools, as compared to 20% in 2006 (Chart 7.1). Looking at the trends, the ASER report estimates that in 2012, about 35% or more of India's primary school children in both urban and rural areas were attending private schools. It goes on to say that in all probability, by 2020, over 50% students will be paying for primary education.[36]

Chart 7.1: Rising Enrolment Share of Private Unaided Schools in Rural India, 1993–2012[37] (%)

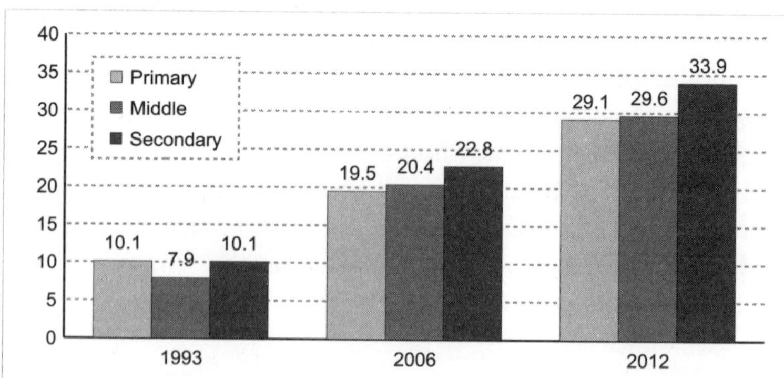

Gold-Plated Primary Schools

Trampling upon the Constitution as it was framed by our founding fathers, school education has now become a roaring business. It costs more to admit a child in an elite private primary, and even pre-primary school, than to put him/her through an IIT or a MBA degree!

The *Economic Times* reported in 2011 that playschools in metros were charging anything between Rs 35,000 and Rs 1 lakh per year, while the fees in primary and secondary schools was anywhere between Rs 50,000 to Rs 5 lakh a year.

Box 7.1: Five Star International Schools in Mumbai

Some of the country's biggest business houses, from the Goenkas, Podars, Somanis, and Ajmeras to Birlas and Ambanis, have hopped on to the school education bandwagon over the past decade. Making huge investments, they have launched five star schools, such as Dhirubhai Ambani International School, Podar World School, BD Somani International School, Aditya Birla Group promoted New Era School and Oberoi International School. These schools offer fully-wired campuses bristling with hi-tech equipment and teaching aids, fully air-conditioned classrooms, low student-teacher ratio of around 15:1, all kinds of extra-curricular facilities like auditoriums, gyms, swimming pools and studios, expat headmasters and affiliation with international examination boards like International Baccalaureate Organisation (IBO), Geneva and Cambridge International Examinations (CIE). Their fees range from anywhere between Rs 5 to Rs 10 lakh a year.

The only shortcoming of these international schools is that given Mumbai's giddy real estate prices, they cannot afford the sprawling campuses which are a distinguishing feature of international schools in cities like Delhi and Bangalore. The latter boast resort-style campuses spread over 40–100 acres, with residential and/or extensive sports facilities such as cricket and hockey fields, horse riding, tennis courts, and athletic tracks.

[Source: "Mumbai's New Genre International Schools", November 2007, http://www.educationworldonline.net.]

That was two years ago. Since then, school fees have more than doubled! An Assocham survey in Delhi-NCR in 2013 found that parents have to keep aside an average budget of between Rs 3 to 8 lakh for educating a single child in private schools. This includes fees, transport, books, uniform, stationery, building fund, educational trips, tuition, extra-curricular activities, etc.

Even that appears cheap, as compared to the fees charged by some of Mumbai's top schools. The fees in Ecole Mondiale, one of Juhu's posh schools, is Rs 15 lakh![38]

The Final Burial of the Constitutional Dream

Thus far, the government had surreptitiously promoted privatisation of elementary education. Now, the Planning Commission, in the Approach Paper to the Twelfth Plan, has shed all inhibitions and declared that the private sector needs to be involved more meaningfully in expanding the reach and improving the quality of elementary education in the country.[39]

In the same breath, the Planning Commission of the Government of India also emphasises that "education is the most important lever" for economic development.[40]

This latter statement of the Planning Commission is in direct contradiction with the previous statement on involving the private sector in the development of elementary education in the country. The Planning Commission is absolutely right in stating that education is the most important lever for economic development. As we have discussed in the Introduction to this book, all developed countries focused on providing free, compulsory, equitable and good quality elementary education to all their children in the initial stages of their development, and later expanded it to secondary and higher secondary education. All the major 'developing countries', including the countries of East Asia and Latin America, also took the same path when they began their development. But what the Planning Commission forgets to add is that all these countries achieved universalisation of elementary and later secondary/higher secondary education entirely through public funding, despite the fact that all these countries are avowedly free market economies.

Praveen Jha, Professor at the Centre for Economic Studies and Planning, Jawaharlal Nehru University, New Delhi and his colleagues make the same point in their study of financing of elementary education in India:

> India's policy makers refuse to learn a powerful lesson from history, which is: a decent quality infrastructure for school education accessible to all sections in society, particularly in the early to middle stages of economic development, has to be primarily the responsibility of the State. Even now, in most OECD countries, only about 10 percent of students attend private primary schools (a section of which are dependent on government support). In Sweden, only about 2 percent of the total expenditure on education is supplied by private sources, and in countries like France, more than 99.5 percent of educational expenditure comes only from the government. There is no historical script that points to any other way, apart from the strong public provisioning in this sector.

They go on to say that in fact, even after having achieved "comparatively very high levels of development and well-being, public provisioning of education (continues to have) a pre-eminent role" in the developed countries.[41]

There is no country in the world that has achieved universalisation of elementary education through the private sector. It can only be achieved in the public sector, through government spending. Despite this global developmental experience, India's ruling classes are bowing to imperialist dictates and ruthlessly implementing World Bank dictated neoliberal educational reforms, reducing government expenditure on education and gradually privatising not just higher education, but school education too. (And yet, they claim that the country is on its way to becoming an economic superpower!)

The conclusion is inescapable: *India's rulers have now finally decided to bury the dream nurtured by the freedom struggle and embedded in the Constitution of providing cost-free, equitable and quality education to all our children.*

Post-Script

The UPA Government had placed the 'Right to Free and Compulsory Education' granted by the Indian Constitution in the coffin for burial, the new BJP Government is hammering in the nails.

Even though the BJP Government has wound up the Planning Commission and replaced it by a new body, the Niti Aayog, the new government continues to tread the path laid out by the Planning Commission in its Eleventh and Twelfth Plans of accelerating privatisation and commercialisation of school education. It is doing this in a very straightforward way, by simply reducing the already low government spending on school education.

During the financial year 2014–15, the Modi–Jaitley Government cut its actual spending (over the budget estimate) on Sarva Shiksha Abhiyan, the main programme for implementing the Right to Education Act and universalising elementary education in the country, by 14%. Even the expenditure on the Mid-Day Meal programme—an important programme whose aim was to stop hunger from keeping children away from schools and improve school enrolment—was slashed, by a whopping 47% (see Table 7.3)! India's ruling classes have become so insensitive and self-centred that they are not even willing to spend a few thousand crores on providing nutritious, wholesome food once a day to the country's children.

Addressing the joint session of Parliament on February 23, 2015 at the beginning of the budget session, President Pranab Mukherjee, outlining the overall orientation of the BJP Government, stated that "Education is the priority of priorities for my government."[42] It has proven to be yet another false claim by the new government. A few days later, Finance Minister Arun Jaitley presented Union Budget 2015–16 to the Lok Sabha. In this first full budget of the BJP Government, he has unashamedly cut spending on Sarva Shiksha Abhiyan by 22% and the Mid-Day Meal programme by 30% over the budget estimates for 2014–15. (Note that these are entirely Central funded schemes.) Jaitley's allocations for these schemes are so low that they are even below the amount spent by the previous UPA Government on these schemes in 2013–14 (Table 7.3). In all probability, the actual amount that will be spent by this heartless government is going to be even lower.[43]

Table 7.3: Budgetary Allocations for Education 2013–14 to 2015–16[44] (*in Rs crore*)

	2013-14 (1)	*2014-15 BE* (2)	*2014-15 RE* (3)	*Reduction (2 – 3), %*	*2015-16 BE* (4)	*Reduction (2 – 4), %*
Ministry of Human Resource Development	71,321	82,771	70,505	14.8	69,075	16.6
Department of School Education and Literacy	46,856	55,115	46,805	15.1	42,220	23.4
of which:						
Sarva Shiksha Abhiyan	24,802	28,258	24,380	13.7	22,000	22.1
Mid-Day Meal Scheme	10,918	13,152	6,973	47	9,236	29.8
Department of Higher Education	24,465	27,656	23,700	14.3	26,855	2.9

NOTES

1. Prachi Srivastava, *Public–Private Partnerships or Privatisation? Questioning the State's Role in Education in India*, http://www.tandfonline.com.
2. Editorial, *Taalim Ki Ladaai*, Bulletin of the All India Forum for Right to Education, Joint issue: September 2012–March 2013, http://aifrte.in.
3. "11th Five Year Plan will be India's Education Plan: PM", *PTI*, December 28, 2007, http://articles.economictimes.indiatimes.com.
4. *Eleventh Five Year Plan, Vol. II: Social Sector*, Planning Commission, Government of India, pp. 1, 9, 16–17, 19, http://planning commission.nic.in.
5. *Towards Faster and More Inclusive Growth: An Approach to the 11th Five Year Plan, 2007–12*, Planning Commission, Government of India, December 2006, pp. 91, 101, http://planning commission.nic.in.
6. Jandhyala B.G. Tilak, "On Allocating 6 Percent of GDP to Education",

Economic and Political Weekly, February 18, 2006, available on internet at: www.nuepa.org.

7. *Analysis of Budgeted Expenditure on Education 2009–10 to 2011–12*, MHRD, 2013, http://mhrd.gov.in.
8. *Eleventh Five Year Plan, Vol. II: Social Sector*, op. cit., p. 1.
9. Ibid., p. 9.
10. Jandhyala B.G. Tilak, "Financing the Implementation of Right to Education Act", *Budget Track*, September 2010, Centre for Budget and Governance Accountability, New Delhi, www.cbgaindia.org.
11. *Twelfth Five Year Plan: 2012–17, Vol. III: Social Sectors*, Planning Commission, Government of India, p. 54, available on internet at: http://planningcommission.gov.in.
12. *Eleventh Five Year Plan, Vol. II: Social Sector*, op. cit., p. 19.
13. Ibid., p. 8.
14. *Towards Faster and More Inclusive Growth: An Approach to the 11th Five Year Plan, 2007–12*, op. cit., p. 58.
15. *Mid-term Appraisal of the Eleventh Five Year Plan*, Planning Commission, Government of India, 2011, p. 141, http://planning commission.nic.in.
16. Prachi Srivastava, *Public–Private Partnerships or Privatisation? Questioning the State's Role in Education in India*, op. cit.
17. See, for instance: Shishir Prashant, "To Fight Inefficiency, Uttarakhand Adopts PPP Model for its Schools to Fight", October 31, 2012, http://www.business-standard.com; "Haryana Follows Punjab Model to Set up Schools", *Express News Service*, April 6, 2011, http://www.indianexpress.com; *Public Private Partership in School Education*, http://www.azimpremjifoundation.org.
18. *Karnataka Government Shutting Down Government Schools - Dr. Niranjanaradhya V.P.*, October 25, 2011, http://www.haqcrc.org; "Government Eyes Private Assistance to Revamp Karnataka Schools", December 13, 2013, http://www.newindianexpress.com.
19. "Government Schools for PPP Mode in Uttarakhand", February 8, 2013, http://www.linkedin.com; "Dr. Udit Raj: National Convention on Education Policy on 8 September, 2013", Facebook, https://www.facebook.com.
20. "Public-Private Partnership Model Holds Promise for Educating Poor", *TNN*, April 11, 2012, http://articles.timesofindia.india times.com; "Hindustan Zinc to Adopt 92 Schools in Rajasthan", December 5, 2012, http://www.thehindu.com.
21. "Privatising BMC Schools an Assault on Education: Experts", July 23, 2013, http://www.themetrognome.in; "Keep Off Education", *Economic and Political Weekly*, June 8, 2013, http://schoolchoice.in.
22. *Eleventh Five Year Plan, Vol. II: Social Sector*, op. cit., pp. 16–17.

23. Ibid., p. 15; *Mid-term Appraisal of the Eleventh Five Year Plan*, op. cit., p. 126.
24. *Eleventh Five Year Plan, Vol. II: Social Sector*, ibid., p. 15.
25. *Eleventh Five Year Plan, Vol. I: Inclusive Growth*, Planning Commission, Government of India, p. 17, http://planning commission.nic.in.
26. *Mid-term Appraisal of the Eleventh Five Year Plan*, op. cit., p. 126.
27. *Eleventh Five Year Plan, Vol. II: Social Sector*, op. cit., p. 17.
28. J.B.G. Tilak, "Public-Private Partnership in Education", May 24, 2010, http://www.thehindu.com; Aesha Datta, "PPP Model Schools – Worries Over Commercialisation", July 28, 2013, http://www.thehindubusiness line.com.
29. Prachi Srivastava, *Public–Private Partnerships or Privatisation? Questioning the State's Role in Education in India*, op. cit.
30. *Mid-term Appraisal of the Eleventh Five Year Plan*, op. cit., p. 141.
31. *Unni Krishnan, J.P. and Ors. Etc. ... vs State of Andhra Pradesh and Ors. ... on 4 February, 1993*, http://www.indiankanoon.org.
32. *Mid-Year Analysis: 2010–2011*, Ministry of Finance, Government of India, p. 52, http://finmin.nic.in.
33. *Analytical Tables 2002–03*, DISE, http://dise.in; *Flash Statistics, Elementary Education in India: Progress Towards UEE: DISE 2012–13*, 2013, NUEPA, New Delhi-16, http://dise.in.
34. Figures for 2002–03 calculated from *Analytical Tables 2002–03*, DISE, http://dise.in; and figures for 2012–13 taken from: *Flash Statistics, Elementary Education in India: Progress Towards UEE: DISE 2012–13*, 2013, NUEPA, New Delhi-16, http://dise.in; Note that the data, especially the absolute numbers, given here has some limitations, but it gives a broad idea of the extent of privatisation that has taken place. The number of private unaided schools for 2002–03 is an underestimate, as the DISE survey of 2002–03 is much less comprehensive as compared to the 2012–13 survey; similarly, the data for both 2002–03 and 2012–13 excludes unrecognised private schools, whose number is also considerable, and has gone up over the years—the 2012–13 survey mentions that there are at least around 35,000 unrecognised schools and recognised and unrecognised madrasas, with the actual number probably being much more. Therefore, rather than the absolute figures, the percentages give a better idea of the extent of privatisation of elementary education.
35. *Annual Status of Education Report (Rural) 2012: Provisional*, January 17, 2013, ASER Centre, New Delhi, available on internet at http://www.asercentre.org.
36. *Annual Status of Education Report (Rural) 2012: Provisional*, ibid., p. 4.

37. Data for Chart taken from Tables 5.3 and 7.2.
38. "Pre-school in Mumbai Could Cost You Rs 7 lakh a Year", December 7, 2010, http://www.ndtv.com; "Child Education: A Dream Unfulfilled! - Parents Need to Keep Aside Rs. 3 to 8 Lakh for Nursery Admission: ASSOCHAM", February 25, 2013, http://www.assocham.org; Nupur Anand, "Education: Now, Take a Loan to Pay School Fee", *ET Bureau*, April 11, 2011, http://articles.economictimes.indiatimes.com; Shreya Bhandary, "Ecole Mondiale World School in Trouble Again", *TNN*, July 13, 2012, http://timesofindia.indiatimes.com.
39. *Faster, Sustainable and More Inclusive Growth: An Approach to the Twelfth Five Year Plan (2012–17)*, Planning Commission, Government of India, p. 97, http://planningcommission.gov.in.
40. *Twelfth Five Year Plan: 2012–17, Vol. III: Social Sectors*, op. cit., p. 47.
41. Praveen Jha et al., *Public Provisioning for Elementary Education in India*, Sage Publications, 2008, p. 37, http://books.google.co.in.
42. "President Pranab Mukherjee Speech to the Joint Session of Parliament", February 23, 2015, http://www.thehindu.com.
43. As discussed in our booklet *Budget 2015–16: What Is in It for the People?* (published by Lokayat, Pune, available on Lokayat website, lokayat.org.in), the government has over-estimated its tax revenues for 2015–16, and therefore, it will have to reduce its actual expenditures to achieve its fiscal deficit target—the axe will obviously fall on social sector spending.
44. Source for Table: Union Budget 2015–16 documents, available at: "Union Budget 2015–2016", http://indiabudget.nic.in.

8

HIGHER EDUCATION IN INDIA DURING THE BRITISH COLONIAL PERIOD

During the British colonial period, the rulers consciously made no attempt to promote higher education in India, beyond meeting their immediate needs of producing the small number of educated people needed to staff the lower rungs of their administration. The limited higher education system introduced by them was thus an integral element of the underdevelopment of India.

The first 'Europeanised' institution of higher learning in India was however not set up by the East India Company, but by Raja Ram Mohan Roy and a number of other anglicised elites of Bengal. They established the Hindu College in Calcutta in 1817, that was later renamed Presidency College. Over the next decades, several English colleges were set up both by Christian missionaries and the East India Company. Thus, the Mission College at Serampore (Hooghly district, West Bengal) was founded by the English missionaries Carey, Marshman and Ward in 1818; Bishop's College at Sibpur (Calcutta) by the Church of England in 1820; and the Scottish Church College also at Calcutta by the Scottish missionary Alexander Duff. The East India Company established the Sanskrit College at Calcutta in 1825, the Hooghly College at Chinsurah (Hooghly district, West Bengal) in 1836, Elphinstone College at Mumbai in 1834 and Madras Christian College at Madras in 1837. By 1855, there were 281 high schools and 28 colleges. Thus the British education system gradually supplanted the pre-colonial indigenous system of education and imposed a new language and curricula. Education in these new colleges became a passport for jobs in the colonial administrative and judicial system.

As the number of colleges increased, the need arose for regulating their work, holding examinations, and establishing a common standard. In 1854, Charles Wood, then President of the Board of Control of the East India Company, sent a despatch to Lord Dalhousie, the then Governor-General of India, recommending establishment of education departments in every province, streamlining education from primary to university level, and establishment of universities in the Presidency towns of Bombay, Madras and Calcutta. In accordance with his instructions, the Government of India passed Acts of Incorporation of all three universities in 1857. The main function of these universities was to conduct examinations and award degrees, while teaching work was done in the affiliated colleges.

It took the British another 30 years to establish universities at Allahabad (in 1857) and Lahore (in 1882). The Mohammedan Anglo-Oriental College at Aligarh was established in 1875, which later developed into the Aligarh Muslim University in 1920. The first university to deviate from the affiliating model was the Banaras Hindu University, set up in 1916—it was a unitary, residential and teaching university. Subsequently, more such teaching and residential universities were set up. The University of Mysore, also established in 1916, was the first university in a princely state.

By 1947, there were 21 universities in the Indian subcontinent. Partition left 19 universities and 496 colleges in India. With the partition of Punjab, and Punjab University (Lahore) going over to West Pakistan, India established the Panjab University soon after independence. Thus, by the end of 1947, there were 20 universities in India.

Most of the colleges set up during the colonial period were 'arts' colleges, whose primary function was to produce civil servants and white collar workers, imbued in Western culture; therefore, priority was given to the study of English language and literature. The curriculum was skewed towards the West and ignored Indian history, culture and philosophy. The British made only a very limited attempt to impart scientific and technical education to Indians—only to the extent needed by them for their limited public works such as roads, canals, bridges and railways (the British were not interested in industrialising India); and here too, the aim was to produce only skilled technicians to work at the lower grades like craftsmen and sub-overseers; all the engineers were recruited from Britain. Consequently, in 1947, of the total of 496 colleges, 420 colleges were 'arts' colleges.[1]

Nationalistic Education

Nationalistic Indians were dissatisfied with the British colonial education system; they wanted to set up schools and colleges that inculcated patriotic sentiments. And so, in 1884, at the initiative of nationalist stalwarts like Vishnushastri Chiplunkar, Bal Gangadhar Tilak, V.S. Apte and Gopal Ganesh Agarkar, the Deccan Education Society was founded which set up the Fergusson College in Poona in 1885. Mahatma Gandhi founded a series of national universities during the first non-cooperation movement in 1920–1922. These included the Gujarat Vidyapeeth, Kashi Vidyapeeth, Bihar Vidyapeeth, Tilak Maharashtra Vidyapeeth and Jamia Millia Islamia. Hindi or the vernacular languages were the medium of instruction in these universities. Meanwhile, Rabindranath Tagore founded Visva-Bharati University in 1921 at Shantiniketan. In another pioneering initiative, D.K. Karve started a women's university, the first of its kind, in 1918 at Poona.*

The socio-religious reform movements of the late 19th century too set up several colleges, partly in response to the colleges set up by the Christian missionaries. Thus, the Arya Samaj set up the Dayanand Anglo-Vedic College (DAV) at Lahore in 1886. Subsequently, more such colleges were set up.

Simultaneously, Indian nationalist leaders and businessmen also set up higher education institutions for imparting training in pure sciences and engineering. The leaders of the Swadeshi Movement in Bengal established a college for granting diplomas in mechanical and engineering courses in 1907 (later shifted to Jadavpur). Jamshedji Tata set up the Indian Institute of Science at Bangalore in 1911; it primarily focused on postgraduate teaching and research in pure and applied chemistry, biochemistry and electrical technology. Pandit

* *These universities are obviously not included in the list of 20 official universities in India at the time of independence.*

Madan Mohan Malviya took the initiative to start the first degree classes in mechanical, electrical and metallurgical engineering at the Banaras Hindu University in 1917.[2]

While all these nationalistic higher educational institutions played an extremely useful role, they could not provide a viable indigenous alternative to the Macaulayan system that had already got established, primarily because they were too few in number compared to the educational institutions set up by the British (which of course were also not many in number).

State of Indian Higher Education in 1947

At the time of independence in 1947, there were just 20 universities (3 Central and 17 state) and 496 colleges in the country.[3] Total enrolment in higher education was very low; there were a total of around 1 lakh students studying in these colleges and universities in 1947. The total enrolment per lakh of population was a mere 30.3. Even this limited enrolment was hugely distorted, with women, scheduled castes and scheduled tribes virtually excluded from higher education—for instance, the enrolment of women in higher education was a mere 1.24% of the total enrolment in 1916–17 and it had risen to 9.35% by 1947.[4]

The whole orientation of the higher education system under the British was to produce graduate flunkeys—office functionaries and clerks—to meet the needs of the colonial administration. Hence, most of this enrolment, more than two-thirds, was concentrated in general and liberal education; engineering and medicine accounted for just 6% and 8% of the total enrolment, respectively. Even this limited enrolment in engineering and medicine had been achieved only during the immediate three decades before independence: in 1916–17, there were a mere 1,139 students enrolled in engineering and 2,481 students enrolled in medicine, and in 1947, these numbers were 6,437 and 8,850 respectively.[5]

* * *

From the above mentioned efforts of our freedom fighters and social reformers to spread higher education in the country, it is obvious that one of the important dreams of our freedom struggle was that in independent India, as the country developed, the policy makers would take steps to ensure that affordable and equitable higher education became available to all children. This dream was encapsulated by our Constitution makers in Article 41 of the Indian Constitution:

> The State shall, within the limits of its economic capacity and development, make effective provision for securing the right to ... (all levels of) education ...

Further, Article 46 directed:

> The State shall promote with special care the educational ... interests of the weaker sections of the people, and, in particular, of the Scheduled Castes and the Scheduled Tribes ...

NOTES

1. Compiled from: *Kavita A. Sharma, Sixty Years of the University Grants Commission*, University Grants Commission, New Delhi, http://www.ugc.ac.in; *Challenges of Education in 21st Century*, Indian Economic Association, Annual Conference, http://books.google.co.in; *An Overview of Technical Education in India and the Origin of IITs*, http://shodhganga.inflibnet.ac.in; and articles from Wikipedia.
2. Compiled from: Kavita A. Sharma, *Sixty Years of the University Grants Commission*, ibid.; *Challenges of Education in 21st Century*, ibid.; *An Overview of Technical Education in India and the Origin of IITs*, ibid.; and articles from Wikipedia.
3. Deepti Gupta, Navneet Gupta, "Higher Education in India: Structure, Statistics and Challenges", *Journal of Education and Practice*, Vol. 3, No. 2, 2012, http://www.iiste.org.
4. Shaloo Sharma, *History and Development of Higher Education in India, 5 Vols.*, pp. 238, 244, http://books.google.co.in; Note: Several other sources give the figure for student enrolment in higher education as 2 lakhs in 1947.
5. Shaloo Sharma, ibid., p. 240.

9

HIGHER EDUCATION IN INDEPENDENT INDIA: THE NEHRUVIAN PERIOD

Objectives

Why do we need colleges and universities, or to put it another way, why do we need higher education? Many people will laugh at this question, as the answer is so obvious—'for a job'. Indeed, this is the perspective of most people towards higher education today. It assumes that a college/university is a place where students acquire the necessary skills necessary for getting a job in the job market. And therefore, most people have come to accept that higher education would have to be paid for, the fees being commensurate with the 'value' of the degree being acquired—the more the market price of the degree, measured in terms of its potential to fetch the student a high paying job (such as an engineering or medical or management degree), the higher the fees.

But readers of this book would be surprised to know that this was not the perspective of our educationists and policy makers at the time of independence. Thus, for instance, delivering the Convocation Address at the Allahabad University in 1946, Jawaharlal Nehru stated:

> A university stands for humanism, for tolerance, for reason, for progress, for the adventure of ideas and for the search for truth .... If the universities discharge their duty adequately, then, it is well with the nation and the people.[1]

This remained the opinion of the country's political leadership, policy makers and academicians in the immediate decades after independence, up to the 1970s. Higher education was seen as a channel for promoting the values of justice, liberty, equality and fraternity enshrined in the Preamble of the Constitution of India. This was clearly stated in the report of the Committee on 'Model Act' for Universities (1961–64):

> The function of the universities is not only to preserve, disseminate and advance knowledge but to furnish intellectual leadership and moral tone to society.

and

> (while an) autonomous institution may not always achieve these ideals; but it is certain that a university which is not autonomous is hardly likely ever to achieve these great objectives.[2]

Probably one of the most lucid and insightful elucidations regarding the "general objectives of university education" was given by the Kothari Education Commission (1964–66):

> First and foremost, they must learn to strive to serve as the 'conscience of the nation', as assessors of the national way of life, and this responsibility becomes all the greater in the absence of an enlightened public opinion ... (U)niversities are pre-eminently the forum for a critical assessment of society—sympathetic, objective, unafraid ...[3]

All this supposedly falls within the domain of the social sciences and the humanities; does it mean that we are supposed to give a primacy to these disciplines over natural sciences? No, it is not a question of emphasising one set of disciplines as compared to the other; it is a question of creating an atmosphere in the universities wherein there is an awareness of, a concern for, the social conditions and problems of our country; where teachers and students together address the challenges before the country to build a society in accordance with the spirit embodied in the Preamble and the Directive Principles of the Indian Constitution.

For universities to perform this most important social role, one of the most important conditions is that they should have complete autonomy. This was emphasised by the University Education Commission set up in 1948 under the Chairmanship of Dr. Sarvapalli

Radhakrishnan, and repeated by several subsequent committees on higher education. Thus, the report of the Committee on 'Model Act' for Universities (1964), recommended:

> If such a community (teachers and students) is to discharge its duties to itself and to the nation, the governance of the university must essentially be in its own hands. The teachers should have in practice an effective voice in the determination of the policies and the management of the affairs of the university; their participation should be real and meaningful and not merely formal and constitutional.[4]

The Kothari Commission comprehensively examined the principles of governance of institutions of higher education that were essential for maintaining their academic freedom, and stated:

> The character of a university as a society of teachers and students engaged in the pursuit of learning and discovery, distinguishes fundamentally the regulation of its affairs from, say, the profit-motivated management of commercial or industrial concerns or the administration of a government department.... Rules, regulations and techniques that hamper the achievement of the real purposes of the university should be modified or scrapped ...[5]

The Gajendragadkar Committee on Governance of Universities and Colleges (1971) also recommended student participation in academic and administrative decision-making to enhance the 'sense of belonging' within the academic community.[6]

The Kothari Commission was emphatic that it was not enough that universities have mere 'institutional autonomy', but that they should also have complete 'academic freedom'; it stated that teachers must have the freedom "to hold and express their views, however radical, within the classroom (and outside) provided they are careful to present the different aspects of a problem without confusing teaching with 'propaganda' in favour of their own particular views."[7]

Necessity of Public Funding

For universities to discharge this role, it is essential that they be publicly funded.

Private investors are only going to invest in education for making a profit; for them, there is no difference between investing in higher education and investing in making soaps and cars. When private for-profit institutions provide education, education becomes a commodity, a product on sale, and students become consumers who buy education. If students have to buy education, that is, if they have to pay fees for education, their main interest in pursuing higher education will be to get a job; quality of education will then be measured by its potential of getting them a high-paying job; and like in a shopping mall, the consumer's (student's) ability to pay will determine the quality of goods (education) delivered.

Private universities will prefer to offer courses that are marketable and revenue-generating such as engineering and management courses, and not courses in areas like the natural and social sciences. This is exactly opposite to the vision of our founding fathers and the Kothari Commission regarding what universities should be. Therefore, if higher education is privately funded, the entire orientation of the education system changes.

Private funding affects higher education in other ways too. Private universities will be interested in strong, centralised administrative control and curbing autonomy; they will be keen on enforcing 'discipline' and stifling academic freedom, dissent and debate.

Therefore, if universities are to be a place where teachers and students jointly work to address the problems facing the country, if they are to be oriented towards the task of nation-building, if they are to serve as critical assessors of society, as 'conscience of the nation', then, not only should they be adequately protected against external pressures, including political and bureaucratic pressures, most importantly, they must be State-funded.

Growth of Higher Education, 1947–90

After independence, there was a rapid growth of higher educational institutions in the country. Over the four decades from 1950–51 to 1990–91, both the number of universities and the number of colleges went up by several times: the number of universities increased from 30 to 190, and colleges from 695 to 7,346. Enrolment in higher education zoomed, going up from 3.97 lakh in 1950–51 to 49.25 lakh in 1990–91. The number of teachers also rose from 24,000 to 2,63,000 over these four decades (Table 9.1).

Table 9.1: Growth of Higher Education in India, 1947–91[8]

	*Universities**	*Colleges*	*Enrolment (in '000)*	*Teachers (in '000)*
1950–51	30	695	397	24
1960–61	55	1542	1050	60
1970–71	103	3604	1954	129
1980–81	133	4722	2752	193
1990–91	190	7346	4925	263

*Includes Central and State Universities, Deemed Universities, Institutes of National Importance, and Private Universities

[Note: Figures of student enrolment and teaching staff (1970–71 onwards) pertain to regular courses in universities and colleges (excluding polytechnics, other diploma awarding institutions and non-formal systems of higher education)]

Chart 9.1: Growth of Student Enrolment in Higher Education[9] (*'000*)

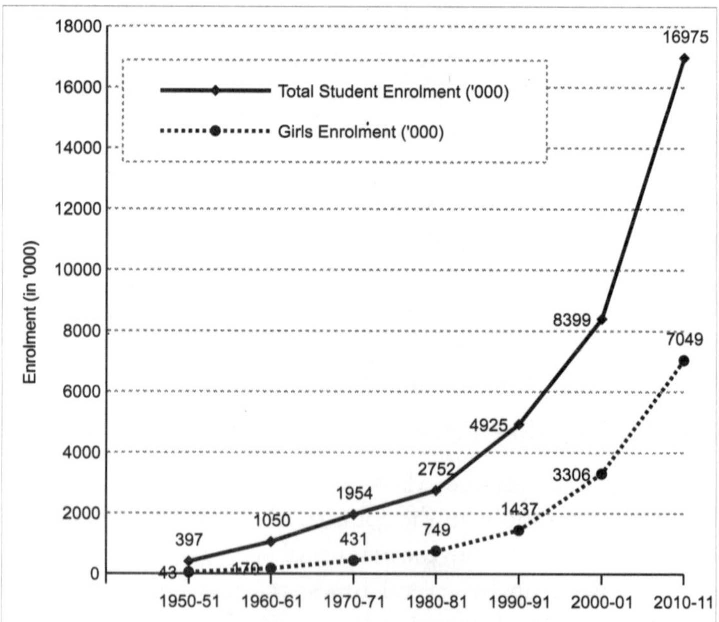

Even more remarkable was the growth in enrolment of girls in higher education. Their share in total enrolment went up from 10.8% in 1950–51 to 29% in 1990–91. In absolute numbers, the number of girls in higher education went up from 43,000 to 14,37,000 over this period.[10]

Government figures indicate that the enrolment of scheduled castes and scheduled tribe students in higher education more than doubled over the period 1957 to 1987, from 1.07 lakh to 2.53 lakh. However, as a percentage of total enrolment, the number of SC/ST students in higher education actually declined over this period, from 12.4% in 1957 to 6.8% in 1987; it then rose to 10.6% in 1990–91.[11]

Crisis

Despite the lofty objectives of higher education voiced by Nehru and other leaders of independent India, India's higher education system was never really able to break out of the Macaulayan mould set by the British (for reasons discussed in Chapter 3). As the Nehruvian model gradually sank into crisis, the idealism present in society during the initial years after independence also dissipated. The vibrant intellectual atmosphere that was present during the early post-independence years in the universities gradually decayed; and instead of being places where teachers and students jointly address the challenges of 'nation-building', universities gradually became mere graduate producing factories producing qualified workers for the range of jobs available in society.

As discussed in Chapter 4, the independent India's new rulers did not really make a serious effort to fight the feudal values entrenched in Indian society for the past nearly 2000 years. An important reason for a more democratic capitalist society in Europe is the long struggle waged by the rising middle classes against superstitions, prejudice and other forms of feudal backwardness. Because of this intense struggle that spanned more than 500 years, democratic values are more strongly entrenched in those societies. However, in India, the rising capitalist and middle classes compromised with medieval backwardness, due to their inherent weakness and fear of the masses. This had its impact on the various modern institutions created after independence, including educational institutions. Despite the efforts of our educational thinkers like Maulana Abul Kalam Azad, Dr. S. Radhakrishnan and Dr. Zakir Husain, our universities continued to be plagued by political interference, the feudal mentality of patronage and dependence did not end, and the intellectual elites instead of animating universities undermined them by their allegiance to norms of patronage—promoting people of their caste/community/region.

Table 9.2: Expenditure on Higher Education as % of GNP[12]

Year	*Percentage*
1950–51	0.19
1960–61	0.39
1970–71	0.77
1980–81	0.98
1990–91	0.46

The second and equally important reason for the gradual decay of the higher education system in India was that the Indian ruling classes made very inadequate public investment in education. To repeat what we have mentioned in Chapter 3, during the first two decades after independence, the Indian government spent less than 2% of the GDP on education; after that, it slowly rose, but only to a maximum of 4% of the GDP by 1990. It is true that within this limited expenditure on education, the government laid more emphasis on promoting higher education. (We have discussed this in greater detail in Chapter 3). Of the total public expenditure on education, the government spent as much as 30–50% on university and technical education during the period 1956–85 (see Chapter 3, Table 3.2); and in absolute terms, the total expenditure on higher education touched a high of 1% of the GNP in 1980–81 (before falling off sharply to less than 0.5% of the GNP in the mid-1980s, see Table 9.2). Therefore, as discussed in the previous section, there did take place some expansion of higher education in the country during the first few decades after independence. However, this expansion was on a very low base; and was very inadequate as compared to our actual needs. The Gross Enrolment Ratio in higher education, that is, the total enrolment in higher education as a percentage of the total youth population in the age group of 18–22, was only 6% in 1989–90.[13]

☆ ☆ ☆

By the 1980s, the Nehruvian economic model was in deep crisis. The Indian ruling classes experimented with partial liberalisation of the economy in the 1980s, and then went in for full-fledged globalisation of the economy in the 1990s. As we have seen in the previous chapters, the new policies have totally changed the entire orientation of the school education system in the country. The neoliberal educational reforms have severely impacted the higher education sector too—they have given an entirely new dimension to the crisis gripping the higher education sector ...

NOTES

1. Amlanjyoti Goswami, *Higher Education Law and Privately-Funded University Education in India: Towards a Vision?*, www.idfc.com.
2. *Report of the Committee on 'Model Act' for Universities*, http://www.teindia.nic.in.
3. *Education and National Development: Report of the Education Commission, 1964–66, Vol. 3: Higher Education*, p. 555, http://www.teindia.nic.in.
4. "General Constitution Underlying University Organisation", in *Report of the Committee on 'Model Act' for Universities*, op. cit.
5. *Education and National Development: Report of the Education Commission, 1964–66, Vol. 3: Higher Education*, op. cit., p. 643.
6. Prof. Madhu Prasad in: *Betraying the Constitution: Tailoring Higher Education to the Market*, paper presented at the Seminar– "Emerging Crisis in Higher Education", organised by Pune University Teachers Association and Lokayat, Gokhale Institute of Politics and Economics, September 25, 2010.
7. *Education and National Development: Report of the Education Commission, 1964–66, Vol. 3: Higher Education*, op. cit., p. 644; also cited by Prof. Madhu Prasad, ibid.
8. *Higher Education in India at a Glance*, UGC, February 2012, http://www.ugc.ac.in.; Note that other sources give different statistics, also citing the UGC. See for example: Deepti Gupta, Navneet Gupta, "Higher Education in India: Structure, Statistics and Challenges",

Journal of Education and Practice, Vol. 3, No. 2, 2012, http://www.iiste.org; and also: Ved Prakash, "Trends in Growth and Financing of Higher Education in India", *Economic and Political Weekly*, August 4, 2007, http://eledu.net.

9. *Higher Education in India at a Glance*, UGC, ibid.
10. Ibid.
11. Figures for 1957 and 1987 calculated from statistics given in: Dr. Vijender Sharma, *Crisis of Higher Education in India*, Chapter 2, http://indiaeducrisis.wordpress.com; figures for 1990–91 taken from: Ved Prakash, "Trends in Growth and Financing of Higher Education in India", ibid.
12. Figures for 1950–51 to 1980–81 taken from Dr. Vijender Sharma, *Crisis of Higher Education in India*, ibid., Chapter 3; figure for 1990–91 from: *Report of the CABE Committee on Financing of Higher Education in India*, June 2005, p. 24, http://www.teindia.nic.in.
13. *Higher Education in India: Twelfth Five Year Plan (2012–2017) and Beyond*, Ernst and Young and FICCI, 2012, p. 8, http://www.ey.com.

10

HIGHER EDUCATION AND GLOBALISATION

Neoliberal Winds: NPE-1986

In the early 1980s, the Indian government went in for a major loan from the IMF. In the dog-eat-dog world of global capitalism, 'there is no free lunch'. The loan came with conditionalities, that impacted every sector of the economy, including the education sector too.

In 1986, the World Bank came out with a document, *Report on Financing Higher Education in Developing Countries*, that explicitly stated that in view of the general shortage of funds, it was better that governments devote their limited resources to financing primary education, and end subsidies for higher education. The World Bank argued that since only the relatively better off students were able to enter higher education, subsidising them makes for inequality and not egalitarianism; if the same subsidy were shifted instead to primary education, the effect would be towards equality.

This thinking had its influence on the National Policy of Education of 1986 (NPE-1986). NPE-1986 can be said to have laid the foundations for an entirely new orientation to India's education policy in that for the first time, the Government of India announced that it was abandoning its Constitutional commitment to provide equality of opportunity for all children from school to higher education. On the one hand, the NPE-1986 paid lip-service to the nation-building role of higher education: "Higher education provides people with an opportunity to reflect on the critical social, economic, cultural, moral and spiritual issues facing humanity. It contributes to national development through dissemination of specialised knowledge and skills." Simultaneously, it also paved the way for the policy of commercialisation of higher education that was to be aggressively pursued in later years by stating that the resources for higher education should be raised through "mobilising donations", "raising fees", "effecting some savings by efficient use of facilities", etc. The policy document clearly stated that all these measures will "reduce the burden on State resources" and create "a greater sense of responsibility within the educational system."[1] The NPE-1986 was revised in 1992, and along with that, a revised Programme of Action was also drawn up, which was even more brazen in its recommendations:

> All institutions will be encouraged to achieve maximum self-reliance by generating resources through measures like enhancement of fees coupled with provision of soft loans to the needy students; consultancy; testing; sponsored projects; community contributions; institutional chairs; raising donations for infrastructural development with a provision for tax exemption; establishment of industrial foundations; charging fees for specific facilities such as laboratory, library, games, magazines, etc.[2]

The government set up two committees to recommend measures through which universities could raise their own resources. In 1992, the University Grants Commission (UGC)* set up the Punnayya Committee to look into the funding of Central universities. The Committee submitted its report titled *UGC Funding of Institutions of Higher Education* in November 1993. While stating that "the State must continue to accept the major responsibility for funding the essential maintenance and development requirements of universities", the report nevertheless recommended that universities should raise their own resources, which should constitute "at least 15% of the total recurring expenditure (Plan and Non-Plan) at the end of the

---

* *University Grants Commission (UGC): A statutory organisation set up by the Union government in 1956, with mandate for coordination, determination and maintenance of standards of university education.*

first five years and at least 25% at the end of ten years." It suggested a number of ways through which universities could raise their own resources. Thus, it recommended: "The universities may initiate measures to rent out their facilities such as auditoria, classrooms, computer services, playgrounds, guest houses, hostels, lawns, messes, etc." Another mechanism of raising resources suggested by the Committee was raising tuition fees and other fees to be paid by the students. It recommended that these fees should be regularly and periodically adjusted to the rise in costs and "the revision of fees must be related in a meaningful manner to the recurring cost of the course of study and employment opportunities offered by the course, that is, that the tuition fees will be different within an university for different courses of study."[3]

Similarly, in 1994, the All India Council for Technical Education (AICTE)[†] set up the Swaminathan Committee to look into possibilities of resource mobilisation in technical education, essentially through cost-recovery from students. The committee's recommendations included:

(i) reducing the share of salaries in recurring expenditure from the present level of 80% to 60%;
(ii) enhancing fees to recover at least 20% of the recurring expenditure;
(iii) reducing share of regular faculty to 60% and appointing the remaining staff on contract basis;
(iv) increasing the staff-student ratio.[4]

Implicit in all these policy documents is the assumption that the aim of higher education is to impart market-oriented skills to students so as to make them employable. In other words, the nation building task of higher education was now being formally abandoned. Higher education was now no longer being seen as benefiting society as a whole, it was now only seen as a means of getting a job, thus creating

† *All India Council for Technical Education (AICTE): A statutory body responsible for planning and coordinated development of the technical education and management education system in India.*

the ground for the government to argue that it should no longer be subsidised. In other words, since higher education was now meant for individual profit (that is, for getting a job), those who individually profit should pay for it. This was precisely the logic put forth by the government over the next decade, thus paving the way for a subsequent policy of aggressively promoting commercialisation of higher education.

Elementary Education vs. Higher Education

In 1994, the World Bank came up with another policy document on higher education, *Higher Education: The Lessons of Experience*. This stated that: "Indeed it is arguable that higher education should not have the highest-priority claim on incremental public resources available for education in many developing countries, especially those that have not yet achieved adequate access, equity and quality at the primary and secondary levels. This is ... because the social rates of return on investments in primary and secondary education usually exceed the returns on higher education." The World Bank therefore advocated strong participation of the private sector in higher education. While stating that governments must establish a general framework for the functioning of private institutions, the World Bank advised "the avoidance of regulation on the cost of enrolment and tuition". It further recommended that the representatives of the private business sector should be included in "government agencies that work with public and private universities."[5]

Complying with World Bank orders, the Ministry of Finance of the Government of India brought out a discussion paper on *Government Subsidies in India* in May 1997. The paper suggested that subsidies are normally to be advocated when the social benefits of a particular service are greater than the sum total of private benefits to the individual consumers of that service. It went on to classify social and economic services into 'merit' and 'non-merit' services, 'merit' services being those where there is a substantial gap between the social benefits of the service and its private valuations, and 'non-merit' services being those where there is no significant gap between the two; and argued for reduction in subsidies to non-merit services. The paper considered elementary education to be a 'merit service' as its benefits "spread well beyond the immediate recipients". On the other hand, it categorised higher education as a 'non-merit service'. It stated: "A significant portion of subsidies in higher education is appropriated by the middle to high income groups", because there is a "shortage of seats in this sector", which are therefore filled by "entrance examination, interview, group discussion, etc., where the poorer sections of society are easily competed out" by the "better-off sections of society". Therefore, it recommended that subsidies provided to higher education be reduced, and the government pursue a strategy of cost-recovery through user charges. It suggested setting "a target of reducing subsidy rate for non-merit subsidies from 90% to 50% in three years, with a further goal of reducing it to 25% in another two years."[6]

The paper fragments education, making a distinction between elementary and higher education, and assumes that while elementary education benefits society as a whole, the benefits of higher education accrue primarily to the recipients, and that society at large does not benefit. This is directly opposite to the perspective of our educationists and political leaders in the early decades after independence, who had visualised universities to be places where teachers and students jointly work on behalf of the people, "furnish intellectual leadership and moral tone to society", serve "as the 'conscience of the nation'", as "assessors of the national way of life" ...

This fragmentation of education, defining elementary education as a merit good and higher education as non-merit good, and counterposing one against the other while allocating resources, actually undermines the idea of an integrated system of education, which was one of the founding principles of the freedom struggle and which had subsequently been established through three decades of public education policy. Way back in 1895, Surendranath Banerjee had stated in his presidential address to the Poona session of the Indian National Congress, "We are not in favour of higher education versus primary education. We are in favour of all education, high and low. They act and react upon each other. They are part and parcel of a common and indissoluble system." The Kothari Commission too made exactly the same point: "(T)he provision of universal primary education is vital on grounds of social justice and to help the process of transformation of the national economy. Again, development of higher education and research is central to the entire developmental programme; and without an adequate provision for higher education there will be no adequate supply of competent teachers for primary and secondary education. What we want is a balanced growth of education." And so it had favoured equal distribution of resources amongst all the three branches of education in the long run, one-third to elementary, one-third to secondary and the remaining one-third to higher education.[7]

Reduction in Public Funding of Higher Education

Ignoring the wise words of its own Kothari Commission, and dutifully implementing the dictates of the World Bank, one of the first things the Government of India did as a part of the World Bank dictated Structural Adjustment Programme was to make steep cuts in public funding of higher education.

Chart 10.1: Share of Higher and Technical Education in Total Plan Exp. on Education in Five Year Plans in India[8]

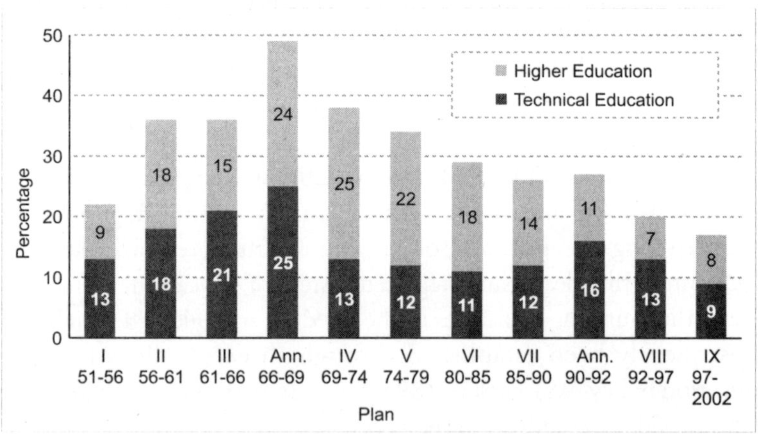

Five Year Plans set new directions for development—quantitative expansion, improvement in quality, innovations. Allocations for higher education, that had steadily increased from 9% in the First Five Year Plan to 25% in the Fourth Five Year Plan (1969–74), fell to all time lows in the Eighth (1992–97) and the Ninth (1997–2002) Plan periods. Hardly 7% to 8% of the total Plan expenditure on education was devoted to higher education. Likewise, allocation for technical education too fell after the first three Plans. In the Ninth Plan (1997–2002), allocations for both higher and technical education as proportion of total Plan expenditure on education were below the allocations made in the First Five Year Plan (Chart 10.1).

With the government ignoring its promise to increase total expenditure on education to 6% of the GNP, this cut in government expenditure on higher education resulted in a sharp fall in expenditure on higher education as a percentage of GNP during the 1990s. By 2001–02, the total government expenditure on higher and technical education as a percentage of the GNP had fallen to just around 0.5%, as compared to between 1% and 2.5% for many developed countries (whose GNP is much more and population much less as compared to India).[9]

Table 10.1: Higher and Technical Education: Relative Priorities[10]

	Govt. Expenditure on Higher Education as		*Govt. Expenditure on Technical Education as*	
	% of GNP	*% of Total Govt. Revenue Exp.*	*% of GNP*	*% of Total Govt. Revenue Exp.*
1990–91	0.46	1.58	0.15	0.51
2001–02	0.39	1.31	0.12	0.41

Table 10.2: Public Expenditure on Higher Education Per Student[11]

	In Current Prices (Rs)	*In 1993–94 Prices (Rs)*	*Index*
1990–91	5652	7676	100
1995–96	6944	5812	75.7
2002–03 RE	9446	5522	71.9

Share of higher education as a proportion of total government expenditure tells us about the relative priority assigned to higher education by the government, as the government has more control over its own expenditure as compared to the national income. As shown in Table 10.1, this too has declined during the 1990s.

This cutback in public expenditure on higher education is also reflected in a drastic decline in public expenditure per student in real prices, both in general higher education and technical and professional education—it had fallen by 30% over the decade 1991–2002 (Table 10.2).

Consequence: Decline in Quality, Fee-hikes ...

After putting a squeeze on government grants, in 2000, the Ministry for Human Resource Development took the next logical step by asking universities and colleges to generate at least 7% of their maintenance grant through internal resources (that is, through fee hike and other sources), with one percent increase every year till it reaches 15%. The MHRD further decided that fees should vary from course to course, 20% of the seats could be filled by foreign and NRI students, 75% of the recurring cost of library, laboratory, sports and computer facilities should be recovered from the students, and hostel fees should be immediately revised to recover actual recurring cost and a part of capital cost.[12]

An important casualty of this reduction in public funding on higher education was decline in quality of education; there were steep cuts in budget allocations for libraries, laboratories, faculty improvement programmes, research, and so on. Faculty recruitment in universities and colleges came to a halt for more than a decade.[13] This was explicitly admitted in the report of the Committee on *Financing of Higher and Technical Education*, set up by the Central Advisory Board of Education (CABE) in 2004 to examine in detail critical issues related to financing of higher and technical education. The Committee, commenting on the consequences of the decline in government funding for higher and technical education during the 1990s, stated:

> The financially unsatisfactory situation in higher education gets clearly reflected in the physical infrastructure of our higher education institutions. It is common knowledge that many institutions of higher education suffer from severe inadequacy of

> physical resources such as buildings, classrooms, libraries, laboratories, etc., not to speak of high tech modern equipment ... The situation is far from satisfactory in many universities, including in some of the best universities, whether Central or state. The situation is worse in affiliated colleges, where 90% of the undergraduate students and 34% of the postgraduate students study.[14]

The CABE Committee pointed out that because of the reduction in funding by the government, universities and colleges "have made very significant upward revisions in fee levels in recent years". Apart from tuition fees, they have also been "introducing different kinds of fees", such as "entrance examination fee, admission fee, registration fee, eligibility fee, library fee, laboratory fee, sports fee, convocation fee, certificate fee, fee for marks statement, etc." The Committee illustrated this point with an example: in 1999–2000, in Bangalore University, tuition fee amounted to only 2.2% of the total recurring income, while income from all fees accounted for above 40%.

Taking advantage of the neoliberal atmosphere, universities/ colleges have not only introduced various kinds of fees, they have also hiked them by several times. Fee increase in technical institutions like IITs and IIMs has been particularly steep. In case of hostel fees and other such 'student welfare' services, almost full cost recovery is being attempted, with the result that fee rise in such items has been very high.

To generate additional resources, many universities and colleges have launched 'self-financing' courses. These have been introduced even in disciplines like Economics, Political Science, Botany, Zoology, etc., courses that ought to be provided as normal courses in these institutions. Exploiting the high demand for higher education, the fees charged are often much higher than the cost. In addition, universities and colleges have also set up postgraduate centres, some of which are solely self-financing.

The CABE Committee comments:

> As a result, many universities are able to generate substantial resources, much above the recommendation made by Dr. Justice

Punnayya Committee! A recent study found that out of 39 universities studied, more than half a dozen universities raised fee rates in such a way that they could generate more than 50% of the total recurring income of the respective universities from student fees in the late 1990s; and another 13 universities could generate more than 20%.[15]

Equity Compromised

Another consequence of the neoliberal reforms is that the government is scaling down its already limited efforts to promote equity. Granting scholarships is one way of promoting equity in higher education. Despite this well-known truism, and even though scholarships constitute a very small percentage of the total government expenditure on higher education, steep cuts have been made in this budget too. The total government expenditure on scholarships both in higher education and technical education was 20% less in 2002–03 compared to 1990–91 (Table 10.3).

Table 10.3: Public Expenditure on Scholarships in Higher and Technical Education[16]

	Higher Education		*Technical Education*	
	In 1993–94 Prices (Rs cr)	*% of Total Expenditure on Higher Education*	*In 1993–94 Prices (Rs cr)*	*% of Total Expenditure on Higher Education*
1990–91	15.35	0.49	2.72	0.45
1999–2000	15.85	0.15	1.08	0.12
2002–03 RE	12.17	0.29	2.26	0.25

Increasing Disparities in Access to Higher Education

We have seen in the previous chapters how, despite the pretensions of the Right to Education Act, the government is not at all concerned with providing free and compulsory elementary education to all children. Neoliberal policies in education are gradually resulting in privatisation of elementary education, with the result that barely 60% of the children who enrol in Class 1 complete Class VIII; worse, due to the dismal quality of education being provided, only a small fraction of these can truly be said to have completed basic schooling.

For those fortunate enough to complete Class VIII, they would obviously want to continue their studies and complete at least higher secondary education. But with the government declaring that it simply does not have the resources to provide affordable secondary and higher secondary education, these levels of education are rapidly getting privatised, and fees are rising. Therefore, it has become very difficult for children from the poorer sections of society to access secondary and higher secondary school. With the result that just around 16% of the children enrolling in Class I cross Class XII.

Obviously, a large majority of the children who are dropping out of school would be children from the poorer and more disadvantaged sections of society.

For those children from the lower strata of society who somehow complete Class XII and want to pursue college education, the neoliberal transformation of the higher education system has made it very difficult for them to seek admission in a degree/diploma course. Under World Bank dictates, the government is reducing spending on higher education, and college/university fees are being hiked. As we discussed in the next chapter, higher education is increasingly becoming a business. The government is not willing to give many scholarships for children from the economically poorer sections for pursuing higher education; the main scheme it has proposed for making higher education accessible for children from the poorer sections of society is bank loans. As the CABE committee on financing of higher education points out in its report, these education loans are operated by banks on commercial lines and are like car loans and housing loans—on top of it, the interest rate on student loans is more than that for car loans! These loans come with collateral and other conditions attached, making it very difficult for students from weaker sections of society to benefit from student loan schemes.[17]

Therefore, higher education in the country is gradually becoming a preserve of children from the better-off strata of society. The poorer/weaker sections are finding it increasingly difficult to send their children to colleges/universities. This has been highlighted in a study sponsored by the UGC itself. We summarise its findings below.

Continuing Exclusion of Poor, Dalits, Muslims and Women from Education

Access to higher education is measured in term of Gross Enrolment Ratio (GER), defined as the ratio of persons enrolled in higher education institutions to the total number of persons in the age-group of 18 to 23 years.

The UGC study shows that there are wide disparities in access to higher education for different sections of society. Further, the figures given in the report are for 2004–05; since then the situation must only have worsened, as neoliberal transformation of education has further accelerated since then.*

The NSS data for 2004–05 estimates the enrolment rate for those pursuing degree courses and above to be 10.84. However, this all-India average masks a huge difference in GER between the rural and urban areas. The GER for rural areas was 6.74%, one-third of that for urban areas at 19.88% (Chart 10.2)![18]

There is also a wide disparity in access to degree level higher education for different social groups. GER for scheduled caste students was 6.52, for scheduled tribe students was 6.57, and for other backward castes was 8.77, compared to 17.22 for the upper castes—that is, GER for SC/ST students was three times less as compared to upper castes.[19] The same data also shows that GER for Muslim students at the graduate level was 6.84—very near the level of SC and ST students, a fact also pointed out by the Sachar Committee (Chart 10.2).

* *There are three different sources of data which provide information on enrolment in higher education in India: i) Selected Educational Statistics (SES), published by MHRD; ii) National Sample Survey data; iii) Population Census of India data. SES data for 2006–07 estimates the GER to be 9.7% (for degree+diploma; and 8.8% only for degree). The GER derived from NSS data for 2004–05 is on the higher side—12.59% (10.84% for graduate, 1.75% for diploma), and GER from the Population Census data is even higher, 13.6% for 2001. The analysis here is based on NSS data of 2004–05.*

Chart 10.2: GER for Graduates by Social Groups: Age Group 18–23, Year 2004–05[20]

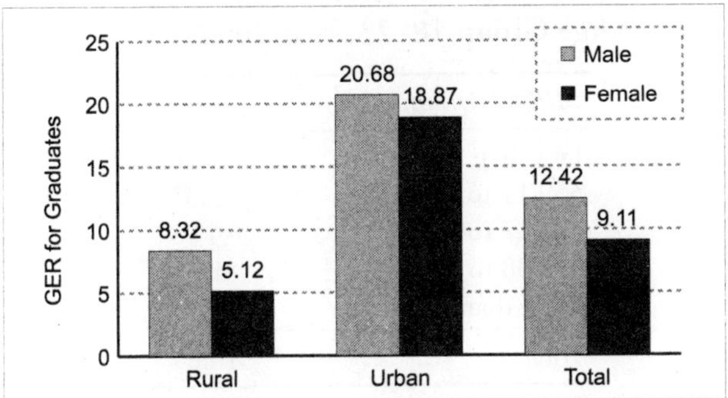

Chart 10.3: GER for Graduates by Gender: Age Group 18–23, Year 2004–05[21]

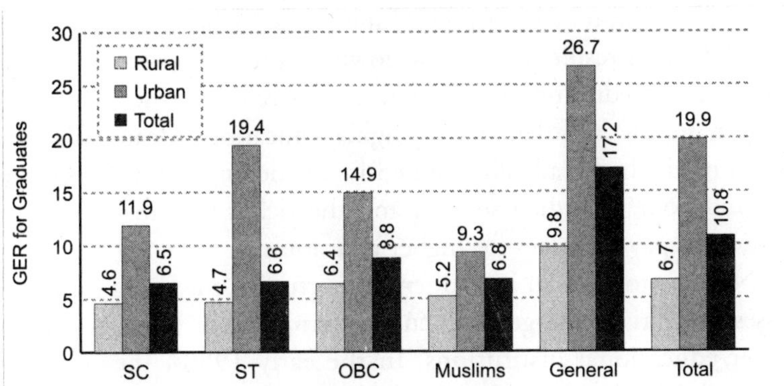

The NSS data reveals that at graduate level, women had a lower GER compared to men, the difference being three percentage points at the all-India level (males 12.42, females 9.11) (Chart 10.3). The rural-urban divide continues here too—women in urban areas had a GER nearly four times that for rural women, while for urban men it was two-and-a-half times that for rural men (Chart 10.3).[22]

Finally, as is obviously to be expected, there is a wide gap between the rich and the poor in access to higher education. NSS data clearly shows that as the income level rises, the enrolment rate goes up. As Table 10.4 shows, the GER for the highest quintile was 18 times the

GER for the poorest section in 2004-05.

Table 10.4: GER for Graduates by Income Level: Age Group 18–23, Year 2004–05[23]

MPCE Quintile*	*Total*
Less than 359.1	1.46
359.11 to 461.14	3.37
461.17 to 587.33	4.88
587.38 to 830.44	9.81
More than 830.5	27.43
Total	10.84

**Monthly per capita expenditure actually measures household expenditure, but obviously, the different quintiles reflect different income levels.*

Gradual Expansion of Private Higher Education

The reduction in government funding for higher education since the 1980s had resulted in a slowdown in the expansion of public funded higher education in the country. There thus arose a huge gap between supply and demand of higher education. Meanwhile, the Nehru model had gradually resulted in a widening gulf between the rich and poor in Indian society, and the richer sections were in a position to pay high fees for higher education.

Not one to miss an investment opportunity, the rising capitalist classes pressurised the government to permit them to open private higher educational institutions. In the early 1980s, the states of Karnataka, Andhra Pradesh, Maharashtra and Tamil Nadu took the decision to permit private registered trusts and societies to establish and run professional educational institutions on a self-financing basis. The first private unaided colleges that were set up offered degree programmes in engineering, followed by programmes in architecture, pharmacy, management, hotel management, computer applications, medicine, nursing, dentistry, physiotherapy and teacher education. Over time, similar colleges started in other states too.[24]

The opening of private unaided colleges picked up pace in the 1990s, and by 2001, private unaided institutions (colleges + universities) accounted for nearly a quarter of the total number of institutions and nearly 22% of the total enrolment (Table 10.5 and Chart 10.4).

Table 10.5: Higher Educational Institutions and Enrolment, 2000–01[25] (*by type of management*)

Type	*Universities*	*Colleges*	*Total*	*Enrolment ('000)*
Government	245	4097	4342	3443
Private Aided	–	5507	5507	3134
Private Unaided	21	3202	3223	1822
Total	266	12806	13072	8399

Chart 10.4: Higher Educational Institutions and Enrolment, 2000–01 (*by type of management, %*)

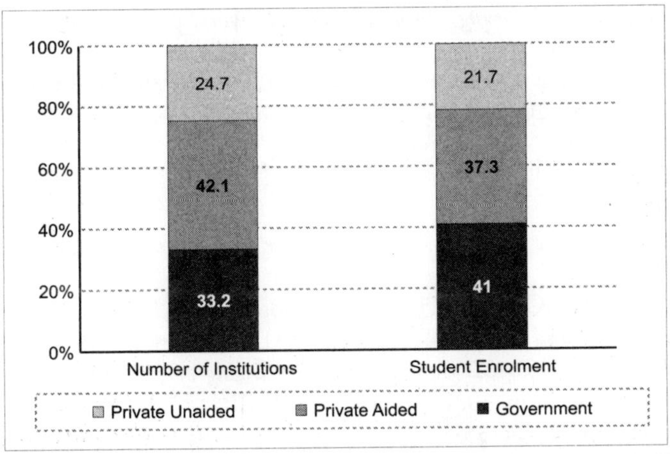

By the turn of the century, the ground had been prepared for full-scale commodification of the higher education sector in the country ...

NOTES

1. Dr. Vijender Sharma, *Crisis of Higher Education in India,* Chapter 1, http://indiaeducrisis.wordpress.com.
2. *National Policy on Education, 1986: Programme of Action 1992,* Ministry of Human Resource Development, p. 81, http://mhrd.gov.in.

3. *UGC Funding of Institutions of Higher Education: Report of Justice Dr. K. Punnayya Committee, 1992–93*, pp. 77–79, www.ugc.ac.in; see also: Dr. Vijender Sharma, *Crisis of Higher Education in India,* op. cit., Chapter 3.
4. N.V. Varghese, "Reforming Education Financing", http://www.india-seminar.com.
5. Dr. Vijender Sharma, *Crisis of Higher Education in India*, op. cit., Chapter 1; for the World Bank report, see: *Higher Education: The Lessons of Experience*, http://siteresources.worldbank.org.
6. K.B. Powar, *Indian Higher Education: A Conglomerate of Concepts, Facts and Practices*, p. 196, http://books.google.co.in; Dr. Vijender Sharma, ibid.
7. Jandhyala B.G. Tilak, "The Kothari Commission and Financing of Education", *Economic and Political Weekly*, March 10, 2007, http://www.rteforumindia.org; *Report of the Education Commission, 1964–66, Vol. 4: Planning, Administration, Finance*, p. 941, http://www.teindia.nic.in.
8. *Report of the CABE Committee on Financing of Higher Education in India*, June 2005, p. 26, http://www.teindia.nic.in.
9. Ibid., p. 24.
10. Ibid.
11. Ibid., p. 26.
12. Dr. Vijender Sharma, *Crisis of Higher Education in India,* op. cit., Chapter 3.
13. Jandhyala B.G. Tilak, "Higher Education Policy in India in Transition", *Economic and Political Weekly*, March 31, 2012, http://www.eledu.net.
14. *Report of the CABE Committee on Financing of Higher Education in India*, op. cit., p. 30.
15. Ibid., pp. 32, 34–35.
16. Ibid., p. 29.
17. Ibid., p. 36.; see also: Dr. Harsh Gandhar, "Educational Loan Scheme of Scheduled Commercial Banks in India: An Assessment", 2010, www.skirec.com.
18. *Higher Education in India: Issues Related to Expansion, Inclusiveness, Quality and Finance*, UGC, New Delhi, November 2008, pp. 25, 83, 87, 117, www.ugc.ac.in.
19. Ibid., pp. 25, 87.
20. Ibid., pp. 25, 87, 90.
21. Ibid., pp. 25, 87.
22. Ibid., pp. 25, 87.

23. Dr. Sukhdeo Thorat, *Emerging Issues in Indian Higher Education—Approach and Strategy under the 11th Plan*, ACU Conference, Hyderabad, November 28, 2008, p. 20, http://hyderabad2008.acu.ac.uk.
24. Pawan Agarwal, "Higher Education and the Labour Market in India", in Justin Yifu Lin, Boris Pleskovic (ed.), *Annual World Bank Conference on Development Economics*, books.google.co.in.
25. Source: University Grants Commission; taken from: "A Policy Note on the Grant-in-Aid System in Indian Education", World Bank, November 2003, p. 17, www.aiiserver.com; and Pawan Agarwal, *Higher Education in India—The Need for Change*, ICRIER Working Paper, June 2006, p. 156, www.icrier.org. Note: There is a discrepancy in the data, as in Table 10.5, the number of universities in 2001 totals 266, whereas in Chart 11.1 in Chapter 11, it is 256.

11

THE 'BUSINESS' OF HIGHER EDUCATION

The turn of the century marked a new turn in the overall orientation of the higher education system in India. In February 2000, bowing to the pressure of the developed countries and their corporations, the member states of the World Trade Organisation (WTO) began negotiations to expand the 1995 General Agreement on Trade in Services (GATS), which is an integral part of the WTO. (When the Doha Round of the WTO trade negotiations began in November 2001, the services negotiations became a part of what is known as 'single undertaking' under the Doha Round, wherein negotiations for all the subjects are to be concluded as a part of a single package, and cannot be agreed upon piecemeal.) The purpose of these talks was to pressurise the third world countries to privatise essential public services such as education, health and water, and throw them open to investment by multinational corporations from the West. Services is the fastest growing sector of the world economy, and within it, health, education and water are considered to be the most lucrative of all services. The global healthcare market is considered to be worth 3.5 trillion dollars, while education is estimated to be a 2 trillion and water a 1 trillion dollar annual market. Western corporations dominate global trade in services (Table 11.1); if new initiatives under GATS as a part of the Doha Round of trade negotiations are concluded and the third world countries make significant liberalising commitments in the service sector, it would obviously mean windfall profits for these corporations.[1]

In the case of higher education, the international market for trade in higher education was valued at more than $30 billion in 1998. This was overwhelmingly dominated by the USA and UK, both of whom earned $11.4 billion each from foreign students in 2001. Third came Australia, which earned over $2 billion.[2] With the present global education services market being just 1.5% of the potential, obviously, the developed countries were keen that third world countries like India privatise their higher education sector and open it up to foreign education providers.

Table 11.1: World Export and Import of Services, 2000[3]
(*in billion Euros and % of world total*)

	Exports	*Imports*
EU-15	291.1 (24.3%)	286.1 (23.8%)
USA	297.8 (24.9%)	215.7 (17.9%)
Japan	74.1 (6.2%)	125.5 (10.4%)

For the developed countries, the higher education sector in India is a particularly attractive market. There were more than 250 universities and 12,800 colleges in India in 2000–01, making it one of the largest networks of higher education systems in the developing world. Even with respect to technical education, a wide network had been established. As of 2003, there were seven technological institutions of high standard (IITs), six institutions of management of high quality (IIMs), around 1000 colleges of engineering, technology and architecture, 759 medical colleges, 873 teacher training colleges, and 1,982 other professional and technical institutions in agriculture, law, management, computer applications and information technology. There were 1,173 polytechnics. These figures do not include the vast network of research and development institutions spread across the country. While in absolute terms the student enrolment in these institutions was huge, nevertheless, in terms of the Gross Enrolment Ratio (number of students as a percent proportion of the youth population in the age group 17–23/18–24), it was quite low. The GER in India in 2002–03 was only around 8–9, which was lower than the average GER for the lower middle income countries of the world (average 15), and much lower than several developing countries like Mexico, Chile, Thailand, Malaysia and Brazil where it was above 20. The GER for developed countries was above

60, with several countries having a GER above 70. Therefore, there was a huge potential for expanding the higher education sector in India.[4]

The Boss Changes Tack

As discussed in the previous chapter, World Bank recommendations in the mid-1980s and early 1990s made the Government of India give priority to elementary education and restrict funding to higher education, pushing the latter into deep crisis. The government had in fact declared in the 1993–94 *Annual Report* of the Ministry of Human Resource Development:

> The higher education system in the country is now sufficiently developed to meet the nation's requirements. The unmet demand for higher education is not considered economically viable.[5]

Having succeeded in making the government higher education system sick, the World Bank now changed tack, and convened a Task Force on higher education. Its report, *Higher Education in Developing Countries: Peril and Promise,* was released in March 2000. Emphasising the importance of higher education in today's knowledge-based global economy, the Task Force pointed out that "narrow—and in our view, misleading—economic analysis has contributed to the view that public investment in universities and colleges brings meagre returns compared to investment in primary and secondary schools" and this has led many developing countries to assign a low priority to higher education since the 1980s. The Task Force urged upon the developing countries to take urgent action to "expand the quantity and improve the quality of higher education". It recommended that for this, the "strengths of all players—public and private—must be used", and suggested "a mixed funding model to maximise the financial input of the private sector, philanthropic individuals and institutions, and students." Simultaneously, it also called for "more consistent and productive public funding mechanisms". It advocated that governments play the role of supervisors, since that is something that markets will not do. Finally, it also warned that since markets require profits, there is a danger that courses like basic sciences and humanities are likely to be underprovided, and governments will need to make special efforts to encourage them.[6]

The Ambani–Birla Report

The same year (2000) saw the release of another report which too had a major impact on the higher education sector in India, *A Policy Framework for Reforms in Education*. This report was shockingly not the product of any committee of academics, but was drafted by industrialists Mukesh Ambani (Convenor) and Kumarmangalam Birla (Member); and they were invited to do so, not by the Ministry for Human Resource Development or the UGC, but Prime Minister Vajpayee's Council on Trade and Industry!

Ambani–Birla were brazen in their recommendations. They stated that we must "fundamentally change our mindset" of "seeing education as a component of social development". They advocated privatisation of universities in India and strict enforcement of the 'users-pay' principle in higher education, with loans and grants for the economically and socially backward sections of society, to make investment in the education sector profitable for investors. They wanted the government to encourage leading industrial houses to set up universities in areas like science, technology and management where there is potential for making profits, and recommended that the State play an active role in disciplines like "oriental languages, archaeology, palaeontology, religion and philosophy" where the private sector may not be interested in investing as scholars in these fields "do not command a market".

The report estimated that corporate investment could double the number of post-secondary institutions by 2015.

Ambani–Birla also wanted to "market India as a destination for affordable and high quality education"; in other words, they wanted India to open up its higher education sector for foreign students from whom high fees can be charged. Simultaneously, they also pushed for "foreign direct investment in education".[7]

The Ambani–Birla report drew strong condemnation from academicians and teachers unions, forcing the government to shelve the report. However, its recommendations have continued to influence the policy framework in higher education.[8]

Box 11.1: How the American University was Killed, in Five Easy Steps

The US had a fairly enlightened education policy in the 1950s and 60s, based on affordability and free access to universities. "Universities were the very heart of intense public discourse, passionate learning, and vocal citizen involvement in the issues of the times. The Liberal Arts stood at the centre of a college education, and students were exposed to philosophy, anthropology, literature, history, sociology, world religions, foreign languages and cultures." This was also the period, beginning in the late 1950s into the 60s, of "uprisings and growing numbers of citizens taking part in popular dissent—against the Vietnam War, against racism, against destruction of the environment in a growing corporatised culture, against misogyny, against homophobia." ... "The American "corporations" ... "didn't like the outcome of the 60s". They realised that these revolts incubated on university campuses, and "would have liked nothing more than to shut down the universities. Destroy them outright. But a country claiming to have democratic values can't just shut down its universities. That would reveal something about that country which would not support the image they are determined to portray—that of a country of freedom, justice, opportunity for all." So, how did the corporates go about "kill(ing) the universities of the country without showing (their) hand?" They did that in five easy steps.

i) Defund public higher education;
ii) Deprofessionalise and impoverish the professors, and create a surplus of underemployed and unemployed PhDs;
iii) Move in a managerial/administrative class to take over governance of the university;
iv) Move in corporate culture and corporate money;
v) Destroy the students.

"Within one generation, in five easy steps, not only have the scholars and intellectuals of the country been silenced and nearly wiped out, but the entire institution has been hijacked, and recreated as a machine through which future generations will ALL be impoverished, indebted and silenced. Now, low wage migrant professors teach repetitive courses they did not design to students who travel through on a kind of conveyor belt, only to be spit out, indebted and desperate, into a jobless economy. The only people immediately benefiting inside this system are the administrative class—whores to the corporatised colonisers, earning money in this system in order to oversee this travesty. But the most important thing to keep in mind is this: The real winners, the only people truly benefiting from the big-picture meltdown of the American university are those people who, in the 1960s, saw those vibrant college campuses as a threat to their established power."

[Article posted on the internet by: 'Junct Rebellion', an organisation established to raise awareness about the demise of the American university system. The full article can be accessed at: "How the American University was Killed, in Five Easy Steps", August 12, 2012, https://junctrebellion.wordpress.com.]

National Knowledge Commission Report

In 2005, the Government of India constituted the National Knowledge Commission (NKC) to recommend policy reforms to "build excellence in the educational system to meet the knowledge challenges of the 21st century and increase India's competitive advantage in fields of knowledge."[9] The Commission was chaired by Sam Pitroda, an NRI known for his open loyalties to neoliberalism. The working of this Commission was a one-man show; Sam Pitroda so blatantly ignored the other members of the Commission that the Vice-Chairman of the Commission, Dr. P.M. Bhargava, a renowned scientist, resigned in protest.[10] The Commission submitted its *Report to the Nation 2006* in January 2007. The Commission's recommendations cover a wide range of areas, from education to e-governance, However, its accent is on higher education, where its prescriptions are along the same lines as the Ambani-Birla report, that basically views the sole objective of education to be placement in the job market. If that is the purpose, it logically follows that higher education need not be publicly funded, and should be privatised.

The NKC recommends the establishment of 1,500 universities by 2015, as well as 50 'National Universities' providing "education of the highest standard". Simultaneously, it points out that "the size and composition of university courts, academic councils, and executive councils slows down decision-making processes." Therefore, it recommends that Vice-Chancellors of universities should function like chief executive officers, university courts should be dispensed with, and in lieu of academic council meetings there should be standing committees taking decisions, all in the name of expeditiousness of decision-making. These suggestions would effectively convert universities into highly authoritarian institutions. Furthermore, these authoritarian institutions need not necessarily be in the government sector, they can be run by the private sector or as public–private partnerships. To facilitate the entry of the private sector into higher education, the NKC recommends that a regulatory authority replace the UGC. The NKC's proposals in short clearly envisage a substantial privatisation of higher education in the country.[11]

To draw talent into the academic profession, the NKC suggests the introduction of "incentives and rewards for performance".[12] This will introduce a new 'caste-system' (to use a phrase coined by Prof. Prabhat Patnaik) on our campuses. On the one hand, there will be an upper caste of highly paid teachers with PhDs from Harvard–Oxford–Cambridge, who will be oriented only towards pursuing their careers rather than having an "ambition to make an impact on the quality of social thinking and endeavour"[13]; who will be more interested in climbing the 'stairs of hierarchy' in the university rather than contributing to building an institution that furnishes "intellectual leadership and moral tone to society".[14] And on the other hand, a lot of our universities and teachers will be considered second-grade. They will be low in morale, lacking in self-confidence, full of cynicism, and drained of whatever enthusiasm they originally had, and whatever creativity they were originally capable of. It will therefore destroy whatever little democratic atmosphere that remains on our campuses, and will be a surest recipe for the destruction of quality in our higher education system.

The Eleventh Plan

The World Bank report of 2000, and its virtual endorsement by India's leading industrialists in the form of the Ambani–Birla report (which reads almost like an Indianised version of the former) and by the National Knowledge Commission saw the Indian government

Box 11.2: The Dismantling of Higher Education in Andhra Pradesh

One of the first states to assiduously implement World Bank mandated reforms in higher education was Andhra Pradesh. The state government took a massive loan from the World Bank, and as a part of the conditionalities, systematically went about dismantling the publicly funded higher education system in the State, which had some of the best universities in the country—the Osmania and Andhra University. Block grants to universities was cut, adversely affecting the quality of libraries, laboratories and infrastructure. They were asked to raise their own funds through self-financing courses like management, professional and vocational courses. The Science Faculty was incentivised to go in for consultancy and patenting. Disciplines like Arts, Humanities, Social Sciences and Basic Sciences were underfunded and the number of faculty in each discipline was reduced to the bare minimum. Fresh recruitment of faculty was stopped. In place of permanent faculty, these universities started employing part-time, under-paid and under-qualified faculty. With such faculty remaining temporary and insecure for decades, obviously it could not have a commitment towards teaching, nor could it indulge in passionate research. The publicly funded universities, including the Osmania and Andhra Universities, have thus been pushed to the verge of collapse. On the other hand, there has been a spectacular rise of private universities and colleges all over the State, particularly in professional education, catering to the better-off sections of society.

[Source: G. Haragopal, "The Story of Dismantling of Higher Education in India", in Ravi Kumar (ed.), "Education, State and Market: Anatomy of Neoliberal Impact", pp. 66–67, Aakar Books, New Delhi, 2014.]

make an about turn in its policy on higher education. This new orientation was visible in the Eleventh Plan.

Echoing the language of the World Bank, the 'approach paper' to the Eleventh Plan called for a major effort to expand the country's higher education system, stating that:

> Only about 10% of the relevant age group go to universities whereas in many developing countries, the figure is between 20

> and 25%. There is an overwhelming need to undertake major expansion to increase access to higher education.[15]

Accordingly, the Eleventh Five Year Plan announced a "focus on the pressing need to expand capacity in our institutions of higher education and technical and professional education (engineering, medicine, law, etc.) ... We must aim at increasing the GER to 15% by the end of the Plan and reach 21% by the end of the Twelfth Plan."[16] And so it proposed the establishment of 30 new central universities, including 14 world class universities, 8 new Indian Institutes of Technology (IITs), 7 Indian Institutes of Management (IIMs), 3 Indian Institutes of Science Education and Research, 10 National Institutes of Technology, 20 Indian Institutes of Information Technology, 2 Schools of Planning and Architecture, 1,000 polytechnics and 370 colleges for general education.[17]

As discussed in Chapter 7, while the Eleventh Plan claimed to be an 'Education Plan', it actually pushed for privatisation of even elementary education. In the case of higher education, its recommendations were even more brazen. The Eleventh Plan document stated:

> A welcome development during the Tenth Plan is that the share of private unaided higher education institutions increased from 42.6% in 2001 to 63.21% in 2006. Their share of enrolments also increased from 32.89% to 51.53% in the same period. This trend is likely to continue in the Eleventh Plan ...

The Eleventh Plan proposed to achieve a GER of 15% (in higher education) by 2011–12, for which it estimated that an additional enrolment of 8.7 lakh students in universities and 61.3 lakh in colleges would be required. The Plan document went on to say: "it is reasonable to expect that about half of incremental enrolment targeted for higher education will come from private providers"![18]

The Planning Commission suggested that many of the large number of higher educational institutions proposed to be set up under the Eleventh Five Year Plan be set up either in the private sector or through PPP: "Since the establishment of world class institutions involves considerable expenditure on creating facilities, the scope for public–private participation in setting up these universities will be carefully explored.... The scope for setting up institutions of higher education in the private sector must also be explored."[19] According to some austere estimates, the large number of premier higher educational institutions proposed to be set up under the Eleventh Plan required an investment of the order of Rs 252,000 crore. However, the financial allocation made in the Eleventh Plan towards setting up these institutions was barely 12% of this amount, implying that the government expected the remaining amount to be put in by the private sector.[20]

Additionally, the Planning Commission called for granting financial autonomy to higher educational institutions, so that they can "mobilise resources from user fees, review fee-structures, consultancy services, and donations." It also argued that since "most university students come from the top 10% of the population by income levels", they can afford to pay higher fees, and therefore fees in colleges and universities should be gradually increased to levels that cover a reasonable part of the running cost, and that fees in professional courses could be much higher. Further, that "the new norms could be implemented in new institutions from the start."[21]

This brazen promotion of the entry of the private sector into the higher education sector and giving it a free rein to hike fees and make unrestricted profits has led to a huge private sector boom in higher education over the past decade.

The Private Sector Takes Off

From 190 in 1990–91 and 256 in 2000–01, the number of universities* in India rose to 700 by 2012–13, a two-and-a-half fold increase in just 12 years. And the number of colleges zoomed to 35,539 in 2011–12, from 7,346 in 1990–91 and 12,806 in 2000–01 (see Charts 11.1 and 11.2).

This increase was mainly driven by a huge increase in the number of private higher educational institutions. As can be seen from Chart 11.3, the total number of private (unaided) universities and colleges

* *Universities includes Deemed Universities and Institutions of National Importance.*

Chart 11.1: Number of Universities in India, 1950–2013[22]

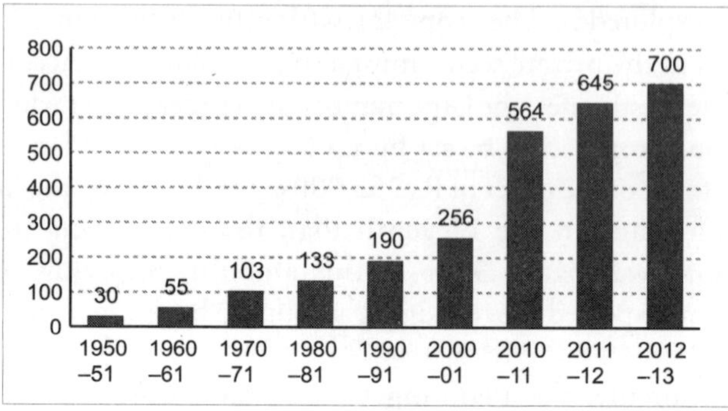

Chart 11.2: Number of Colleges in India, 1950–2012[23]

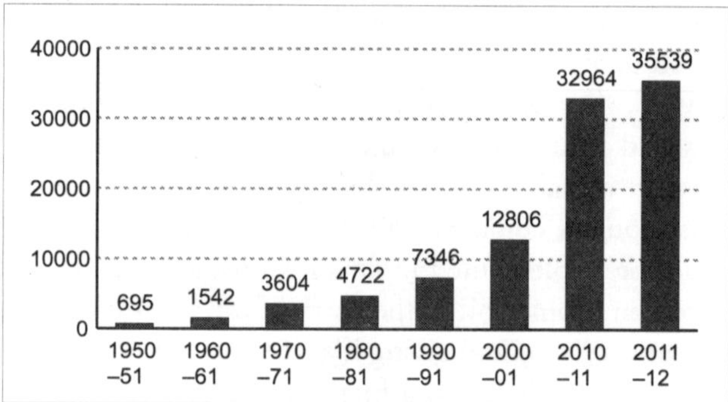

Chart 11.3: Increase in Number of Private Unaided Universities and Colleges, 2001–12

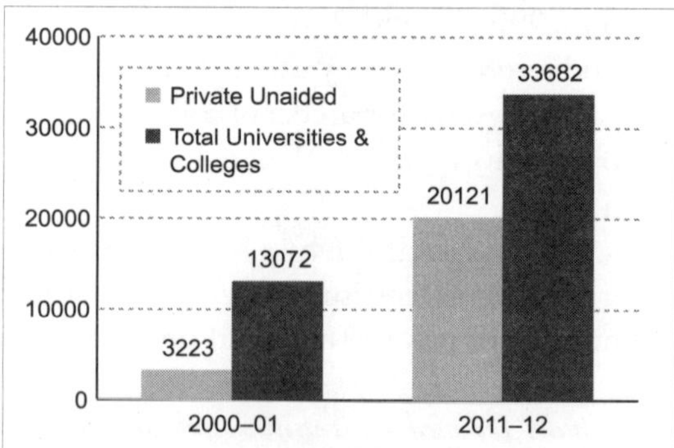

shot up by more than six times in the past decade, and now account for nearly 60% of all universities and colleges combined, as compared to less than 25% in 2001.[24] There are now nearly 200 private universities and deemed universities, compared to almost nil a decade ago.

A significant part of this increase, both in private higher educational institutions as well as in total number of higher educational institutions, took place during the Eleventh Plan period (2007–12). Ninety-eight private state universities, 17 private deemed universities and 7,818 private colleges were set up during the Plan period. Simultaneously, in accordance with World Bank recommendations, the government also made a huge push to set up Central institutions of higher education. The Central government established 65 new degree-granting institutions during the Eleventh Plan period, the highest ever in a single Plan period. Apart from that, it also supported the states to set up 45 model degree colleges during this period.[25]

The total number of higher educational institutions (HEIs), including both degree and diploma granting institutions, increased by a whopping 58% during the Eleventh Plan period (2007–12), from 29,384 to 46,430 (Table 11.2). The total number of private (unaided) HEIs (degree + diploma) now account for two-thirds of all institutions (Chart 11.4).

Table 11.2: Number of Higher Educational Institutions and Student Enrolment, India, 2011–12[26]

	Central	*State*	*Private Unaided*	*Total*
Universities	152	316	191	659
Colleges	69	13,024	19,930	33,023
Diploma Institutions	–	3,207	9,541	12,748
Total number of HEIs	221	16,547	29,662	46,430
Percentage	0.5	35.6	63.9	100
Enrolment (lakhs)	5.63	84.0	128.23	217.86
Percentage	2.6	38.5	58.9	100

Correspondingly, the total student enrolment (degree + diploma) has more than tripled over the past decade, going up from around 70 lakh in 2000–01 to more than 217 lakh in 2011–12. Private institutions now account for nearly 60% of the total student enrolment (Table 11.2, Chart 11.4).[27]

This huge private sector-led boom in higher education has resulted in a near doubling of the Gross Enrolment Ratio (taking into consideration only students in degree and diploma courses, and not those in distance learning courses) over the past 12 years. It has gone up from 8.3 in 2000–01 to 10.4 in 2006–07 to 15.2 in 2011–12.[28]

Chart 11.4: Higher Educational Institutions and Student Enrolment, 2000–01 and 2011–12[29]

(by type of management, %)

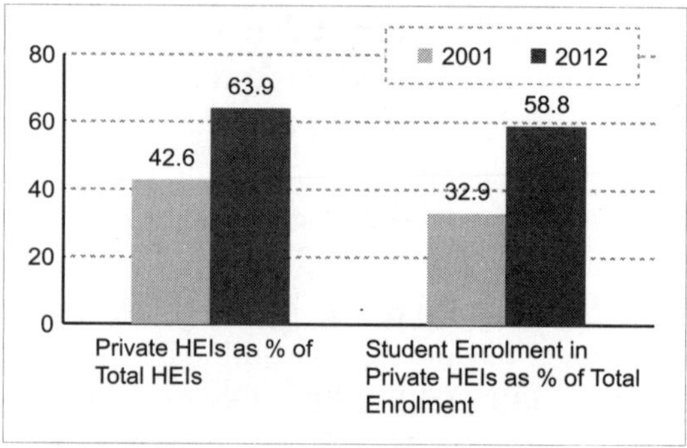

Quality by the Wayside

The government has great faith in the regulatory power of free markets. And so it has allowed this great private sector-led boom in higher education to take place in a completely unregulated way. The minimum norms that an institution needs to fulfil to gain recognition as a 'university' or a 'deemed university' or an 'engineering college' or a 'science college' have been considerably relaxed, or they have been ignored, allowing higher education institutions to sprout up all over the country like mushrooms.

Of course, the government needs to show that it is seeking to maintain some semblance of quality. And so in 1994, some years after the beginnings of globalisation, the government established the National Assessment and Accreditation Council (NAAC) to evaluate, assess and accredit higher education institutions in the country. NAAC functions as an autonomous body under the UGC. It assesses

Box 11.3: National Assessment and Accreditation Council (NAAC)

NAAC assesses and accredits universities and colleges on the basis of the following seven criteria:

i) organisation and governance;
ii) infrastructural facilities and support services (library, laboratory, instrumentation, computer facilities, etc.);
iii) quality of teaching and learning;
iv) curriculum design and review;
v) student services;
vi) research, publications and consultancy/extension activities;
vii) innovative practices.

The institutions are given the grades A, B or C.

[Source: "NAAC – National Assessment and Accreditation Council", http://www.seaastandards.org.]

universities and colleges on the basis of a number of criteria (see Box 11.3) and grades the institutions.[30]

However, accreditation for higher educational institutions is mandatory only for those colleges and universities that receive UGC grants. Most colleges that have opened in recent years are private self-financing colleges; for them, getting assessed by NAAC is voluntary. Even from a purely business point of view, which is obviously how private institutions examine any issue, getting themselves accredited by NAAC is a very profitable proposition provided they get a high grade—they can then attract students from rich families, charge them high fees and make huge profits. However, most private colleges and universities have such poor physical infrastructure and are so deficient in terms of quality and quantity of teachers that they have preferred not to get themselves accredited. Therefore, only a small number of higher educational institutions have been graded by NAAC. As of October 2013, of the 630 universities and 33,000 colleges in India, only 179 universities and 5,224 colleges had valid accreditation—that is, less than 30% of the universities and 16% of the colleges had been assessed and accredited by NAAC.

Such is the dismal quality of higher education in India that even of this small number of higher educational institutions that have taken accreditation, only 11% have obtained A grade; the overwhelming number, 89%, have been graded 'average' or 'below average' (Chart 11.5).[31]

Assuming that all colleges and universities not graded by NAAC are either average or below average, this means that of India's 630 universities, only 70 (11% of the total) are A grade universities; while of India's 33,000 colleges, just 554—less than 2%—are top grade.

Chart 11.5: Graded Break-up of Institutions Accredited by NAAC

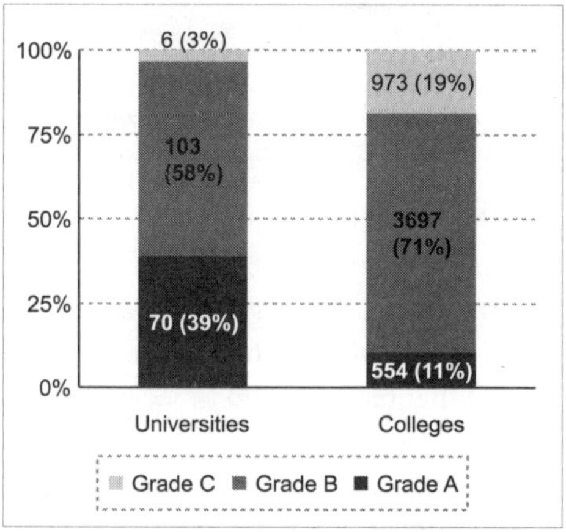

Apart from NAAC, India has another accreditation organisation for professional and technical colleges, that is, engineering and technology, management, architecture and pharmacy colleges, called the National Board of Accreditation (NBA). The NBA was initially established by the All India Council of Technical Education (AICTE), and became an autonomous body in 2010. The difference between NAAC and NBA is that while NAAC assesses physical infrastructure of institutions, faculty, finances, governance, etc., NBA assesses programme and course content.

As discussed above, there has been a boom in professional colleges in India during the past decade. In 2006–07, there were 1,503 engineering colleges which admitted 5.83 lakh students; in 2012, the number of colleges had more than doubled to 3393, with a student capacity of 14.85 lakh seats![32] Similarly, the number of management schools has tripled to 4,500 in the last five years, and their student intake has gone up from 95,000 in 2006–07 to 3.6 lakh in 2011–12.[33]

However, just like the situation for accreditation by NAAC, most engineering and management colleges have not got themselves accredited by NBA. In an unholy alliance with these professional colleges, NBA is not willing to reveal how many colleges it has accredited! NBA's website only gives figures up to May 2009—till then, only 786 engineering institutions out of 1346 had got themselves accredited. Since then, though the number of engineering colleges has more than doubled, there is no update on the website as to how many colleges have got themselves accredited.[34]

The reason is the same like for NAAC—most of them are afraid that their racketeering would get exposed. A survey conducted by the industry body Associated Chambers of Commerce and Industry of India (Assocham) observed that many private schools are a business venture by "some management guru to earn money out of investment." D.S. Rawat, secretary general of Assocham, stated:

> There is no quality control, the placements are not commensurate with fees being charged, the faculty is not good enough and there is no infrastructure.[35]

Commodification of Higher Education

Higher education has now become a commodity in India, a good for sale on the marketplace. Obviously then, like every other commodity—soap, mobile phone, cloth, TV, scooter, car—there would be good quality and bad quality education, depending on the purchasing power of the consumer. Thousands of private colleges have opened in the last few years, some targeted at the children of the elites, others towards the middle and lower middle classes. (There are obviously no private colleges targeting the poor; only those with money can go shopping in the market.) On the one hand, there are colleges

Box 11.4: Five Star Universities

Oasis of Education: Mody Institute of Technology and Science, Lakshmangarh

A few years ago, Lakshmangarh, a small town in Rajasthan's Sikar district, was barren land. Today over 80 species of birds, 14 fountains, five designer buildings, 400 trees and 8,000 students have transformed its landscape and economy. Set up as a state private university in 1998, the all-girls MITS has undergraduate departments of engineering, management studies, arts, science, commerce and law. The 500-acre campus appears as if it is a Bollywood movie set ... the dining hall for students is modelled to resemble Hogwarts, the fictional magic school immortalised in Harry Potter books, with crystal chandeliers, oak tables and a hand-painted ceiling.

Supersize Me: Lovely Professional University, Phagwara

This private university with its 900-acre campus located on the Ludhiana-Jalandhar highway is owned by the Lovely Group. The Group started its journey in 1961 when Baldev Mittal started a small sweet shop in Jalandhar; from sweets they ventured into autos, and then they started this private university in 2005. With its own tram system, Punjab's largest open air theatre, a student-run shopping mall, over 30 ATMs, 90 restaurants, 15 hostels, eight private apartment blocks and a luxury gym, the campus is home to over 40,000 students and staff.

Go Global: KIIT, Bhubaneswar

KIIT was set up in 1997 by Achyut Samanta with a loan of Rs. 25 lakhs from a nationalised bank. Today, it has assets worth Rs. 4,000 crores. This private university is spread over 25 sq km of land, with 20 Wi-Fi-enabled campuses—two of them with solar power backing, multimedia classrooms with 7.5 million sq ft of built-up area, acres of green landscapes, swimming pools, cafeterias and food courts. It now has 18,000 students from across India and 22 other countries, 1,500 faculty members and 2,500 support staff.

[Source: "Five Star Universities", May 27, 2013, http://indiatoday.intoday.in; "A Laddoo King Shapes Academic Careers in Punjab", October 26, 2010, http://www.deccanherald.com.]

with inadequate resources—poorly equipped libraries and laboratories, under-qualified teachers, no sports facilities, badly endowed computer rooms, etc.; and on the other hand, there are five star private universities with luxurious amenities for students, like shopping malls, five star hotels, luxury saunas, designer lounges and touchscreens in classrooms, luxury gymasiums, etc. (see Box 11.4).

An important component of the neoliberal agenda worldwide is casualisation of the workforce so that the capitalist classes can maximise their profits. This is being extended to the education sector too. Colleges and universities are drastically reducing the number of permanent teachers on their rolls, and there has been a huge rise in temporary and ad hoc faculty. A UGC-sponsored study of 47 sample universities from 19 states brought out the dismal fact that in 2007–08, 51% of the teaching positions were lying vacant! The situation in colleges was equally bad. No fewer than 41% of the positions at the Lecturer level, and 18% of those at the Reader level, were lying unfilled.[36]

Super Profits ...

With higher education a business, college fees are going through the roof. Even for a BA or B.Ed. degree, both of which have virtually no job value today, the fees in a private college oriented towards middle class students can be as much as from Rs 20,000 to Rs 50,000 per year. (And in an elite college, like for instance the Flame School for Liberal Education, the course fees for a BA degree can go up to Rs 4 lakh per year.[37]) For a B. Com course, the fees in a middle class private college could be somewhere between Rs 60,000 and Rs 1.2 lakh/year. For a Bachelor of Engineering degree, the fee can range between Rs 1 and 3 lakh and more. (And the price for a management quota seat could go up to a whopping Rs 20 lakh.)[38] An MBA degree in a premium B-School (as they are now called) could cost anywhere between Rs 3 and 10 lakh per year for the two-year course. And if you are cold-blooded enough to be wanting to make money off disease and are aspiring for a seat in a private medical college, that could cost you as much as Rs 30 lakh; there are also colleges offering a combined graduate and postgraduate degree (MBBS + MD) for a cool Rs 1.5 crore.[39]

Scams Unlimited

And then, like in every business, there are also fly-by-night operators, out to make a quick buck.

Fake Degrees

To give one particularly notorious example, after the Chhattisgarh Government passed the Chhattisgarh Private Sector University Act in 2002, a whopping 112 self-financing universities came up in just one year! A UGC inspection found that many of these universities existed only on paper. Some were actually distance learning centres that had taken advantage of the loopholes in the law to declare themselves as universities. Others had hardly any infrastructure worth the name. Some of the degrees they offered were plainly fishy—such as a degree in Member of the International Institute of Medical Sciences (MIMS), a diploma in Cruise Hospitality Management (DCHM) and a BA in Beauty Care and Health Services. The Supreme Court struck down the Act as unconstitutional, putting the future of over 30,000 students in jeopardy. Instead of closing down, many of these universities with the connivance of the state government have resorted to all kinds of tricks to keep their business going.[40]

While the Chhattisgarh scam is probably the biggest, such scams are taking place in all states, ruining the lives of thousands of students tricked into taking admissions into such dubious colleges/universities. Thus, Meghalaya is considered to be the education hub of the North-East. Eight self-financed universities have opened in the State in the last six years through Acts passed by the Meghalaya Assembly. Now, several of them are being investigated for fraud. Last year, the CID sealed the offices of the Shillong based CMJ University after it came to light that since its establishment in 2009, *it had awarded over 4000 fake PhD degrees*. All that one needed to do was pay between Rs 2 and 5 lakh, and the degree would be delivered to your home address. After the scam came to light, the Maharashtra Government did some preliminary investigations and found 36 fake PhD degree holders in the State; while some of them had obtained their phony degrees from CMJ University, others had obtained it from Rajasthan and Tamil

Nadu based universities! After initially showing some zeal, the Maharashtra Government now seems to have stopped further investigation, as no more such cases are being reported in the media. News reports say that a majority of the 4,000 fake PhDs awarded by CMJ University have been distributed to students from Maharashtra; in all probability, these gentlemen must be ensconced in senior positions in private universities and colleges in the State—having PhDs as their instructional staff adds to the market value of these institutions—and so political pressure must have come on the state government to drop its investigation.[41]

Illegal Foreign Tie-ups

Another kind of fraud being indulged in by India's private universities/colleges is collaboration with foreign universities and 'education service providers' operating in India. Cautioning students not to take admission in such courses, an advertisement on the website of AICTE states:

> As per the information available till date, 169 institutions are found to be conducting courses in the field of technical education without obtaining AICTE approval. 104 institutions are conducting technical education programmes in collaboration with foreign universities without AICTE approval.
>
> Students are advised not to take admission in technical education courses run by any institution which has not been approved by AICTE. They are cautioned that joining unapproved programmes can have serious consequences in terms of eligibility for employment, higher studies, etc.

At the foot of this advertisement, two web-links are given which give the names of these unapproved institutions and their programmes. The list includes institutions like ICFAI, IIPM, Ansal Institute of Technology and G.D. Goenka World Institute which regularly issue front page and full page advertisements in national dailies about their programmes and also their tie-ups with foreign universities!

There cannot be more glaring proof that the HRD Ministry and its subordinate, the AICTE, have decided to completely abdicate from their responsibility of regulating higher education! An AICTE regulation of 2005 provides that: "In case it comes to the notice of the Council, that a Foreign University is running diploma or/and degree at undergraduate, postgraduate and research level in technical education in India directly or in collaboration with an Indian partner without obtaining a certificate of registration, the Council shall take immediate steps to initiate action under the Indian Penal Code for criminal breach of trust, misconduct, fraud and cheating and under other relevant Indian laws."[42] AICTE knows the names of these institutions which are indulging in such cheating and fraud, it has even put up their names on its website, yet it is not willing to take action against them. All that it is willing to do is put out an advertisement, warning students not to take admission in such illegal courses!

Illegal Franchisees

To expand their 'customer base' and make more 'profits', private state universities are entering into collaboration with unrecognised for-profit institutions all over the country, through which they offer their degrees to students unable to take admission in a regular course in the university. These centres proceed to advertise that they offer legitimate degrees, as approved outreach centres of the state university. This is illegal on several counts. One, state universities do not have jurisdiction beyond their respective states, so they cannot open such outreach centres beyond their state boundaries. Two, such franchising is illegal, both the UGC and AICTE have banned it. And three, all these centres are for-profit organisations, whereas the law is that a for-profit organisation cannot offer education.

These colleges/outreach centres offer programmes like 'regular weekend classes' or 'online classes', and sometimes even regular classes like in a regular college, and charge hefty fees, which is many times what the student would have paid had he/she taken direct admission in the university. Tens of thousands of students are enrolling in such fraudulent programmes, thinking that they are pursuing regular, approved programmes.

To give a few examples, International Institute of Business Studies (IIBS), Noida offers a Distance Learning (DL) MBA degree from Punjab Technical University (PTU), Jalandhar. IIBS Noida charges Rs 2.95 lakh per student for this degree, whereas a regular MBA from PTU is for Rs 60,000 per annum. Interestingly, the degree that is handed out by IIBS Noida doesn't bear the name of the programme-giver (IIBS) anywhere. IIBS also offers a regular MBA degree from Bharathiar University, Coimbatore for Rs 3.95 lakh. The same Bharathiar University MBA degree is also offered by IBMR Gurgaon for a slightly higher fee of Rs 5 lakh. Likewise, Manonmaniam Sundaranar University, Tirunelveli has appointed Shri Sai Institute in Punjab, Karnavati Education in Gujarat and StrataPro Education Advisory in Delhi as its franchisees.

This massive racketeering is taking place openly; the details of these courses are openly advertised both by the state universities and their franchisees, and information is available on the internet. Yet, all that the UGC has done is to post notices on its website, warning students not to take admission to such courses![43]

These frauds are taking place on such a huge scale that even Prof. Yashpal, who authored the Yashpal Committee report on 'Renovation and Rejuvenation of Higher Education' that implicitly favoured privatisation and commercialisation of higher education,[44] was recently constrained to observe that most private universities are just selling degrees in the name of higher education:

> These so-called universities are practically business centres with nicely done receptions and other allurements to trap degree seekers. These institutes have nothing to do with higher education ... These run only those courses, which generate maximum revenue. A few are selling PhD degrees for cash.[45]

★ ★ ★

The Kothari Commission had stated way back in 1966, during the days when there was still some idealism in Indian society, that:

> Universities are pre-eminently the forum for a critical assessment of society ...

and that

> The character of a university as a society of teachers and students engaged in the pursuit of learning and discovery, distinguishes fundamentally the regulation of its affairs from, say, the profit-motivated management of commercial or industrial concerns or the administration of a government department ...[46]

But now, the university has become precisely that which the Kothari Commission had envisioned it should not be. It is no longer "a society of teachers and students engaged in the pursuit of learning and discovery"; teachers have become mere casual wage workers in an education factory which trains students to take their obedient place in society and become cogs in the wheel—they are trained not to look at what they are doing, not to indulge in critical enquiry, while the wheel spins them around. The university has become a profit-oriented industrial concern...

NOTES

1. Erik Wesselius, *Behind GATS 2000: Corporate Power At Work*, Transnational Institute, Netherlands, 2002, http://www.tni.org.
2. *Internationalisation and Trade in Higher Education: Opportunities and Challenges*, OECD, 2004, pp. 31–32, http://books.google.co.in; Jandhyala B.G. Tilak, *Higher Education: A Public Good or a Commodity for Trade?*, UNESCO, 2009, http://www.kritischestudenten.nl.
3. Erik Wesselius, *Behind GATS 2000: Corporate Power At Work*, op. cit.
4. *Report of the CABE Committee on Financing of Higher Education in India*, June 2005, pp. 9–11, http://www.teindia.nic.in.
5. Madhu Prasad, "Impact of the World Bank on Higher Education", published in: *Neo-Liberal Assault on Higher Education*, booklet published by the All India Forum for Right to Education.
6. "Task Force on Higher Education and Society", http://www.tfhe.net.
7. Dr. Vijender Sharma, *Crisis of Higher Education in India*, Chapter 9, http://indiaeducrisis.wordpress.com.
8. Madhu Prasad, "Impact of the World Bank on Higher Education", op. cit.; Madhu Prasad, "Commoditising Higher Education: The Assault of Neoliberal Barbarism", in Ravi Kumar (ed.), *Education, State and Market: Anatomy of Neoliberal Impact*, Aakar Books, Delhi, 2014, p. 101.
9. *National Knowledge Commission*, Wikipedia, http://en.wikipedia.org.

10. G. Haragopal, "The Story of Dismantling of Higher Education in India", in Ravi Kumar (ed.), *Education, State and Market: Anatomy of Neoliberal Impact*, Aakar Books, Delhi, 2014, pp. 60–61.
11. Vijender Sharma, "Privatisation of Higher Education is the Main Aim", *People's Democracy*, February 18, 2007, http://archives.peoples democracy.in; Prof. Prabhat Patnaik, *Alternative Perspectives on Higher Education in the Context of Globalisation*, August 11, 2007, http://www.nuepa.org.
12. Prof. Prabhat Patnaik, ibid.
13. *Education and National Development: Report of the Education Commission, 1964–66, Vol. 3: Higher Education*, p. 555, http://www.teindia.nic.in.
14. *Report of the Committee on 'Model Act' for Universities*, http://www.teindia.nic.in.
15. *Towards Faster and More Inclusive Growth: An Approach to the 11th Five Year Plan, 2007–2012*, Planning Commission, Government of India, December 2006, pp. 61–62, http://planning-commission.nic.in.
16. *Eleventh Five Year Plan, Vol. I: Inclusive Growth*, Planning Commission, Government of India, p. 17, http://planning-commission.nic.in.
17. *Eleventh Five Year Plan, Vol. II: Social Sector*, Planning Commission, Government of India, pp. 26–27, 29, 34, http://planning commission.nic.in.
18. Ibid., p. 23.
19. *Eleventh Five Year Plan, Vol. I: Inclusive Growth*, op. cit., p. 18.
20. J.B.G. Tilak, "Budget 2010: Neither Vision Nor Policy for Education", *Economic and Political Weekly*, March 27, 2010, http://environmentportal.in.
21. *Eleventh Five Year Plan, Vol. II: Social Sector*, op. cit., pp. 25, 31–32.
22. Dr. M. Abdul Salam, *Higher Education in India at a Glance*, University of Calicut, http://www.slideshare.net; *Higher Education in India at a Glance*, UGC, June 2013, http://www.ugc.ac.in.
23. Dr. M. Abdul Salam, ibid.; *Higher Education in India at a Glance*, UGC, ibid.
24. For 2000–01, same as Table 10.5 in Chapter 10; for 2011–12: *Twelfth Five Year Plan, 2012–2017, Vol. III – Social Sectors*, Planning Commission, Government of India, p. 95, http://planning commission.gov.in. Note that the Twelfth Plan document only talks of private colleges and universities, without stating whether these are private unaided only or include private aided institutions too. Now, the *All India Survey on Higher Education 2011–12 (Provisional)* published by the MHRD, Government of India says that of the total number of

colleges in India, 58% are private unaided. From this, it can be estimated that of the 33,023 colleges mentioned in Twelfth Plan document, 58% or 20,247 are private unaided—which is reasonably close to the figure of 19,930 for 'private' colleges given in the Twelfth Plan. So, we can reasonably conclude that the Twelfth Plan is talking of private unaided colleges and universities when it is talking of 'private' higher educational institutions.

25. *Twelfth Five Year Plan, 2012–2017, Vol. III – Social Sectors*, Planning Commission, Government of India, pp. 94–95, http://planning commission.gov.in.
26. Ibid., pp. 93–94.
27. Ibid., p. 93; *Higher Education in India: Twelfth Five Year Plan (2012–2017) and Beyond*, Ernst and Young, FICCI and Planning Commission, http://www.ey.com. Enrolment figures for 2001 calculated from figures given in Ernst and Young report.
28. *Twelfth Five Year Plan, 2012–2017, Vol. III – Social Sectors*, ibid., p. 93; figure for 2000–01 calculated from GER given in "Private Participation in Higher Education and the Challenges", http://apjor.com, and from this, we have deducted the total students in distance learning given in *Higher Education in India: Twelfth Five Year Plan (2012–2017) and Beyond*, ibid.
29. *Higher Education in India: Twelfth Five Year Plan (2012–2017) and Beyond*, ibid.
30. "NAAC – National Assessment and Accreditation Council", http://www.seaastandards.org; Dr. Vijender Sharma, *Crisis of Higher Education in India*, op. cit., Chapter 6.
31. Manash Pratim Gohain, "Indian Universities Second Grade?", *TNN*, February 21, 2014, http://timesofindia.indiatimes.com. It is not clear why NAAC says that there were 630 universities and 33,000 colleges in India as of October 2013, as the actual number of universities and colleges is more than this figure. Probably NAAC is talking of non-professional educational institutions only.
32. Hemali Chhapia, "Number of Engineers in India Inflated, Says Study", *TNN*, March 6, 2008, http://timesofindia.indiatimes.com; Hemali Chhapia, "AICTE May Bar New Engineering, Management Colleges from 2014", *TNN*, February 28, 2012, http://timesofindia.india times.com.
33. Varun Sinha, "Mismanagement? B-schools in India are Struggling", *NDTV*, January 30, 2013, http://profit.ndtv.com.
34. "The Indian Engineers Coordination Meeting", August 6, 2012, http://xa.yimg.com.

35. Varun Sinha, "Mismanagement? B-schools in India are Struggling", op.cit.
36. *Higher Education in India—Issues Related to Expansion, Inclusiveness, Quality and Finance*, UGC, New Delhi, 2008, pp. 12–13, http://www.ugc.ac.in.
37. "FLAME School of Liberal Education, Fees", http://www.flame.edu.in.
38. Rashmi Belur, "Private Engineering Colleges Go for the Kill", June 17, 2013, http://www.dnaindia.com.
39. See for instance: G. Pramod Kumar, "Study Engineering? If You Don't have Money, Go to Hell!", February 10, 2012, http://www.firstpost.com; "MBA Colleges in Bangalore with Fee Structure", 2012, http://mbacollegesinbangalore.co.in; Veena Venugopal, "The Business of Education", September 15, 2013, http://www.thehindubusinessline.com.
40. Siddharth Narain, "Clampdown on Degree Shops", *Frontline*, March 12–25, 2005, http://hindu.com; "Universities Offering Distance Learning Courses in India—Chhattisgarh", http://simplygovind.blogspot.in.
41. Ratnadip Choudhury, "Pay Rs 70k. Earn a Doctorate from Home", May 18, 2013, http://www.tehelka.com; "CID Seals CMJ University; Office Vandalised", May 2, 2013, http://meghalayatimes.info; Anil Kumar, "CMJ University Latest News", http://codepattern.net; Vaibhav Ganjapure, "Meghalaya University Distributed Over 4,000 PhDs for Rs 2–5 Lakh Each", *TNN*, June 4, 2013, http://timesofindia.indiatimes.com; "Meghalaya Private University Under Scanner", May 15, 2013, http://zeenews.india.com; Vaibhav Ganjapure, "Govt. to Lodge FIR Against CMJ Degree Holders", *TNN*, July 21, 2013, http://timesofindia.indiatimes.com.
42. All the above information taken from: Dr. Vijendra Sharma, "FEI Bill Jeopardises Our Higher Education System", *People's Democracy*, June 21, 2009, http://pd.cpim.org; "AICTE Regulations for Entry and Operation of Foreign Universities/ Institutions Imparting Technical Education in India", May 16, 2005, https://www.bcasonline.org.
43. Urmila Rao, "Students Beware! Degrees for SALE", January 8, 2014, http://www.university.careers360.com.
44. See Vijendra Sharma, "Yashpal Committee Report: Prescriptions Not for Renovation and Rejuvenation of Higher Education", *Debating Education*, August 2009, http://www.scribd.com.
45. "Most Private Universities Sell Degrees: Prof. Yash Pal", October 31, 2011, http://www.indiaeducationreview.com.
46. Quotes from Chapter 9.

12

ACCELERATING NEOLIBERALISM

A business, absolutely. We are in the business of education, and our product is the delivery of quality education. We have customers. I'm telling you, it's a business, period.

– ***Constantine Papadakis,***
President of Drexel University, USA

Opening the Doors to Foreign Institutions

One of the most important conditions imposed on India by the World Bank and India's foreign creditors in order to bail out the Indian economy during the foreign exchange crisis of 1991, was privatisation of essential services, including education, and allowing foreign corporations to enter these sectors too.

A bill to allow foreign educational institutions to enter India was first introduced in the Indian Parliament in 1995, but due to popular opposition, it could not be passed. It was revived in 2007, but again could not go through the proceedings in Parliament.[1]

India's foreign creditors were obviously not happy with this, and they mounted pressure on the Government of India to accelerate the passage of the bill. During Prime Minister Manmohan Singh's visit to the United States in November 2009 soon after coming to power for a second term, the joint statement issued by him and President Obama emphasised the importance of expanding cooperation in higher education, and announced the launching of the Obama–Singh 21st Century Knowledge Initiative to build an enhanced partnership between US and Indian universities. The issue of allowing US universities to open campuses in India was again raised by US Secretary of State Hillary Clinton during her talks with India's HRD Minister Kapil Sibal during his visit to Washington in June 2010.[2]

Box 12.1: The Business of International Education

International education has become big business, with perhaps three million students studying outside their own countries, and billions of pounds, euros and dollars being generated from tuition, living expenses, branch campuses, franchises and much else. No one knows how many branch campuses exist, but estimates are in the hundreds, almost all in developing or middle income countries. The market is large, growing and basically unregulated. It is indeed the Wild West or, more accurately, the Wild East.

[Source: Philip G. Altbach, "The 'Global Market' Bubble", February 14, 2008, http://www.timeshighereducation.co.uk.]

UK Prime Minister David Cameron also raised the issue during his visit to India in July 2010 with a big trade delegation. He candidly stated:

> Education is not just vital for national success, it is one of the best growth businesses of the 21st century. I want us in Britain and India to pool some of our advantages for our mutual benefit.[3]

Foreign Educational Institutions Bill, 2010

With due obeisance, the UPA Government began work to reintroduce the Bill after making suitable amendments. A fresh Bill, the Foreign Educational Institutions (Regulation of Entry and Operations) Bill was approved by the Cabinet and introduced in the Parliament in May 2010. With the UPA Government trundling from one crisis to another, it has fortunately not yet been able to get the Parliament to pass the Bill. Nevertheless, a look at the provisions of the Bill give an insight to the extent to which our rulers are willing to genuflect before Dollar Almighty and the high priests in Washington.

After the Cabinet cleared the Bill, the HRD Minister Kapil Sibal stated:

> This is a milestone which will enhance choices, increase competition and benchmark quality.[4]

In other words, the government is hoping that with the passage of the Bill:

(i) the entry of foreign educational institutions (FEIs) will expand the choices available to Indian students;
(ii) the entry of foreign institutions will result in competition which will improve quality and efficiency of domestic institutions; and
(iii) most importantly, the entry of top ranking foreign institutions into the country will 'benchmark quality'.

All these arguments are untenable. Let us examine them one by one.

Whose Choices Will the Bill Enhance?

As mentioned in the previous chapters, our Gross Enrolment Ratio for higher education is much lower than many developing countries, and far below the developed countries, with barely 15–16% of our students able to access higher education, the majority dropping out due to poverty. The foreign universities are obviously coming here for making profits, not to provide cheap education to Indian students, and therefore they will only increase the choices for the children of the elite. Their entry is not going to lead to an increase in opportunities for accessing higher education for the majority of our students.

Does Competition Necessarily Lead to Better Quality?

This is a typical 'one size fits all' argument given by the neoliberal lobby, which sees competition as the panacea for all problems. The fundamental theoretical problem with this argument is that it applies the theory of free capitalism or small-scale capitalism—wherein small firms engaged in cut-throat competition with each other, leading to fall in prices and improved quality/new technologies—to today's era of monopoly capitalism, where the giant firm has superseded the small firm. But this is not the place to discuss economic theories,[5] so let us leave this aside.

If it were indeed true that competition leads to better quality in higher education, then higher education would have been in the private sector in the developed countries. But that is not so! In nearly all West European countries, from France to Germany, Italy, Spain, Norway and Finland, higher education institutions, including the most prestigious ones, are largely public funded.[6] The USA is probably the only developed country which has a fairly large private higher education sector. But even here, there is a huge network of high quality publicly funded higher education institutions (like the University of California), which together account for nearly three quarters of all student enrolment—proving that publicly funded higher educational institutions can provide high quality education. Even the icons of private institutions in the US like Harvard, Princeton, Caltech, John Hopkins, Yale and MIT are non-profit institutions, motivated primarily by philanthropy.[7]

Not just global experience, the Indian experience too proves that high quality higher education is best provided when it is publicly funded. The best higher education and research institutions in India are all in the public sector. Apart from the IITs and IIMs, these include AIIMS, JNU, Delhi University, Indian Institute of Science, TIFR, BARC, ISRO, Centre of Cellular & Molecular Biology and IUCAA—just to name a few.

The argument that we need competition from foreign for-profit education providers to improve the quality of our higher education institutions actually bypasses the real issue. It is true that the quality of India's publicly funded higher education institutions, including some of our best institutions, has been deteriorating in recent times, but the real reason for that is that the government is gradually reducing its funding for these institutions, forcing them to raise student fees, employ teachers on contract basis, reduce investment in academic support services like libraries and laboratories, cutback research facilities, reduce student support services and raise their charges, etc. Therefore, what we need for improving the quality of our higher educational institutions is not the entry of foreign educational institutions, but increased government funding.

Will FEIs Benchmark Quality?

This brings us to the third argument: What kind of quality will the foreign educational institutions (FEIs) benchmark for India? Even the *Economic Times* (March 17, 2009) was constrained to note in an editorial titled "University of California, Ghazipur?":

> But such a law is unlikely to open the floodgates for foreign providers of quality education.... Only second rate outfits ... are likely to invest in Indian campuses.[8]

That is absolutely correct. It is only the two-tier and three-tier universities which would be interested in coming to India to exploit the huge market here. They will offer low quality programmes, even unaccredited programmes, taking advantage of the loopholes in our rules and regulations and weak regulatory mechanism. Commenting on developing countries opening up their higher education sectors in a big way in recent years to higher education institutions from the developed countries, Philip Altbach, the well known American educationist and director of the Centre for International Higher Education at Boston College, USA, stated some time ago:

> Institutions using the term "American" and often teaching in English are proliferating throughout the developing world, joined recently by institutions with "German," "French," or "Canadian" in their names.... Many of (these sellers are) sleazy recruiters, degree packagers, low-end private institutions seeking to stave off bankruptcy through the export market ...[9]

Even if some top ranking universities do come to India, they will only come, as Philip Altbach points out in his above mentioned article, because they are "forced by government funding cutbacks to enter foreign markets for profit making." In recent years, as governments of developed countries have reduced their higher education expenditures, some top ranking universities have opened special wings whose mandate is to go abroad to raise resources on a business mode; such branches of these universities may come to India, so that they can make money and cross-subsidise the education of local students in their home countries. However, the quality of education that will be offered by their branches in the developing countries will be far inferior compared to the education imparted in their parent universities. This was admitted in a joint document of the World Bank and UNESCO (The Task Force, 2000). It pointed out that prestigious universities from developed nations are offering shabby courses in poor and developing countries, using their renowned names, without assuring equivalent quality.[10] J.B.G. Tilak, the eminent Indian educationist, points out:

> There is no evidence of any developing country having prospered educationally or economically by relying on foreign universities. In fact, the evidence is abundant to show that strong and vibrant higher education systems are built mainly by the governments and with public funds.[11]

And yet the National Knowledge Commission and the Yashpal Committee have recommended opening up of the Indian higher education scene to foreign universities. The bankruptcy of some of our country's leading intellectuals is amazing!

Main Features of the Bill

Despite so much evidence that it is not the top-grade but rather the low-end private educational institutions from the developed countries which are keen to open branches in developing countries, and which will only be offering low quality courses while seeking to maximise their profits, the Government of India is rolling out the red carpet for them. The Foreign Educational Institutions (Regulation of Entry and Operations) Bill gives foreign educational institutions complete freedom to do what they want, with virtually no government supervision. The role of the government is confined to granting permission to set up the institution. The government will have no role in administration—admissions (forget about reservations), fee policies, etc.; it will have no role in recruitment of faculty or other staff—domestic or foreign, their qualifications, salary structure, etc.; it will have no role in academic aspects—curriculum, methods of teaching, evaluation and examination system, recognition of degrees, etc.; it will have no role of any kind in the governance of the institution. There will be no accreditation, assessment or examination by any Indian body. There is no provision for any kind of social control and they will be accountable to none. The government's faith in the goodness of foreign educational institutions is touching!

To promote the entry of foreign institutions, the Bill guarantees speedy processing of applications. The Bill sets minimal conditions for foreign educational institutions to get permission to set up shop in India (such as that they must deposit Rs 50 crore as corpus fund), and also provides for exemption from these conditions![12]

The stated objective of the Bill is "to provide for regulation of entry and operation of foreign educational institutions ..."[13] But it does precisely the opposite—it allows foreign educational institutions to enter and operate in the country without any regulation and supervision!

That is globalisation in operation. Barely six decades after we won our independence through the sacrifices of millions of our people, Delhi's Mughals are once again allowing foreign corporate armies to impudently enter the country and trample over even our most sacred spaces, the 'conscience of the nation', our universities.

Enacting Enabling Legislation to Accelerate Reforms

If the post-independence education policy framework is to be dismantled, privatisation of higher education accelerated, and entry of foreign educational institutions smoothened, an entirely new legislative framework needs to be enacted (apart from the Foreign Educational Institutions Bill). Accordingly, the UPA Government introduced three Bills in the budget session of Parliament, in May 2010. These were related to prevention and prohibition of malpractices, establishment of a tribunal to fast-track adjudication, and mandatory assessment and accreditation. A fourth Bill, for the constitution of the National Commission for Higher Education and Research (NCHER), was introduced in December 2011. And a fifth Bill, regarding setting up of 'innovation universities', was tabled in Parliament in 2012. We briefly discuss each of these Bills below.

(i) The Prohibition of Unfair Practices in Technical Educational Institutions, Medical Educational Institutions and Universities Bill, 2010

Ever since commercialisation of education began in the country, the corrupt practices indulged in by private institutions are legion.

However, the Bill confines itself only to technical and medical colleges/universities; other universities/colleges imparting general and professional education are excluded from the ambit of the bill. Even for these institutions, it restricts itself only to a few selected issues, leaving out most of the 'unfair' practices adopted by private higher educational providers. Thus, for example:

- Regarding student fees, the Bill allows institutions to charge any fees they want, the only condition being that they must declare it in their prospectus. In other words, it legalises high fees!
- It is silent about unrecognised institutions offering degrees and diplomas—they can continue doing so.
- It does not say anything about recognised institutions functioning with less than the required number of teachers; having under-qualified teachers; operating with inadequate infrastructure, including laboratories, libraries, playgrounds, etc.; medical colleges functioning with less than the minimum number of patient beds—all these practices too can continue.
- Underpayment of salaries to teachers, a widely prevalent practice, does not attract any penalty under the Bill—after all, this is a necessary component of neoliberalism.
- The Bill provides for monetary penalties up to Rs 50 lakh for many of the offences listed in the Bill, a pittance considering that technical institutions charge a capitation fee of Rs 15-20 lakh per student for admission. So, even if they are caught, they really don't have to worry.[14]

In the name of prohibiting malpractices, the Bill thus gives legal sanction to many of the malpractices indulged in by private educational institutions!

(ii) The Educational Tribunals Bill, 2010

This Bill recognises that there has been a rapid growth in litigations involving students/teachers/other employees and managements of institutions, statutory bodies and even the Union and state governments, in matters relating to education. Its ostensible aim is to speedily resolve these disputes, for which it provides establishment of a two-tier judicial structure at state and national levels—State Educational Tribunals and a National Educational Tribunal above them. The Bill specifically prohibits civil courts from entertaining any suit relating to any issue which comes under the purview of the Educational Tribunals. There is only a provision for appeal against the decisions of the National Educational Tribunal in the Supreme Court, making such an appeal very costly, and beyond the reach of most students/teachers/other employees.

The real purpose of the Bill gets revealed on a closer examination. Like the Unfair Practices Bill discussed above, this Bill too is vaguely worded; it does not define the scope and nature of unfair practices, nor does it exhaustively list such practices. It is also not clear whether students can go to the Tribunals against unfair practices of the institutions or governments—the Bill is vague on this. Therefore, the real purpose of the Bill seems to be to prevent students, teachers and other employees from going to courts, and thus provide foreign educational institutions a conducive atmosphere for indulging in their 'education business' without having to worry about too much litigation.[15]

(iii) National Accreditation Regulatory Authority For Higher Educational Institutions Bill, 2010

With private education institutions coming up by the thousands all across the country over the past decade, cheating and scams are also on the rise.

The 'free market' way of checking these malpractices is to do a quality assessment of these institutions and grade them (just like there are rating agencies to grade private companies on the basis of which investors can decide where to invest their money). By comparing the fees charged by the various private higher education institutions and their ratings, a student can decide which course/institution best suits his/her budget and accordingly take admission.

And so the government introduced the National Accreditation Regulatory Authority For Higher Educational Institutions Bill in Parliament in May 2010. The Bill proposes to make it mandatory for all institutions imparting education beyond twelve years of schooling to get themselves accredited. Since it is beyond the capacity of our present accreditation institutions, the NAAC and NBA, to accredit all the higher education institutions in India, the Bill proposes to set up a new authority, the National Accreditation Regulatory Authority (NARA), which will create a network of public and private accreditation agencies (in addition to NAAC and NBA) to speed up the job of assessment and accreditation. The very purpose of the Bill is to privatise the accreditation system. NARA will register, monitor and audit the functioning of these accreditation agencies. The Central government can exempt institutions from the provisions of the Bill, including mandatory accreditation.[16]

(iv) The Draft Bill for the NCHER

This is an amazing bill! The government is proposing to replace all the regulatory bodies in higher education (with the exception of medical and agricultural education) that have been set up by Parliament at various points in time, such as the UGC, AICTE, National Council for Teacher Education (NCTE), the Council of Architecture, etc., by a single overarching authority called the National Commission for Higher Education and Research (NCHER).

The various bodies that the NCHER is supposed to subsume, such as the UGC, AICTE, NCTE, etc. were all set up through Acts of Parliament as autonomous statutory bodies with lofty goals and objectives. But during the last several decades, they were rarely allowed to function autonomously, and some of them were in fact practically treated as subordinate departments of the government; they were not provided sufficient funds, and not sufficient professional staff either. As a result, most of them have practically become defunct. Instead of taking the appropriate measures needed to make these bodies effective, the Bill proposes to replace all these bodies with a single body.

According to the Bill, the NCHER will have wide-ranging powers and will combine all functions in itself—academic as well as non-academic. It will "develop", "identify", "specify" and even "monitor" policies, requirements, minimum conditions, norms and standards on almost every aspect of the university. This covers not only issues related to establishing of universities and their governance and funding, but also issues related to all academic operations, from awarding of degrees and diplomas, to workload, development of curriculum, quality, etc. Thus, while the Bill proclaims that the objective of setting up the NCHER is "to promote autonomy of higher educational institutions for the free pursuit of knowledge and innovation", in reality, it actually takes away whatever autonomy they have today. (Of course, this applies only to public universities; the autonomy of private universities will not be affected; as we discuss below regarding the Universities for Research and Innovation Bill, private universities/ foreign universities have been kept out of the purview of the NCHER.)

What is the reason for creating such a powerful, if not an authoritarian, body? The proposal for creating the NCHER is basically based on the National Knowledge Commission (NKC) recommendations on higher education submitted to the Prime Minister in 2006. The NKC report brazenly favours privatisation, commercialisation and internationalisation of higher education. It argues that the existence of several regulatory bodies in higher education creates tough entry barriers and a cumbersome system of authorising entry. Replacing them by a single overarching authority will facilitate the easy setting up of new universities and colleges by the private sector. It will thus help the rapid growth of the private sector in higher education, and will also facilitate entry of foreign institutions into India.[17]

(v) Universities for Research and Innovation Bill, 2012

This Bill was introduced in Parliament in May 2012.[18] The ostensible aim of this bill is to facilitate the setting up of the 14 innovation universities promised in the Eleventh Five Year Plan. These Universities for Innovation are expected to be very special universities, which would be universally recognised for quality teaching, learning and research. According to the draft bill, these universities "would be at the fount of making India the global knowledge hub and set benchmarks for excellence for other institutions of higher learning."[19]

However, the real aim of this Bill appears to be to provide an alternative route for foreign universities to enter India, as the Foreign

Educational Institutions Bill is held up in Parliament. During his visit to the United States in June 2010, the HRD Minister Kapil Sibal had discussed the possibility of US varsities setting up some innovation universities in India. The UK Higher Education and Science Minister David Willetts has also gone on record to say that UK universities are interested in collaborating in the setting up of these universities.[20]

According to the Bill, "acclaimed" Indian institutions with 25 years standing or foreign institutions with 50 years standing, or private bodies—registered societies, trusts or companies registered under Section 25 of the Companies Act—can set up innovation universities. Though these universities are supposed to be not-for-profit entities, they will not be under the purview of the Comptroller and Auditor General of India and will appoint their own auditors. This, plus the fact that a profit-making company can set up an Innovation University, indicates that these universities will actually be for-profit entities.

The Central government will provide public funds to these innovation universities in the form of land, contribution to capital investment, grants for supporting research and so on. Despite that, the Bill provides that they will have complete autonomy with respect to their core academic, administrative and financial aspects, with absolutely no government regulation, supervision, monitoring or social control.

These universities are supposed to be so special that they are to be above all laws of the land. The existing rules of the UGC or any other public body in higher education will not be applicable to them. They will not be touched by any of the Bills pending in Parliament discussed above, like the Educational Tribunals Bill, the Bill prohibiting unfair practices, and the NCHER Bill.

As discussed above, the Foreign Educational Institutions Bill, 2010 gives foreign educational institutions seeking to enter India a lot of autonomy. For foreign universities entering India as 'Innovation Universities', the 'Universities for Research and Innovation Bill, 2012' gives them even more freedom and power, and also provides them with a loophole through which they can be profit-earning; not only that, it also contains provisions for transfer of substantial public funds to these universities.[21]

An Unprecendented Situation

The spate of legislation waiting for ratification in Parliament is indicative of where education is headed. Never before in the history of India have so many proposals in the form of bills been brought before Parliament in one go. All these bills directly or indirectly negate the Constitutional mandate and its egalitarian vision. Sixty years of educational endeavours of Indian society are on the verge of being devoured by imperialist and corporate interests ...

Twelfth Five Year Plan: Further "Encouraging Private Participation"

The approach paper of the Eleventh Five Year Plan was titled *Towards Inclusive Growth*. It led to rapid growth of the private sector in higher education in India. The draft approach paper to the Twelfth Five Year Plan is titled *Faster, Sustainable and More Inclusive Growth*.[22] That is, the Twelfth Plan aims to do exactly the same, at a faster pace.

The Twelfth Plan approach paper unequivocally declares that the role of the private sector in higher education needs to be enhanced. In the very first chapter, it announces: "Private initiatives in higher education, including viable and innovative PPP models, will therefore be actively promoted."[23]

The approach paper makes a number of explicit proposals for "Encouraging Private Participation" in future plans for expansion of higher education in the country. We discuss these proposals below.

(i) Institutions of higher education "should be encouraged to raise their own funds through various legitimate means".[24]

What does this mean? During the last two decades, higher education institutions have been encouraged, or even required, to generate more resources and they have been doing this mostly through steep increases in student fees and other charges; the government is now proposing that they increase their fees yet more, making higher education the preserve of students from rich families only.

Box 12.2: Government Subsidies to Private Higher Educational Institutions

A recent report by the Institute of Costs and Works Accountants of India (ICWAI) revealed that Prawara Medical Trust's (of the education–sugar baron Balasaheb Vikhe Patil) dental and medical colleges at Loni (Maharashtra), Vidya Shikshan Prasarak Mandal's (of education baron Ranjeet Deshmukh) dental college at Nagpur; and the Annasaheb Chudaman Patil dental and medical colleges at Dhule (Maharashtra) have received land free of cost; the state government also granted them concession in property tax.

[Source: Siddhartha D. Kashyap, "18 Medical Colleges Took Government Favours", TNN, May 26, 2004, http://timesofindia.indiatimes.com.]

(ii) "Innovative Public–Private Partnerships (PPP) should be explored and developed".[25]

PPP, better described as a policy of "private enrichment and public pauperisation", effectively means that while the costs and risks are borne by the public, guaranteed profits go to the private partners. All the 20 new IITs that the government is planning to set up are going to be under the PPP mode.[26] One of the new 'innovations' in 'PPP in higher education' being considered by the government is transferring well-functioning public sector universities to the private sector![27]

(iii) "Deserving" private institutions should be provided "access to public funds in the form of loans, financial aid for students and competitive funding for research".[28]

This takes the cake!

Note that here, the Planning Commission is talking of giving public funds to private unaided institutions, not private aided institutions which follow government rules and regulations and are subject to government control; in contrast, the private unaided institutions have their own rules and regulations and are the least regulated by the government—they are de facto profit-making institutions.

Not many know that the government already gives a huge amount of backdoor funding to the private sector 'unaided' higher education institutions. They have been given land at concessional rates and even free (see Box 12.2). Apart from this, they are also given grants for research, for organising conferences and seminars, and so on. As if this was not enough, the UGC, at a meeting on September 27, 2010, decided to provide grants to private self-financing deemed universities and state private self-financing universities. The influence of the private sector on the UGC—the highest body overseeing the functioning of higher educational institutions in the country — can be gauged from the fact that of the six members who attended this meeting, three were representatives of private deemed universities![29]

Now, for the Twelfth Plan, the Planning Commission is proposing yet more liberal funding of the private sector educational institutions. In this context, it is important to note that the best institutions of higher education in the world in terms of quality and standards are public institutions or private institutions that are guided by principles of philanthropy. India's private self-financing higher education institutions are known to be for-profit institutions, that are basically oriented towards providing education to only those who can afford high fees. Despite this, the government proposes to provide liberal public funds to these institutions, while reducing funds for even the top grade public sector higher educational institutions like the IITs, because of which students' fees in these institutions have gone through the roof.[30]

(iv) "The 'not-for-profit' tag in the higher education sector should, perhaps, be re-examined in a more pragmatic manner".[31]

The gloves are off! Though private educational institutions in India are supposed to be charitable or not-for-profit institutions, it is well known that many of the newer private institutions opened in the last two decades are vulgarly profit-making institutions, which are least regulated by and least accountable to the government. The government now wants to give formal recognition to this reality, and allow private higher education institutions to indulge in open, naked, profiteering.

The Approach Paper acknowledges that "private higher education accounts for about four-fifths of enrolment in professional higher education and one-third overall."* These proportions are much higher compared to figures in advanced countries. Even in the US, which has the highest proportion of private higher education institutions amongst the developed countries, hardly one-fourth of the students in higher education are enrolled in private institutions.[32] Despite such obscenely high levels of privatisation of higher education, the government wants to further accelerate commercialisation of education! The Approach Paper says: "This growth trend is likely to continue in the Twelfth Plan."[33]

We Need to Save Our Universities

The Planning Commission's vision proposal for the Twelfth Five Year Plan embodies the essence of neoliberalism in higher education. It envisages not just accelerated privatisation of higher education. It visualises creating conditions so that the private sector can earn windfall profits. It even advocates naked transfer of public funds to corporate houses, so that they can maximise their earnings!

The Planning Commission says that the growth trend seen in the Eleventh Plan would continue in the Twelfth Plan. The Eleventh Plan saw elitist private higher education institutions with ultra-modern and lavish amenities sprouting up all across the country, charging exorbitant fees and catering to the children of the rich. On the other hand, accessing higher education is becoming increasingly difficult for children from poor families—the few who somehow manage to go past Class XII and take admission in colleges are only able to take admission in shabby government-funded colleges whose conditions are rapidly deteriorating due to cutbacks in government-funding. The Planning Commission unashamedly admits that this segregation in higher education is going to worsen in the coming years.

This new model of educational development is detrimental to national development in several ways. It will adversely affect the growth of a balanced system of higher education, and will result in rapid extinction of some of the important disciplines of study that serve as

* *If enrolments in self-financing courses in public higher education institutions are also added, these proportions would be much higher.*

the basic foundation for the development of any humane society. Only the marketable and revenue-generating courses of study will survive. This has already started happening in India, where all those who can afford to pursue higher education are seeking to take admission in fields like engineering education, management education, fashion technology, and so on, while there is a falling demand for courses in natural sciences, social sciences, humanities, languages, etc.

Commercialisation of higher education will destroy the very nature of universities as centres of creation and dissemination of knowledge in a spirit of academic freedom with special stress on independent research. With universities becoming profit–oriented institutions, run by corporate houses, the priority, quality and content of higher education and research will now be determined by corporate interests, and not broad public interests.

More importantly, the commodification of higher education transforms the entire relationship between the educated and the rest of society. The Kothari Commission had visualised the function of the university to be an institution that would provide society with competent men and women trained in various professions, who will also be cultivated individuals, imbued with a sense of social purpose.[34] However, a private higher education institution oriented towards profit-making cannot instil such a sense of social purpose in the students studying in its portals. Such an institution ruptures the organic relationship between the individual and the society/collective. Students graduating from such institutions will not consider themselves to be a part of society to which they must contribute so that the well-being of the entire collective is promoted. On the contrary, they will look at everything, including life objectives, from a cost-benefit perspective. They will look at society as a market place from where they have to not only recover their cost of higher education, but also from which they must extract the maximum possible benefits for themselves.

This will also lead to an erosion of all the finer values/relationships in society, like doctor and patient, engineer and ethics, architect and aesthetics, scientist and mass needs, teacher and pupil, and so on—something that has already begun in Indian society.

The Kothari Commission had visualised the universities to be institutions that promote the path of national development laid out in the directive principles of the Indian Constitution. It had envisaged that the university would promote equality and social justice.[35] Neoliberal transformation of higher education means this objective too now goes out of the window, with universities themselves becoming institutions promoting segregation in education.

To conclude, higher educational institutions are not just centres of learning, that engage vigorously and fearlessly in the pursuit of truth, that interpret old knowledge and beliefs in the light of new needs and discoveries, that preserve and promote much cherished attitudes and values. They also play a key role in nation-building; they are centres where a society can mould its younger generation to take up the tasks of building a more humane, democratic and harmonious society. Globalisation, privatisation, WTO–enforced GATS, is now threatening to destroy these institutions. Philip Altbach, the renowned US educationist and professor, has cautioned:[36]

> Universities are indeed special institutions with a long history and a societal mission that deserve support. Subjecting academe to the rigours of a WTO–enforced marketplace would destroy one of the most valuable institutions in any society.

We must join hands to prevent our higher education institutions from being transformed into business firms and higher education from being transformed into a commodity to be bought and sold on the marketplace ...

NOTES

1. "It's a Jungle Out There", October 25, 2012, http://www.timeshighereducation.co.uk; Jandhyala B.G. Tilak, "Policy Crisis in Higher Education: Reform or Deform?" *Social Scientist*, Vol. 38, Nos. 9–12, September–December 2010, p. 65, available on internet at: http://thechalkcorner.wordpress.com.
2. Dr. Vijender Sharma, *Facilitating Trade in Higher Education*, 2010, http://muta.in; *The Full Text of the Joint Statement by PM Manmohan Singh and President Obama*, November 25, 2009, http://news.rediff.com.
3. Dr. Vijender Sharma, ibid.
4. "Will the Foreign Education Bill Help?", *Business Standard*, March 24, 2010, http://www.business-standard.com.
5. For more on this subject, see Paul Baran and Paul Sweezy, *Monopoly*

Capital, Monthly Review Press, New York.

6. *Public University*, Wikipedia, accessed on March 25, 2014, http://en.wikipedia.org.
7. Lester M.M. Salamon (ed.), *The State of Nonprofit America*, p. 138, http://books.google.co.in; Anil Sadgopal, "Foreign Universities Bill is a Bill to Sell Education Out by Degrees", March 21, 2010, http://www.dnaindia.com.
8. Cited in: Devender Sharma, "Educating India, in a B-Grade American Style", March 16, 2010, http://devinder-sharma.blogspot.in.
9. Philip G. Altbach, *The Subprime Market and International Higher Education*, 2008, http://www.cautbulletin.ca.
10. Angela C. de Siqueira, "The Regulation of Education Through the WTO/GATS", *Journal for Critical Education Policy Studies*, March 2005, http://firgoa.usc.es; Jandhyala B.G. Tilak, "Policy Crisis in Higher Education: Reform or Deform?" op. cit., p. 66.
11. Jandhyala B.G. Tilak, ibid., p. 67.
12. Ibid., pp. 68–69.
13. Ibid., p. 71.
14. Ibid., pp. 65–71; Dr. Vijender Sharma, "Facilitating Trade in Higher Education", op. cit.
15. Jandhyala B.G. Tilak, ibid., pp. 75–78; Dr. Vijender Sharma, ibid.
16. Dr. Vijender Sharma, ibid.; "Autonomous Accreditation Body for Colleges Soon", *Deccan Herald*, March 10, 2014, http://www.deccanherald.com.
17. Jandhyala B.G. Tilak, "The Proposed NCHER: A Solution Worse Than the Disease?", *Economic and Political Weekly*, May 1, 2010, http://www.epw.in.
18. Jandhyala B.G. Tilak, "Islands of Autonomy Without Accountability", *The Hindu*, June 28, 2012, http://www.thehindu.com.
19. Jandhyala B.G. Tilak, "Policy Crisis in Higher Education: Reform or Deform?" op. cit., p. 79.
20. Dr. Vijender Sharma, "Facilitating Trade in Higher Education", op. cit.; "US Institutions to Partner for Proposed Innovation Varsities", *PTI*, June 3, 2010, http://articles.economictimes.indiatimes.com.
21. Jandhyala B.G. Tilak, "Islands of Autonomy Without Accountability", op. cit.; Jandhyala B.G. Tilak, "Policy Crisis in Higher Education: Reform or Deform?" op. cit., pp. 78–82; Dr. Vijender Sharma, ibid.
22. *Faster, Sustainable and More Inclusive Growth: An Approach to the Twelfth Five Year Plan (2012–17)*, Planning Commission, Government of India, http://planningcommission.gov.in.

23. Ibid., pp. 8–9.
24. Ibid., p. 101.
25. Ibid., p. 102.
26. "Government Approves Scheme for Setting Up 20 IITs in PPP Mode", December 5, 2012, http://articles.economictimes.indiatimes.com.
27. For example, see: "Four Year Undergraduate Programme Aims to Privatise Education: Arundhati Roy", June 1, 2013, http://timesofindia.indiatimes.com.
28. *Faster, Sustainable and More Inclusive Growth: An Approach to the Twelfth Five Year Plan (2012–17)*, op. cit., p. 102.
29. Basant Kumar Mohanty, "Deemed to Get UGC Aid – Education Regulator Funds for Self-financed Campuses", *The Telegraph*, December 4, 2010, http://www.telegraphindia.com.
30. See for instance: "IITs Becoming Self-Financing Institutes: Protest Against Privatisation of Higher Education", June 7, 2013, http://beta.bodhicommons.org.
31. *Faster, Sustainable and More Inclusive Growth: An Approach to the Twelfth Five Year Plan (2012–17)*, op. cit., p. 102.
32. Jandhyala B.G. Tilak, "Higher Education Policy in India in Transition", *Economic and Political Weekly*, March 31, 2012, http://www.epw.in.
33. *Faster, Sustainable and More Inclusive Growth: An Approach to the Twelfth Five Year Plan (2012–17)*, op. cit., p. 102.
34. *Education and National Development: Report of the Education Commission, 1964–66, Vol. 3: Higher Education*, p. 553, http://www.teindia.nic.in.
35. Ibid.
36. Cited in: J.B.G. Tilak, *Higher Education: A Public Good or a Commodity for Trade?*, UNESCO, 2009, http://www.kritischestudenten.nl.

13

IS THERE AN ALTERNATIVE TO PRIVATISATION OF EDUCATION?

Many people who are supporters of capitalist competition and individualism nevertheless agree that all children in society should be provided genuinely free, compulsory and equitable education of good quality.

However, simultaneously, they also argue that there is no alternative to sending children to private schools because, firstly, government schools are of poor quality and have poor learning outcomes; and secondly, that in any case, the government does not have sufficient money to improve the quality of government schools.

We discuss the second argument, whether the government really does not have the money for education, in the next chapter. We examine the first argument here.*

Can the Government Provide Good Quality Education in the Public Sector?

The truth is, all developed countries, and most middle income developing countries that are aspiring to join the ranks of the developed countries (from South Korea to Brazil) have well-funded public (i.e. government) education systems, which provide excellent quality (by

* *In this and the following chapter, we discuss only this question: Is there an alternative to privatisation of school education? If it is possible to build such an alternative, and we have a society sensitive enough to be concerned about providing genuinely free, compulsory, equitable and good quality school education to all children, then obviously it will ensure that higher education also be accessible to all young people irrespective of their family background.*

Indian standards) free and compulsory education to all children—at least elementary and secondary education, and in most countries, higher secondary education too. All these countries are capitalist countries, and many of them have private schools too. But their policy makers realise that the private sector will only invest in education for profit. This means that if all children, irrespective of their family background and income levels, are to be provided equitable and good quality education, that can only be done in the public sector, that is, the government will have to take the responsibility for that. And so, in all these countries, not only does the government invest heavily in public education, policy makers are also concerned about the performance of government schools, strive to continuously improve the quality of instruction given in these schools, and also implement systems to ensure that each and every child benefits from excellent instruction.

If these countries can provide good quality education in the public sector, and have school systems that have achieved high and socially equitable distribution of learning outcomes, then why can't we also strive for the same, instead of privatising our public education system?

Actually, in India too, when the government so desires, it does run good schools! After all, even today, the government-run Kendriya Vidyalayas and Navodaya Vidyalayas are considered to be amongst the best run schools in the country. And these school networks are not small: there are 1,093 Kendriya Vidyalayas in the country having more than 11 lakh students on their rolls, while more than 1.8 lakh students study in the 595 Navodaya Vidyalayas located in rural areas across the country.[1] So the problem in India is not that the government cannot run good schools; the problem is, it does not want to run all its schools well.

What most people don't realise is: the government has deliberately allowed the condition of government-run schools to deteriorate. Till the late 1980s, there were very few private schools in the country, and most children, even of the middle and upper classes, used to study in government schools. Virtually all the eminent intellectuals and academicians in the country today aged 50 and above have studied in government schools.

This is not to say that the government schools were in an excellent condition in those days. There was much scope for improvement. For that, a key requirement was that the government increase its expenditure on education to at least 6% of the GDP, that had been recommended by the Kothari Commission way back in 1966 but had been never implemented by the government, and, along with that, energise and restructure the entire public-funded school education system in the country.

Instead, in the early 1990s, the government accepted World Bank conditionalities, and began a deliberate assault on the government school system, by starving it of funds, and rapidly replacing the cadre of regular and trained teachers by para-teachers, i.e. under-qualified, ill-trained and under-paid young persons appointed on short-term contracts. This resulted in a rapid deterioration in the quality of government schools. Simultaneously, in the name of expansion, a parallel stream of all kinds of non-formal education was promoted.

The decline in quality of government schools, resulting in low learning levels, has shaken the faith of the people in the capability of the government to provide good quality education to children, and they have begun withdrawing their children from the public-funded school system. Those who can afford it have begun to send their children to private schools that are mushrooming all over the country. This in turn has provided an alibi for the government to shut down or privatise its schools. This was the precise objective of the World Bank dictated neoliberal reforms, and they have more than succeeded in their objective.

Conclusion

The conclusion is obvious: if the government wants, it can improve the government school system. Not only that, if it so wishes, it can make the public school system very good, and bring all the schools in the country to the level of at least the Kendriya Vidyalayas.

If the government is seriously concerned about developing the country from the bottom up, that is, if it is indeed concerned about involving the poorest of the poor in the development process and mobilising their energies for the development of the country, this is one of the most important steps it needs to take: it must act, and act urgently and decisively, to improve the government school system.

How to Improve the Quality of Government Schools?

The way to improve government schools was recently demonstrated by a senior government official. In June 2011, when the new academic year began and schools began admitting students, the Collector of Erode (in Tamil Nadu), Dr. R. Anandakumar, went to the Tamil-medium Panchayat Union (government) School at Kumalankuttai near the Collectorate, stood in the queue along with other parents, and got his daughter Gopika admitted to the school. The Collector also told the headmistress that his child would not be bringing her lunch from home and would take the mid-day meal served in the school.[2]

Anandakumar had indeed taken a pathbreaking step. It was the first time a government official had sent her/his child to the Kumalankuttai Panchayat Union primary school. Even teachers of the school did not admit their children to this school. Most of the 250 children in the school hailed from poor families—dyeing unit workers, auto drivers, daily-wage labourers and weavers.

What happened next is revealing and provides the cue for improving the government school system. As soon as news spread that the Collector's child was studying in the school, panchayat officials inspected the school to ensure that it had all basic facilities in place—till then, they had not been concerned, since after all, it was only the children of the marginalised who were studying in the Panchayat school![3] The punctuality of the teachers improved. The sanitary staff began visiting the school and cleaning the toilets twice a day.[4]

This means that once senior bureaucrats, MPs, MLAs, school and college teachers, middle and upper middle classes start sending their children to government schools, automatically, the school inspection machinery will crank up, school infrastructure and facilities will start improving, pressure will mount on the government to employ trained, regular and well-paid teachers in schools, teachers will start teaching and the problem of teacher absenteeism will vanish. Public pressure will mount on the State to increase its allocations for education.

[Of course, this is only the first step in the long road to improving the government school system in the country. Along with this, the government would need to substantially hike its educational expenditure, replace all para-teachers with regular trained teachers, and so on. But the key step, the most crucial step, to qualitatively improving the government school system is that everyone, the rich and the poor alike, must send their children to the same schools.]

What we have described above is known as the common school system.

The Common School System

The establishment of common schools in all localities in the country had been recommended way back in 1966 by the Kothari Education Commission. A common school (also called neighbourhood school) is a school where all children living in a locality/area, irrespective of their class, caste, religious or linguistic background, study together in the same school situated in their locality.

The Kothari Commission argued that:

> (T)he establishment of such schools will compel rich, privileged and powerful classes to take an interest in the system of public education and thereby bring about its early improvement.[5]

The Collector of Erode probably had not heard of the Kothari Commission recommendations regarding common schools. But by putting his daughter in the neighbourhood Panchayat Union school, he was in essence implementing its recommendations. As the Kothari Commission had pointed out in its perceptive report, it immediately compelled the "rich, privileged and powerful classes to take an interest in the system of public education"; the local officials took immediate action to ensure that the school had all basic facilities in place.

The second argument advanced given by the Commission while calling for establishment of neighbourhood schools is equally important. The Commission said that the common school system is essential to "bring the different social classes and groups together and thus promote the emergence of an egalitarian and integrated society." It warned that since this was not happening at present, "education itself is tending to increase social segregation and to perpetuate and widen class distinctions." It added, "This is bad not only for the children of the poor but also for the children of the rich and the privileged groups," as by "segregating their children, such privileged parents prevent them from sharing the life and experiences of the children of the poor and coming into contact with the realities of life." The Commission contended that:

> If these evils are to be eliminated and the education system is to become a powerful instrument of national development in general, and social and national integration in particular, we must move towards the goal of a common school system of public education.[6]

The Commission's warning is proving to be prophetic. The failure of India's ruling classes to build a more egalitarian educational system has gradually led to a situation wherein the rich are now brazenly building a separate five star education system for their children, while the poor are condemned to teach their children in dilapidated single-room schools staffed by a single under-paid and ill-trained contract teacher. And at the same time, the rich have become so insensitive and divorced from the life realities of the common people of the country, that they take pride in splurging Rs 250 crore on a wedding while debating whether the country's poverty line should be Rs 25 or Rs 30 a day; and the country's richest man builds himself a 27-storey house, the most expensive house in the world, in a city where 400,000 people sleep homeless on the streets.

The common school system will also lay the foundation for building a more socially integrated society. More than 60 years after independence, Indian society continues to be racked by caste divisions; it is probably the most important factor inhibiting our development. Political reservations have delivered some empowerment and mobility to the oppressed castes, and so there are Dalit MPs, MLAs, even an occasional Dalit Chief Minister and President of India. But this advancement has been very limited, caste divisions within society continue to be very strong, and very little social integration has taken place at the grassroot level. One of its most important manifestations is that in the cultural sphere, upper castes continue to dominate society.

A survey by the Centre for the Study of Developing Societies of 315 important decision-makers in 37 Delhi-based publications and television channels found that there was not a single Dalit or Adivasi amongst them.[7] In the USA, the African-Americans have similar histories of slavery and oppression as the Dalits in India. Even though their general condition continues to be vastly inferior to the white population, American society has become integrated enough to provide conditions for the rise of black icons who are celebrated across race barriers. But Indian society has yet to produce its Dalit Muhammed Alis, Michael Jordans, Tiger Woods, Carl Lewis, Michael Jacksons, Oprah Winfreys, Denzer Washingtons and Serena Williams (the list is endless).

The failure of our policy makers to ensure compulsory education for all children has led to a situation where just 8% of the Dalit children cross the Class XII barrier. Had the government implemented the Kothari Commission recommendations and ensured that all children in a neighbourhood compulsorily study together in a common school, it would definitely have led to greater social integration in Indian society. Unfortunately, Indian society is now moving in the opposite direction, with the upper caste upper classes divorcing themselves from the rest of the people and building a separate education system for their children. It will only further accentuate the caste divisions in our society.

The Kothari Commission had pointed out that a neighbourhood school system exists "in different forms and to varying degrees" in many developed countries, like the USA, France and the Scandinavian countries. It would not be an exaggeration to say that one of the key reasons for the huge strides in cultural and social development in all developed countries is their implementation of the common school system; without providing compulsory good quality education to all children, it is not possible to unleash their inherent creative potential, and without doing that, no society can genuinely develop.[8]

Essential Features of the Common School System

If India is to genuinely provide free, compulsory, equitable, good quality education to all children, that can only be done through establishing a publicly funded common school system as recommended by the Kothari Commission. Such a common school system would need to have the following essential features:

- It should extend to entire school education, that is, from pre-primary to Class XII stage.
- All schools, including private schools, must become neighbourhood schools; the government/local body would specify the neighbourhood for each school with a view to optimising socio-cultural diversity among children in each school.
- Schools will not be allowed to screen students, take interviews or interact with parents to decide which children to admit. They will compulsorily have to admit all children in their defined neighbourhood.
- All schools, whether privately managed or government-run, will have to provide genuinely free elementary education to all children. This means not just free tuition fees; schools must not be allowed to charge any other fees such as library fees, computer fees, exam fees, etc.—all these facilities must be provided to students free. Additionally, schools must also provide all the other things needed by the child, such as uniforms, textbooks and notebooks, school bags, and all necessary educational aids like pencils, pens and geometry boxes, free of cost.
- Of course, providing compulsory elementary education for all children requires that the country take firm steps to genuinely abolish child labour, and provide suitable facilities such as residential schools for children of migrant labour—a very large number of out-of-school children belong to such families.
- While it may not have been possible to provide free education at the secondary and higher secondary level at the time of independence, today, definitely, the country has enough financial resources to provide genuinely free education to all children up to Class XII (see Chapter 14 for more on this).

- The government must define common minimum norms and standards for both state-funded and private schools for aspects like: school land and buildings; number, size and design of classrooms; drinking water and toilets; mid-day meals; playground and sports; performing and fine arts facilities; teaching aids; libraries; laboratories; computers; number of teachers; teacher qualifications; teacher salaries; pupil–teacher ratio; etc.
- An essential feature of the common school system is that schools respond to local conditions while deciding curriculum, methods of teaching and teaching aids, language of teaching, etc. In a country like India with so much linguistic, cultural, religious and ethnic diversity, this is a must, implying that each school, or a cluster of schools, must be different, must take into consideration the local situation. This would be in complete contrast to and would mean challenging the present rigid school system, imposed by the Board Examinations (from CBSE/ICSE to State Boards).
- For this to be possible, schools would have to be managed in a decentralised way—only then will it be possible to meet the above mentioned condition of schools being able to respond to local conditions. This decentralisation is irrespective of whether the school is government-funded or not. In developed countries like the USA and Canada, the school system is entirely funded by the state governments but it is entirely managed locally in a decentralised mode. For decentralised management of schools, school management committees also need to be involved, with the majority of members being parents of students, along with appropriate linkages with local bodies.
- This decentralisation and flexibility would have to take place within an overall common curriculum framework that would need to be evolved by the government, within which there must be sufficient flexibility related to texts, teaching aids, evaluation parameters and procedures, school calendar, etc.
- The government would also need to evolve a uniform

language policy, taking into consideration the linguistic diversity in our country, the importance of educating children in the initial years in their mother tongue, and the increasing significance of English in pursuing careers.

- The government would have to allocate funds for improving the quality of teacher education, and also set up systems for in-service training of teachers. And of course, the system of appointing para-teachers would have to be completely abolished.

Lessons from the World's Best Performing School Systems

Just implementing 'neighbourhood schools' will not be enough to improve the quality of government schools. Several studies of the world's best performing school systems—such as the school systems of Australia, Belgium, Canada, Finland, Hong Kong, Japan, Netherlands, New Zealand, Singapore and South Korea—have pointed out that the most important feature which made these school systems achieve excellence consistently throughout the education system was the quality of their teachers and the high quality of instruction given in schools. This conclusion is not surprising, and is in conformity with several other studies that show that students placed with high-performing teachers progress much faster compared to those placed with low-performing teachers.

Numerous studies have shown that all the high performing school systems in the world in general have the following common features:

(i) *The quality of an education system cannot exceed the quality of its teachers*: They attract able people into the teaching profession through effective selection processes, and give them good salaries.

(ii) *The only way to improve outcomes is to improve instruction*: They put in considerable effort to develop these people into effective instructors; and also select the right people from amongst the best teachers to be principals.

(iii) *They put in place systems to monitor the performance of schools*, and intervene when they do not meet expectations; they also

> keep a tab on students falling behind, and provide targeted support to improve the child's performance and ensure that no child is left behind.[9]

This is much different from what happens in our schools, where only those not able to get good jobs elsewhere enter the teaching profession, where now ill-trained young people are being appointed as para-teachers on low salaries, where the school inspection system is terrible with officials being the least concerned about the quality of instruction, where if a child falls behind, he/she is failed, and eventually pushed out of school.

All this can be changed. But for that, the key is that the government must hugely increase its expenditure on education, so that:

(i) the infrastructure and facilities in all schools can be improved to at least the level of Kendriya Vidyalayas; and

(ii) well-trained teachers on decent salaries are appointed in all schools (this also means abolishment of contract teaching, and regularisation of all teachers in private schools)—only if decent salaries are given, and job security assured, will able and motivated young people be attracted to the teaching profession.

But the government claims that its social sector expenditure is already very high, and it cannot afford to spend more money on education. Is this indeed true? Does the government really not have the money? We discuss this in the next chapter.

NOTES

1. Latest figures from their websites.
2. Anil Sadgopal, "Neoliberal Act", *Frontline*, July 2–15, 2011, http://www.frontline.in
3. Gopu Mohan, "In Tamil Nadu Govt. School Where Poor Kids Go, a New Face: The Collector's Daughter", June 19, 2011, http://archive.indianexpress.com.
4. "Collector Admits Daughter to Panchayat School", *Press Trust of India*, June 19, 2011, http://www.ndtv.com.
5. *Report of the Education Commission, 1964–66: Vol. 2 – School Education*,

National Council of Educational Research and Training, 1970, p. 471, http://www.teindia.nic.in.

6. *Report of the Education Commission, 1964–66: Vol. I – General Problems*, National Council of Educational Research and Training, 1970, pp. 14–15, http://www.teindia.nic.in; Anil Sadgopal, "Common School System and the Future of India", *Radical Notes*, February 28, 2008, http://radicalnotes.com; "Common School System", Centre for Education and Documentation, http://www.doccentre.net.
7. Nissim Mannathukkaren, "The Echoing Silence of Caste", *The Hindu*, April 15, 2014, Hubli Edition.
8. Anil Sadgopal, "Common School System and the Future of India", op. cit.
9. "How the World's Best-performing School Systems Come Out on Top", September 2007, http://mckinseyonsociety.com; "What We Can Learn from Finland's Successful School Reform", http://www.nea.org.

14

IS THE GOVERNMENT REALLY SO POOR?

Those who take the meat from the table
Teach contentment.
Those for whom the taxes are destined
Demand sacrifice.
Those who eat their fill speak to the hungry
Of wonderful times to come.
Those who lead the country into the abyss
Call ruling too difficult
For ordinary folk

– ***Bertolt Brecht***

As we have pointed out earlier, it can be argued, with some justification, that at the time of framing of the Constitution in 1949, the country was too poor to guarantee free education to all children up to the higher secondary, that is, Class XII.

Today, seven decades later, so much wealth generation and development has taken place in the country that our leading mainstream politicians from Atal Bihari Vajpayee to Manmohan Singh (and now Narendra Modi), economists from Montek Singh Ahluwalia to Raghuram Rajan, and corporate honchos from Mukesh Ambani to Ratan Tata, are all claiming that India is not only an economic superpower in the making, it is even headed towards becoming a knowledge superpower. Assuming there is some substance in these claims, there is no reason why at least today a 'future economic superpower/knowledge superpower' cannot guarantee free and compulsory school education up to the age of 18 for all its children, and at least affordable higher education to all children wanting to pursue it. But such is the self-centredness and narcissism of our ruling classes and elites, that they are not willing to spend a fraction of this wealth on providing even free elementary education to all our children!

The Government of India will express shock at our above statement. It claims the exact opposite, that it is spending huge sums on providing subsidies to the poor. In fact, the government claims that its social expenditure, that is, expenditure on providing cheap welfare services—education, health, food, drinking water, etc.—to the people has reached such high levels that it has become "unsustainable".[1] To quote the then Finance Minister Pranab Mukherjee a few days before he was due to present the Union Budget 2012–13, "As finance minister when I think of the enormity of the subsidies to be provided, I lose my sleep."[2]

That the Indian government's expenditure on subsidies has gone through the roof, that the government's expenditure minus its revenues, called the fiscal deficit, has reached unsustainable levels and needs to be curtailed, is accepted economic wisdom today. All the leading economic advisors to the Government of India, each and every economist associated with international financial institutions, every renowned management guru—are in agreement that India needs to rein in its fiscal deficit if India is to maintain its growth rate and become an economic superpower in the near future (see Box 14.1).[3] The Indian Parliament even passed a law in 2003 requiring the reduction of the fiscal deficit to 3% of the GDP by 2008. This deadline was subsequently suspended because of the 2007 international financial crisis. Nevertheless, P. Chidambaram, the Finance Minister in the UPA Government that recently demitted office, promised to bring down the fiscal deficit to this level by 2016–17.[4] He brought down the fiscal deficit from 4.9% in 2012–13 to 4.5% in 2013–14; and then set a target for further reducing it to 4.1% for the year 2014–15 in his interim budget presented just before the 2014 Lok Sabha elections.[5]

Now, a new BJP-led NDA Government is in power at the Centre. The new Finance Minister Arun Jaitley, soon after being sworn in, declared that the immediate focus of the government will be on curbing the fiscal deficit.[6] In his first budget speech, he vowed to adhere to the "daunting" fiscal deficit target of 4.1% of the GDP for the year

Box 14.1: The Fiscal Deficit Gospel

- **Kaushik Basu, World Bank Chief Economist and Former Chief Economic Advisor in the Finance Ministry, Government of India** (2012): "Government's top across politicians together are mature enough that they realise that the path of fiscal consolidation is extremely important."
- **C. Rangarajan, Chairman, Prime Minister's Economic Advisory Council (2013):** "I think there has been an effort to reduce subsidies (given by the government). We need to do more."
- **Raghuram Rajan, Former Director, Research Department, IMF and presently Governor, RBI:** "The government has to be commended for its efforts to revive growth, narrow the current account deficit, and meet fiscal targets ... going forward, however, we need to continue on the path of fiscal consolidation—constantly improving the sustainability and quality of fiscal adjustment."

[Sources: See Endnote 3.]

2014–15 set by his predecessor.[7] In his next budget presented on February 28, 2015, he declared that the target for 2014–15 had been achieved, and that the fiscal deficit would be further brought down to 3.9% in 2015–16, to 3.6% in 2016–17 and 3% by 2017–18.[8]

Chart 14.1: Fiscal Deficit of the Central Government *(% of GDP)*[9]

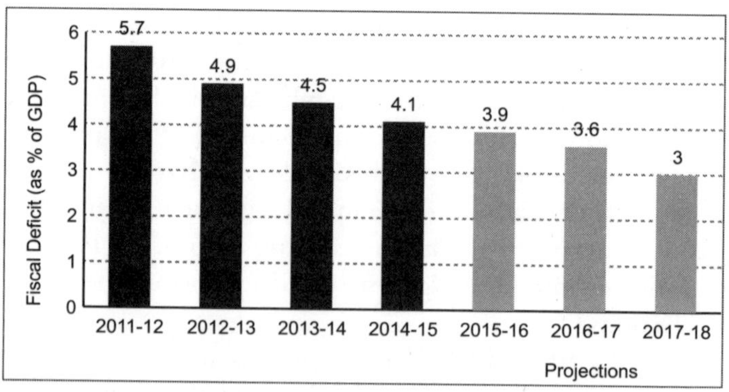

Every news channel and newspaper every other day carries a newsreport highlighting the disaster that awaits us if we don't control our fiscal deficit. And so, most people have come to accept this as a gospel truth.

Fiscal Deficit

Fiscal deficit is just another term for government borrowings of various types. The government borrows when its expenditures exceed its receipts of all types.

- Fiscal Deficit = Government expenditures – Receipts
- Receipts = Tax Revenues + Non-tax Revenues + Non-debt Capital Receipts

Receipts include tax revenues, non-tax revenues and non-debt capital receipts. Tax revenues include direct taxes (income tax, corporation tax, etc.) and indirect taxes (customs duties, excise duties, sales tax, etc.). Non-tax revenues include profits of public sector enterprises, interest receipts on loans given by the government (to public sector enterprises, state governments, etc.), and income such as sale of spectrum. Non-debt capital receipts include disinvestment income and return of loans.

The Humbug of Finance

The fact is, and this may sound unbelievable to most of our readers, the economic theory that the government must balance its expenditure with its income, that is, must bring down its fiscal deficit to near zero, is plain humbug. John Maynard Keynes, considered by many to be the greatest economist of the 20th century, had convincingly demolished it long ago in his opus *The General Theory of Employment, Interest and Money* published in 1936. Keynes argued that in an economy where there is unemployment, it means economic resources (labour, machinery, etc.) are lying idle due to lack of demand. In such an economy, the government can, and in fact should, expand public works and generate employment by borrowing, that is, enlarging the fiscal deficit. Far from there being any adverse effect of this on private sector expenditure, such government action in fact would stimulate private sector expenditure through the 'multiplier' effect (the employment created due to government investment would stimulate demand, and hence would lead to larger output and employment in the private sector too). It would also not generate any significant inflationary pressures. Keynes went on to show that the fiscal deficit (that is, the additional investment by the government) would eventually result in accrual of an equal amount of savings in private hands (which can be invested). A fiscal deficit in other words finances itself.

Keynes in fact stated that to argue against the mitigation to human suffering that an increased fiscal deficit can provide is sheer "humbug of finance".[10]

Return of the Humbug

All developed countries (especially in Western Europe) and many newly independent countries initially adopted Keynesian economic principles after the Second World War, thus giving rise to what has come to be known as the Welfare State.

During the 1950s–60s, the changed economic conditions after the Second World War and historical conditions led to rapid economic growth in the advanced capitalist countries. However, by the 1970s, the special factors that had caused this growth were mostly on the wane.[11] These economies started to slow down, and entered a long period of stagnation, that has continued till today.

Among the various strategies adopted by the ruling classes of the developed countries to keep the profit accumulation process going, one important strategy was to *withdraw the welfare benefits given to the poor and transfer them to the rich.* To legitimise this assault on the Welfare State, the 'voodoo economics' of the 1920s, dubbed by Keynes as the 'humbug of finance', was revived—that government budgets must be balanced (and hence welfare expenditures must be cut). Josef Steindl, the great Austrian economist, called it a "counter-revolution, the return of the Bourbons" in economics. Meanwhile, transfers to the rich were justified in the name of promoting entrepreneurism. An economic theory was also invented to back it up—'supply-side economics'—which claimed that tax breaks to the wealthy would help boost investment. The theory was of course silent on who would buy the goods thus produced in an economy already in the grip of saturation.*

* *To explain this point further, in an economy gripped by stagnation/recession, the problem is not that the capitalists do not have money to produce goods, the problem is there is a surplus of goods in the market which are not being sold.*

This capitalist offensive on the working classes was first launched in the United States and Britain in the early 1980s during the days when the Conservative Governments of Reagan and Thatcher were in power. Since then, these policies have continued, irrespective of the shade of government in power, and have spread to the rest of Europe as well.[12]

Meanwhile, by this same time, the economies of most third world countries or 'developing countries' had also become crisis-ridden. Their autonomous capitalist development models had started failing.[13] In the early 1980s, several third world countries approached the World Bank (WB) and the International Monetary Fund (IMF) for loans to avoid external account bankruptcy. The IMF–WB readily agreed, but in return, forced these countries to undertake a thorough restructuring of their economies (the so-called 'Structural Adjustment Programme'). One of the important conditionalities imposed on these debt-laden underdeveloped countries was that they implement the Reagan–Thatcher economic model and reduce their fiscal deficit, that is, reduce their subsidies to the poor and privatise welfare services. Simultaneously, they were encouraged to transfer ownership of public resources and public sector institutions to private sector corporations and give the latter 'incentives' to accelerate GDP growth.[14]

While the consequences of this economic model have been catastrophic for the people of these countries,[15] nevertheless, the ruling classes of the third world countries have faithfully implemented this model—as the rich of these countries have not suffered, rather they have benefited by these economic reforms, similar to what is happening in India today.

The Humbug Imposed on India

Till about 1990, hardly anyone in India mentioned the 'fiscal deficit'. The term is not even to be found in the *Economic Survey*

For more on this, see Paul M. Sweezy, Harry Magdoff, "Supply-Side Economics", Monthly Review, March 1981, http://archive.monthlyreview.org; "Notes from the Editors", Monthly Review, October 2010, https://monthlyreview.org.

1989–90. Till then, what used to be discussed was the budget deficit—the printing of money by the central bank to meet government spending needs. [Budget Deficit = Government Expenditures – (Government Tax and Non-tax revenues + Government Borrowings)]

One of the conditionalities of the World Bank dictated SAP imposed on India following the foreign exchange crisis of 1990–91 was that the government must stop the printing of money to finance its deficit, that is, it must phase out its budget deficit. Instead, the WB asked the government to resort to borrowing from the market to meet its deficit—this borrowing is what is called the fiscal deficit;[16] and further, that the government must strive to reduce its fiscal deficit. According to the World Bank, reduction in India's fiscal deficit 'would materially increase growth and reduce inflation.'[17] And so, the term 'fiscal deficit' made its first appearance in the *Economic Survey 1990–91* presented to Parliament by Finance Minister Manmohan Singh on July 20, 1991.[18]

Since then, each and every budget of the Government of India (even though the coalition at the Centre has been changing) has made reduction in fiscal deficit a central task of the budget. The pimps who masquerade as intellectuals have been writing lengthy articles in the media warning of impending doom unless the fiscal deficit is curtailed.

Of course, neither the World Bank, nor any of our Finance Ministers—from Arun Jaitley to P. Chidambaram to Manmohan Singh—have really been concerned about reducing the fiscal deficit. This is obvious from the way they have been handling the various components of the government's expenditures and revenues. The fiscal deficit is the excess of the government's expenditures over receipts. Even a cursory look at the policies being pursued by the Government of India reveals that it is giving away lakhs of crores of rupees as subsidies to the rich. Had it really been concerned about the fiscal deficit, it could have easily reduced these mind-boggling give-aways! But in the new economic lexicon preached by the High Priests in Washington, these concessions are called 'incentives' and are considered essential for 'growth'. On the other hand, the concessions given to the poor, which are aimed at making available essential welfare services like education, health, food, transport, electricity, etc. to them at affordable rates, are given the derisive name 'subsidies' and are being drastically reduced in the name of containing the fiscal deficit. Not only that, these essential services are also being privatised—resulting in fabulous profits for the private sector.

In short, all the hue and cry about high fiscal deficits is just an excuse to cut welfare spending on the poor, and transfer the savings to the rich! *It is India's biggest scam, involving several lakhs of crores of rupees ...*

Part I: Incentives to the Rich

Let us take a look at some of these so-called incentives given to the rich, especially the giant foreign and Indian business houses that today dominate the Indian economy and exercise enormous control over government policies.

(i) Tax Concessions to the Rich

While presenting the 2013–14 budget, Finance Minister P. Chidambaram admitted that the ratio of taxes to GDP in India is "one of the lowest for any large developing country", and that it "will not garner adequate resources for inclusive and sustainable development." However, in the same breath, he also stated that there was very little potential for raising taxes to improve the tax–GDP ratio: "In a constrained economy, there is little room to raise tax rates or large amounts of additional tax revenues."[19]

Chidambaram is a bare-faced liar! Every year, for the past several years, the budget documents have included a statement on the estimated revenue forgone by the government due to exemptions in major taxes levied by the Centre. The budget documents reveal that for the year 2013–14, the government gave away Rs 5.32 lakh crore in tax exemptions/deductions/incentives to the very rich.* These major write-offs are in direct corporate income tax, customs and excise duties:

* *The write-offs as mentioned in the Budget are actually Rs 5.72 lakh crore. From that, we have deducted the Rs 40,000 crore forgone on personal income tax, since this write-off benefits a wider group of people.*

corporate tax concessions amounted to Rs 76,116 crore, more than twice that sum (Rs 1,95,679 crore) was forgone in excise duty, and well over three times the sum was sacrificed in customs duty (Rs 2,60,714 crore).[20]

Had Chidambaram really been concerned about reducing the fiscal deficit, he could have reduced these tax concessions given to India's richie rich. The total tax concessions given by him to the wealthy in 2013–14 of Rs 5,32,509 crore is more than our fiscal deficit for that year (Rs 5,24,539 crore).[21]

Successive governments at the Centre have been doling out these concessions to the 'corporate needy and the undernourished rich' for the last several years, ever since the economic reforms began. But we have data on revenue forgone only from 2005–06 (as it is only from 2006–07 that the Budget documents started carrying these figures). They reveal that over the nine-year period 2005–06 to 2013–14, the tax write-offs given by the government to the super-rich total a mind-boggling Rs 36.6 lakh crore! To give an idea of the immensity of this figure, it amounts to roughly one-third of our 2013–14 GDP.[22]

These tax concessions are being given to some of the richest people in the world. *Forbes*, the oracle of business journalism, puts out a list of the world's billionaires every year. Its 2013 list included the names of 55 Indians, with an average net worth of around Rs 19,080 crore. Their total net worth was Rs 10.5 lakh crore, double our fiscal deficit for 2013–14.[23]

The obscenity of these tax concessions becomes evident from just a single statistic: in 2013–14, the single biggest chunk of customs duties forgone was on diamonds and gold, accounting for Rs 48,000 crore. The waiver on gold and diamonds in just three years (2011–14) was Rs 1.6 lakh crore—equivalent to 30% of our fiscal deficit for 2013–14. No wonder that three new Indian entrants to Forbes 2013 billionaires list were from the field of jewellery.[24]

India's Tax–GDP Ratio: Lowest in the World

It is because of these huge tax concessions that India's tax–GDP ratio, at 18.5% of GDP, is far below not only the 'advanced economies' (36.7%), but also the 'emerging market and developing economies'

(27.9%). Even the countries of sub-Saharan Africa, considered to be one of the poorest regions in the world, have a tax–GDP ratio of 27% (Chart 14.2). It is thus obvious that there is a huge scope for increasing tax revenues in India.

Chart 14.2: General Government Revenues[25]

(% of GDP, 2007–11)

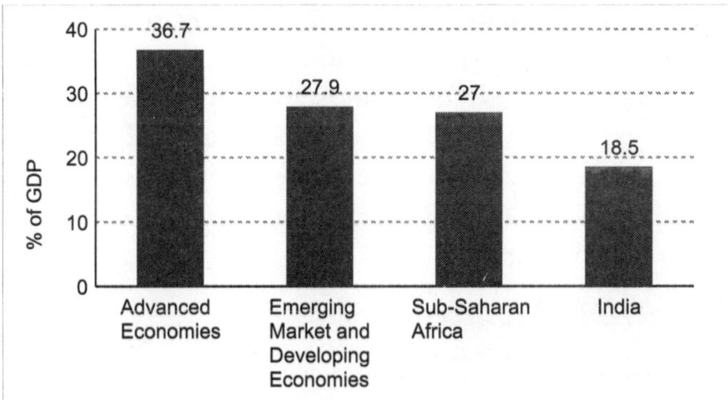

The international credit rating agencies, the IMF and World Bank, the economic czars occupying prestigious chairs in the universities in New York and London, all of whom lecture us every day on the importance of reducing our fiscal deficit—none of them ever talk of our low tax–GDP ratio and the need to increase it to at least the level of the sub-Saharan African countries by reducing the subsidies given to our super-rich.

Why is the government giving such mind-boggling tax concessions to the already wealthy? This is revealed in the presentations made by Finance Minister Chidambaram to foreign investors during his trips to Singapore, Hong Kong, London and Frankfurt in January 2013. Wooing these brigands to invest their monies in India, he stated:

> Among emerging markets India has one of the most favourable tax regimes, a very crucial factor for business growth.[26]

BJP Government: More Tax Concessions to the Rich

The new BJP Government is continuing with these mind-boggling transfers to the corporate trough. The budget documents reveal that it doled out Rs 5.49 lakh crore of tax concessions to the country's super-rich in 2014–15. This is the biggest ever corporate karz maafi in the past ten years for which data is available. The BJP and its intellectual drum-beaters are asserting that its budget is oriented towards benefiting the aam aadmi. The tax concessions include write-offs in customs duty on gold, diamonds and jewellery (all aam aadmi items, of course) worth Rs 75,592 crore.[27]

As if these exemptions are not enough, Jaitley in his latest 2015–16 budget has announced a reduction in corporate tax rates from 30% to 25% over the next four years, starting from the next financial year. This is expected to provide corporates a total tax relief bonanza of Rs 2 lakh crore: Rs 20,000 crore in the first year, Rs 40,000 crore in the second year, Rs 60,000 crore in the third year and Rs 80,000 crore in the fourth year.[28]

(ii) Plundering Resources

(a) Mother of All Scams: KG Basin Gas Scam

Though hydrocarbon reserves of the country belong to the people, bowing to WB conditionalities, the Government of India in 2000 handed over exploration of gas reserves in D-6 block of the Krishna Godavari basin to Reliance Industries Limited (RIL). The Production Sharing Contract with RIL stipulated that RIL is to pay the government only 10% of the total revenue till it recovers 1.5 times its investment; thereafter, the government's share would increase.[29] RIL, in naked collusion with the government, through a series of manipulations, has indulged in absolutely mind-boggling plunder of the country's natural gas wealth. We briefly give three of these frauds below:

- In 2004, the government allowed RIL to over-invoice its capital expenditure in developing the D-6 block from the original estimate of $2.4 billion to $8.8 billion. This 'gold-plating' by RIL is estimated to have caused a loss to the government of at least Rs 37,000 crore.[30]
- In 2003, the public sector National Thermal Power Corporation (NTPC) agreed to buy gas from RIL for its

Box 14.2: The Oil Subsidy Hoax

The government/official economists have been claiming, and the corporate friendly media has been duly propagating, that the public sector oil marketing companies—Indian Oil, BPCL and HPCL—are making heavy losses as the petroleum products are being sold at heavily subsidised rates. The government claims that this subsidy burden is becoming unbearable, and so it is allowing the oil companies to gradually raise the prices of petrol, diesel and gas, to reduce the subsidies it is giving to these companies.

The government is lying! The truth is, there is no net subsidy on petroleum products as a whole. Rather, they are heavily taxed. The government earns more from its taxes on petroleum products than what it gives to the oil companies.

Revenues of the Central government from taxes and duties on petroleum products	Rs 1,36,497 cr
Revenues of state governments from taxes and duties on petroleum products	Rs 88,997 cr
Total tax revenues of the Centre and states	**Rs 2,25,494 cr**
Total subsidies paid by the Central government to the oil companies	Rs 43,926 cr
Net earnings of the Centre and state governments	**Rs 181,568 cr**

Who is subsidising whom?

[Source: "Hike in Petro Price: A Gigantic Fraud", People's Democracy, June 3, 2012, http://pd.cpim.org.]

thermal plants at the rate of $2.34 per unit of gas* for the next 17 years—even though ONGC was supplying gas (to industries such as power and fertiliser) at the rate of $1.83 per unit of gas. (According to one estimate, RIL's cost per unit of gas is $1.43; another estimate puts it at less than $1.)

- And then, in 2007, the government allowed RIL to double the price of gas being supplied by it (to NTPC and other industries) to $4.20 per unit! The total additional profit to RIL due to this price increase—a cool Rs 1,20,000 crore (this

* *One unit of gas = One million British thermal units (mBtu)*

is over and above the profit it was making when it was supplying gas at $2.34 per unit)![31] Three-fourth of the natural gas in the country is consumed by the power and fertiliser industries,[32] implying that this largesse to RIL is one of the reasons for the steep hike in price of electricity and urea fertiliser in recent years.

Adding up these figures, the total profits to RIL and loss to the exchequer from this illegal transfer of our natural gas reserves to RIL is going to be Rs 2 lakh crore at the minimum. This, for gas fields identified by the ONGC, which also has the necessary technology and the expertise needed to explore and develop these gas fields—in other words, there was no need to transfer them to RIL!

(b) The Iron Ore Mining Scam

In 2005, the US–Korean multinational POSCO signed an agreement with the Odisha Government to build a steel plant in the state, along with a captive port and allocation of iron ore mines. The agreement allows POSCO to extract a total of 600 million tons of high grade iron ore for use in its proposed steel plant in the area, and also mine another 400 million tons of iron ore for export to its steel plants in South Korea. While the project is billed as India's largest FDI proposal, it is also going to result in stupendous profits for POSCO. We make a rough estimate of its profits below (for only its mining operations).[33]

- Let us take the cost for extraction, processing and transport for iron ore for POSCO to be a generous Rs 800 per ton. (These costs are Rs 400 per ton for Karnataka.)
- The government has fixed the royalty on the iron ore (to be paid by POSCO to the government) at an absurdly low 10% of the sale price. Taking the market price of iron ore lumps to be Rs 5,000 per ton (an underestimate), this means POSCO will be paying a royalty of Rs 500 for each ton of iron ore mined.
- POSCO therefore stands to make a profit of at least 5,000 – 800 – 500 = Rs 3,700 for each ton of iron ore mined. POSCO will be mining 600 million tons of iron ore for its steel plant

over the next 30 years—giving it a total profit of over Rs 2.22 lakh crore.

- Additionally, POSCO has been allowed to export 400 million tons of iron ore to South Korea—thus giving it an additional profit of Rs 1.48 lakh crore.

All this, just from mining iron ore, that belongs to the people of the country, when we have public sector companies with all the necessary technology and expertise needed to mine it.

That is just the *legal* iron ore mining scam. Apart from this, millions of tons of iron ore are being illegally mined and exported from the country. There are reportedly nearly twice as many illegal mines in the country as legal ones. Illegal iron ore mining scandals have come to light in at least five States—Karnataka, Andhra Pradesh, Chhattisgarh, Odisha and Jharkhand—with the Chief Ministers of at least three States directly involved in these scams.[34]

(c) **The Coal Scam**

Post-globalisation, the government began allocating coal blocks to private companies for private use. As of March 31, 2011, the government had allocated 194 (net) coal blocks to government and private parties. Wonder of wonders, these allocations were not done on the basis of any competitive bidding! When the Comptroller and Auditor General of India (CAG) investigated the coal block allocations to private parties, its report tabled in Parliament on August 17, 2012 contained damning findings. It estimated the financial gains accruing to the private block allottees in respect of the 57 open cast/mixed mines allocated to them to be a gigantic Rs 1.86 lakh crore![35]

(iii) The Great Land Grab

Tens of thousands of acres of land are being handed over to private corporations virtually for free to set up their projects. A few examples:

(a) **Land @ Re 1 per sq metre**

The Gujarat Government allotted a staggering 14,305 acres—equivalent to 5.78 crore square metres—of land in Kutch to billionaire

Gautam Adani controlled Adani Group at prices ranging from Re 1 to Rs 32 per sq metre (average price less than Rs 10 per sq metre). Adani paid less than Rs 60 crore for the huge chunk of land, whose market price was anywhere between Rs 1,000 to Rs 1,500 per sq metre. He then sublet a part of it to other companies, including State-owned Indian Oil, for as much as Rs 780 per sq metre.

Such scams abound in Gujarat. To give a few more examples:[36]

- the state government allotted 8 lakh sq metres (80 hectares) of prime land to Larsen and Toubro in the industrial zone of Hazira in Surat also at Re 1 per sq metre;
- 24,021 hectares were gifted to Archean Chemicals Ltd and 26,746 hectares to Solaris ChemTech in the Rann of Kutch for manufacturing salt and salt-based chemicals, at just Rs 150 per hectare;
- the Essar Group, another Modi favourite, was allotted 2.08 lakh sq metres of Coastal Regulation Zone land and forest land—that cannot be allotted as per Supreme Court guidelines—for a steel plant; as if to atone for this crime, Essar paid Rs 20 lakh as fine and peacefully continues to occupy the land.

(b) The DMIC Corridor

This proposal to construct a 1,483 km-long 'industrial corridor' between Delhi and Mumbai that will pass through six states is probably the biggest land grab in India's history. The $90 billion project includes plans to develop 24 'industrial cities' over an area of 5,000–5,500 sq km, 3 ports, 6 airports, a high-speed freight line, and a 6-lane 'intersection-free' expressway. In the first phase, by 2018, seven cities will be developed, over an area of 2,000 sq km—to put this in perspective, Delhi is around 700 sq km. The main beneficiaries of the project are expected to be Japanese firms, including Mitsubishi, Hitachi, Toshiba and JVC. The government subsidy for phase I: Rs 2,500 crore per city, or Rs 17,500 crore in all.[37]

(iv) Direct Cash Transfers to Corporations

(a) The Costly People's Car

State governments are competing with each other to give thousands of crores of rupees as subsidies to private corporations for setting up projects in their states. After Tata Motors was forced to move out of Singur by a determined people's movement, Modi rolled out the red carpet to welcome Ratan Tata to Gujarat. It was a carpet with gold linings. Here is a brief list of the concessions given to the Tatas for setting up the Nano car project in Gujarat:

- Tata Motors was allotted 1,100 acres of land for the project in Sanand, Gujarat at a discounted price of Rs 900 per sq metre, when its market rate was around Rs 10,000 per sq metre—a total concession of Rs 44,100 crore.
- On top of it, Tata Motors was given the facility of making the payment of Rs 400 crore for the land in eight equal instalments at 8% compound interest with a moratorium of two years.
- The total project cost is projected at Rs 2,200 crore. No financial institution grants a loan of more than 70–80% of the project cost; however, Tatas were given a soft loan of Rs 9,570 crore at an interest of 0.10% per annum, with repayment deferred for 20 years.
- The state government also volunteered to meet the cost of shifting the project, estimated to be Rs 700 crore!
- Tatas were exempted from payment of stamp duty, registration charges and transfer charges.
- The Gujarat Government promised to build a four-lane highway for the facility; it also agreed to acquire land for a railway line leading to the plant, for ancillary industries and for setting up a township for Tata Motors.
- Additionally, it agreed to provide 220 kv and 66 kv substations at the plant's doorstep for free, make provisions for supply of 14,000 cubic litres of water per day to the project site, and provide facilities for disposal of hazardous waste, facility for a transport hub, and a pipeline for supply of natural gas to the project site.

The total cost to the Gujarat exchequer? Rs 33,000 crore over the next 20 years! The installed project capacity is 2.5 lakh small cars per annum, so the plant would be producing 50 lakh cars over these 20 years—implying that for each car produced, tax-payers would be shelling out Rs 66,000![38]

(b) Multi-billion Dollar Transfers to the Car Industry

The Centre too is giving generous dole-outs to the car industry. On January 29, 2007, Prime Minister Manmohan Singh officially released the Automotive Mission Plan (AMP) 2006–16. The Plan, drawn up by the auto industry itself [with each sub-group chaired by the head of a top auto firm (Tata, Mahindra, Maruti)], envisages huge tax concessions and grants for the automobile industry, so as to help the industry increase its turnover from $35 billion to $145 billion and exports from $4.1 billion to $35 billion over the decade 2006–2016. These subsidies include tax holidays, tax deductions on export profits and R&D expenditure, exemption from electricity duty, grants for fundamental research, and so on. Media reports of course called these multi-billion dollar subsidies "incentives for the auto industry so as to make India a hub for automobile industry."[39]

(c) PPPs in Infrastructure Sector

The concept of Public–Private–Partnership (PPP) was originally conceived for the infrastructure sector (it was only later extended to education and other social sectors). The *Economic Survey 2008–09* argued, "Infrastructure projects often have high social, but an unacceptable commercial rate of return. These are generally characterised by substantial investments, long gestation periods, fixed returns, etc.", and therefore, the private sector will only enter the field if it is given suitable financial incentives.[40]

Note that the *Economic Survey* does not claim that the infrastructure projects are necessarily loss-making. It says that the rate of return is 'unacceptable' to the private investor, that is, it is not sufficiently high! And so it wants to give 'incentives' to corporations so that they can earn high profits from their investments.

One of the most common forms of PPP subsidy being given to

private sector corporations investing in infrastructural sectors in India is what the government calls 'Viability Gap Funding' (VGF), wherein, in the name of making their investments 'viable', the Government of India provides a direct subsidy to investors in the infrastructural sector of up to 40% of the project cost![41] And if the investor is somehow able to pad up his project cost, he can then extract an even higher subsidy!

The scale of the PPP scheme is enormous: the cost of projects completed, under implementation or in the pipeline as on March 31, 2012, was nearly Rs 13 lakh crore.[42] These projects are in highways, roads, ports, airports, railways, power, urban infrastructure and other sectors. Assuming that most of these projects are receiving 'investment incentive' grants @ 40% of the investment, the total outflow works out to more than Rs 5 lakh crore.

But the 'VGF Scheme' is just one of the many ways in which lakhs of crores of rupees in subsidies are being given to investors in the infrastructural sectors. To give another example, private corporations building expressways and metro projects are additionally being given vast amounts of real estate for commercial use. Thus, in the case of the infamous Yamuna Expressway built by the Jaypee Group under the PPP model, the Group was allowed to acquire five parcels of land along the expressway, each of 500 hectares, for township projects. The expressway cost the Jaypee Group roughly Rs 13,000 crores. The Group must have got 40% of this, that is, Rs 5,200 crores, as investment subsidy. But the real bonanza for the company was the 2,500 hectares of land allotted to it—it acquired this land from farmers for around Rs 1,500 crore (at the rate of around Rs 5 lakh to 60 lakh per hectare), and its present market value has zoomed to a whopping Rs 1.5 lakh crore (according to a *Forbes* newsreport)! That is some deal.[43]

(v) Firesale of PSUs to the Private Sector

One of the most important elements of the WB-imposed SAP is privatisation of public sector undertakings (PSUs). Governments of all shades that have come to power at the Centre since 1991 have dutifully implemented this diktat and have been gradually selling government equity in public sector companies to private investors; in many firms, the government has even sold majority stake and handed over management control to the private sector. Each and every such disinvestment in these PSUs, built out of the hard-earned savings of the people of the country, has been done at scandalously low prices, resulting in huge losses to the government. This has been so from the very first round of disinvestment carried out in 1991-92—for which the CAG estimated the loss at Rs 3,442 crore, on receipts of just Rs 3,038 crore.[44] Ever since then, each and every privatisation deal has surpassed the record of previous sell-off in terms of the damage inflicted on the national exchequer and the fortuitous gain for the private buyers. Some more examples:

- In 2001, the then NDA Government sold 51% of Bharat Aluminium Company (Balco), the giant public sector aluminium producer, to Sterlite, a company notorious for its environmental abuses and bad safety record. The controlling stake in the company, valued at more than Rs 5,000 crore and with fixed deposits of Rs 350 crore, was handed over to Sterlite for just Rs 550 crore—an amount less than half the value of Balco's captive power plant![45]
- In 2002, the government handed over 25% shares and absolute control of Videsh Sanchar Nigam Ltd (VSNL), the telecommunications giant, to the Tatas for just Rs 1,439 crore. VSNL was a cash-rich company with cash reserves and surplus to the tune of Rs 6,000 crore and had made a profit of Rs 800 crores over the paid-up capital of Rs 285 crore in the year ending 2000. At the time of its sale, VSNL had a market capitalisation of about Rs 10,000 crore. In addition, it had prime properties in all major cities, whose present market value would be several thousands of crores of rupees. Tatas, who were more interested in leveraging the huge resources with VSNL to benefit their priority area of mobile telephony rather than further strengthen VSNL in its core competencies of long distance calls and internet services, very soon pumped out Rs 1,200 crore from VSNL to Tata Teleservices Ltd.[46]

Box 14.3: Sycophancy Unlimited

"You came to India and stayed for 200 years. Now come prepared to invest and stay for another 200 years and there will be huge rewards."

– Finance Minister P. Chidambaram, addressing investors in London

[*Source: Sudesh K. Verma, "FMs Invitation To MNCs Raises Swadeshi Hackles", February 27, 1997, http://www.business-standard.com.*]

India's rulers have become so shameless that they have actually been gloating over this sale of 'family jewels' at throwaway prices. During his roadshows across Asia and Europe in early 2013, the theme of the presentation made by Finance Minister P. Chidambaram before foreign investors was: "Why Global Investors Should Invest in India." One of the arguments he gave was that the government was going to sell off shares in India's leading public sector corporations, and it presented investors with an "[O]pportunity to Reap High Yields".[47]

(vi) Robbing Banks: The Grandmother of All Scams

As if giving them tax concessions, cash transfers, control over the nation's natural resources and profitable public sector enterprises was not enough, the government is allowing private sector corporations to siphon off public sector bank funds too! It is the grandmother of all scams.

Small time bank robbers are put in jail (if caught); ordinary people defaulting on bank loans have their house/scooter/ other assets seized; farmers are driven to suicide for not being able to pay the instalments on their bank loans. But when the super-rich default on their (public sector) bank loans, nothing happens to them, they go scot free, even their names are not disclosed; they continue to enjoy their heated swimming pools, rooftop helipads, foreign homes, fast cars. The banks simply write off their loans. In a presentation made to bankers, Reserve Bank of India deputy governor K.C. Chakrabarty revealed that over the past 13 years (2001–2013), Indian public sector banks have written off a whopping Rs 2 lakh crore of loans, of which more than Rs 1 lakh crore was owed by corporate houses. He went to the extent of saying that while such a hue and cry was made when the Finance

Minister had waived off loans to farmers of Rs 60,000 crore in 2008, the loan waiver given to corporate houses is much more than this.[48]

Loan write-offs, however, make bad news, both for the corporates and the banks/government. So public sector banks are adopting a new stratagem to provide succour to these 'helpless' rich, they 'restructure' their loans. That's the buzz word today, 'Corporate Debt Restructuring' (CDR). Under its name, the payback period may be extended, interest may be waived, a part of the loan may be converted into equity; the corporation is even given another loan to tide over its 'crisis'. Private corporations whose loans have been approved for restructuring include some of India's most well-known names:

- the Andhra Pradesh based infrastructural corporations IVRCL and Coastal Projects (total CDR of Rs 11,000 crore);
- ABG Shipyard, the largest private sector ship builder in India (CDR of Rs 11,000 crore including Rs 1,800 crore as fresh loan);
- Gammon India, India's largest civil engineering construction company (CDR of Rs 14,800 crore);
- Electrosteel Steels (Rs 6,000 crore loan recast);
- Suzlon Energy (Rs 11,000 crore CDR package);
- Orchid Pharma, the leading pharmaceutical company (Rs 3,000 crore CDR package);
- Lanco Infratech, one of India's largest conglomerates (CDR package of Rs 7,000 crore); and so on.[49]

Data provided by the Reserve Bank of India shows that banks, led by State-run lenders, had cumulatively recast loans worth more than Rs 2.5 lakh crore under the CDR mechanism till June 2013. Another report by the industry body FICCI says that the total volume of restructured loans is much more than this, and stood at over Rs 4 lakh crore, as banks restructure loans outside the CDR cell too.[50]

This 'loan restructuring' subsidy being given to India's biggest corporate houses is all set for a massive hike in the coming years. A 2013 Credit Suisse report titled *House of Debt–Revisited* evaluated debt levels at ten of India's biggest corporate houses, including some owned by India's richest billionaires, and came up with stunning numbers: Anil Ambani's Reliance Group has a debt of Rs 1,13,543 crore on its books while London–based mining tycoon Anil Agarwal's Vedanta Group owes Rs 99,610 crore; the Essar Group has run up a debt of Rs 98,412 crore, while Gujarat billionaire Adani's group has a debt burden of Rs 81,122 crores. All other corporate houses investigated—the Jaypee Group, JSW Group, GMR Group, Lanco Group, Videocon Group and GVK Group—also had very high debt levels. The report predicted that banks will likely need to refinance/restructure most of these loans.[51] Its predictions did not take much time to come true. In December 2013, the newspapers reported that the government was considering restructuring the loans of the power companies of some of India's biggest corporate houses, including the Tatas, Reliance, Adani and Essar groups, worth more than Rs 2 lakh crore.[52]

With the government allowing corporate houses to plunder bank funds to the tune of lakhs of crores of rupees, obviously it will have to compensate the banks for this largesse—this roundabout subsidy to corporates has a fancy name called 'recapitalisation'. Over the last seven years, the government has poured in more than Rs 71,000 crore into public sector banks in the name of bank recapitalisation.[53]

(vii) To Recap

Each of these above mentioned 'scams' involves the transfer of anything from Rs 10–50 thousand crore to a few lakh crore of public money to the coffers of big business houses:

- ☞ Tax Concessions to the wealthy (2006–14) ⇒ Rs 36.6 lakh crore;
- ☞ KG Basin Gas Scam ⇒ Rs 2 lakh crore;
- ☞ Posco Iron Ore Mining Scam ⇒ Rs 3.7 lakh crore;
- ☞ Coal Scam ⇒ Rs 1.86 lakh crore;
- ☞ Gujarat Land Scam ⇒ Rs 6,000 crore and counting;
- ☞ DMIC Land 'Subsidy' (Phase 1) ⇒ Rs 17,500 crore;
- ☞ Tata Nano Subsidy ⇒ Rs 33,000 crore;
- ☞ Subsidy to automobile companies in the name of AMP ⇒ Tens of thousands of crores of rupees;
- ☞ PPP subsidy to corporations for infrastructure projects ⇒

Rs 5 lakh crore and counting;
- ☞ Sale of profit-making PSUs ⇒ Thousands of crores of rupees;
- ☞ Bank loan write-offs ⇒ Rs 1 lakh crore;
- ☞ Bank loan restructuring (most of it is eventually written off) ⇒ Rs 2–4 lakh crore.

And the above is just a cursory list. There would be dozens more of such scams.

The 'Bofors Scam' that shook the nation in the 1980s was of only Rs 200 crore. Each of the above mentioned scams is at least a 100 to 1,000 times bigger than the 'Bofors Scam'. However, only a few of these scams have hit the headlines, like the 2G Spectrum Scam and the Coal Scam, primarily because the Supreme Court has intervened in these cases. In most of the other cases of loot of public money by big corporations, the mainstream political parties (except the left parties to an extent), the country's leading intellectuals, and the media houses have chosen to maintain a conspiracy of silence—such is their collusion with big business today. That is why most people have not even heard of these scams. In fact, the country's rulers have become so audacious in their toadying to corporate houses that Prime Minister Manmohan Singh, defending the sale of '2G' telecom licences to corporate barons at a massive loss to the exchequer, compared this giveaway to top corporate firms with subsidies on the subsistence consumption of the poor, implying that it was a subsidy to corporations and therefore cannot be called a loss.[54] And Narendra Modi, when he was the Chief Minister of Gujarat, had the temerity to order an inquiry into who leaked the details of the concessions given to Tata's Nano project![55]

If the Government was Serious About the Fiscal Deficit ...

It is this brazen loot of the nation's wealth that has led to the sharp rise in the wealth of India's uber-rich. Between 1996 and 2008, wealth holdings of Indian billionaires are estimated to have risen from 0.8% to 23% of India's GDP. Of the 55 Indian billionaires in the 2010 Forbes list, nearly half of them are involved in sectors which have seen large scale privatisation and transfer of land and natural wealth (iron and steel, oil and natural gas, commodities, mining and metals, telecom, power, infrastructure and real estate) to private corporate houses.[56]

This vampyrean plunder of the country's wealth and resources by the corporate sector has reached such rapacious proportions that even the RBI Governor Raghuram Rajan, himself an ardent votary of neoliberalism and globalisation, has lambasted the collusion between "venal politicians" and "crony capitalists". After observing that India had the second highest number of billionaires in the world per trillion dollars of GDP (after Russia), he pointed out that "three factors—land, natural resources, and government contracts or licenses—are the predominant sources of the wealth of our billionaires. And all of these factors come from the government."[57]

If the government was indeed serious about containing the fiscal deficit, the simplest way of doing so would have been to curb some of the above mentioned freebies to India's billionaires —withdraw some of the tax concessions given to them, ask them to pay more for their wives' jewellery, get them to pay market prices for the land they purchase, make them repay their bank loans, restrain them from plundering our natural resources...

But that is precisely the point we are trying to make: the government is not really interested in reducing the fiscal deficit.

Part II: Withdrawal of 'Subsidies' to the Poor

If that is so, then why have the IMF–WB and all the governments at the Centre since 1991 been harping upon the necessity of reducing the fiscal deficit? Because it provides them with a theoretical justification for drastically cutting down social sector expenditures of the government, and privatising these sectors. In a deft use of language, while the breathtaking 'subsidies' given to the rich are justified as being necessary 'incentives' for 'growth', the social sector expenditures—whose purpose is to provide the bare means of sustenance to the poor at affordable rates—are condemned as 'subsidies', as being wasteful, inefficient, benefiting the middle classes rather than the poor, promoting parasitism, and so on.*

The neoliberal doctrine that each and every sector of the economy must be profitable is nothing but economic rubbish. A society provides free or low cost food, water, education, health, housing, sport, transport and other essentials to its citizens so that they can live like human beings and develop their abilities to the fullest extent. This 'subsidy' is actually an 'investment' for the future. Human beings are nature's highest creation, their potential is infinite. However, people must be given the appropriate social circumstances and opportunities to realise their inherent potential. When such 'human beings' pool in their energies and engage in collective labour, they can create heaven on earth. The wealth they will create will be many times the 'subsidies' invested on them. This is simple economic commonsense. To give a quote from an absolutely mainstream document in support of our above argument, even the *UN Human Development Report* of 1996 had stressed the vital importance of government policies in "spreading skills and meeting basic social needs" as a "springboard for sustained economic growth."[58]

India: Already at the Bottom

Most developed countries have a very elaborate social security network for their citizens, including unemployment allowance, universal health coverage, free school education and free or cheap university education, old age pension, maternity benefits, disability benefits, family allowance such as child care allowance, allowances for those too poor to make a living, and much more. Governments spend substantial sums for providing these social services to their people. People in the developed countries consider government investments on social security to be their right. In recent years, millions have come out on the streets in these countries to protest government attempts to reduce social sector spending.

The average public social sector expenditure of the 34 countries of the OECD has been around 20% of the GDP for the last many

* *A classic example of this convoluted thinking can be seen in this paper by Arvind Panagariya, Professor of Economics at Columbia University: "Tax Hike or Expenditure Cut?", http://www.columbia.edu.*

years, and for the EU-27 has been even higher at around 30% of the GDP, touching 33% for France in 2013.

The average public social sector expenditure for the 21 countries of Latin America and the Caribbean has risen significantly over the past decade, from an average of 4.8% of the GDP in 2001–02 to 18.6% in 2009–10 (Chart 14.3). This expenditure was as high as 27.8% of the GDP for Argentina, 27.1% for Brazil, and a fantastic 40.7% for Cuba (all figures for 2009).[59]

Chart 14.3: Public Social Sector Expenditures of Developed Countries and India, 2010 (*% of GDP*)

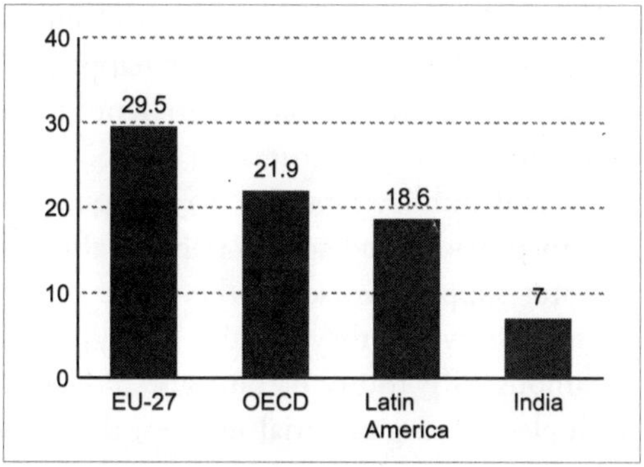

In contrast, the public social sector expenditure of the Government of India is very low! Jaitley and his predecessors in the Finance Ministry and the 'Chicago boys' who are their economic advisors are all blithely lying when they claim that the subsidies to the poor are very high! The total social sector expenditure of the Government of India (Centre and states combined) is barely 7% of the GDP.[60] Of this, the Central government's share is an abysmal 2% of the GDP (Table 14.1).[61]

Table 14.1: India: Total Central and State Governments Expenditure on Social Services (*% of GDP*)[62]

	2005–06	*2010–11*	*2011–12 (RE)*	*2012–13 (BE)*
Total Exp. on Social Services	5.49	6.79	6.89	7.09
Of which: On Education	2.61	3.13	3.25	3.31

It is because of this very low social sector spending that the Human Development Report released by the UNDP ranks India near the bottom with regards to overall human development. *India's Human Development Index ranking fell from 119 in 2010 to 135 in 2014 (in a list of 187 countries)*. According to the *UN Human Development Report 2011*, 53.7% of the Indian population is 'multidimensionally poor'—a measure that captures how many people experience overlapping deprivations in living standards, health and education, and how many deprivations they face on the average.[63]

And yet the WB–IMF and the foreign corporate houses and their concubine governments are pressurising the Government of India to further reduce its social sector expenditure, and Delhi's Badshahs are slavishly implementing their dictates. This is happening not just in the education sector that we have discussed in depth in this book; the government is slashing its expenditures on all social services, from health, electricity and public transport, to the public distribution system designed to provide food to the poor at affordable rates, to even drinking water supply. Worse, in the name of improving the quality of these social services, they are also being privatised—either through the infamous PPP route, or outright. Private corporations are jumping with glee—being essential services, the scope for profits is huge.

We briefly discuss the abysmally low social sector expenditures of the Government of India in the areas of health and food security, and its consequences for the people.

Collapse of the Public Health System

The state of social services in the country was dismal even before the economic reforms began in 1991. The Indian ruling classes have always been very self-centred, to the extent of being shortsighted. All the high-flown talk of socialism was meant to hoodwink the people; the callous elites were never really concerned with the welfare of the ordinary citizens. Hence, public social sector expenditures were low even before the reforms began in 1991.

With the onset of the reforms, the Indian rulers have willingly accepted World Bank instructions and are further reducing the already low government expenditures on providing essential services to the people. This is happening even in the vitally important health care sector too.

The World Health Organisation (WHO) recommends that countries should allocate at least 5% of the GDP for public health services. The advanced countries spend more than this; public health care spending as a percentage of GDP in 27 advanced economies rose from 5% to more than 7% over the period 1990–2008, with spending in 2008 ranging from 5.5% for Australia to 8.7% for France. Public health care spending in several emerging economies is between 3 and 5% of GDP—especially in East European countries and several Latin American countries like Argentina, Brazil and Chile. It is because of these high expenditures on public health services that nearly all OECD countries have universal or near-universal access to health care; the same is the situation in most of Eastern Europe, and several developing countries in Asia, Africa and Latin America, including Costa Rica, Cuba, Argentina, Brazil, South Africa, Kenya, Iraq, Iran, Thailand and Sri Lanka.[64]

In contrast, public health expenditure in India (Centre and states combined) has stagnated at a dismal 0.9–1.2% over the last two decades.[65] According to the WHO, India ranks 171 out of 175 countries in public health spending, and is ranked even below the sub-Saharan countries.[66]

This has forced citizens to bear the brunt of health spending. India has amongst the most privatised health systems in the world—households undertake nearly three-fourths of all the health spending in the country (72%), public spending accounts for just 28%.[67]

Obviously, in such a situation, the poor are going to be the worst sufferers. An appalling 21% of Indians no longer seek medical treatment of any kind for their ailments—up from 11% a decade ago—because they cannot afford it.[68] Despite this terrible situation, the government is not willing to transfer even a wee bit of the subsidies given to the rich towards providing essential healthcare to the poor. An example is government funding for its much vaunted National Rural Health Mission, which was launched in 2005 and was aimed at strengthening the healthcare infrastructure in rural areas. A key component of this Mission was upgrading every district headquarter hospital to provide quality health facilities to all by 2012. However, this has remained only on paper, with the government allocating only a minuscule 19.6% of the recommended outlay (Rs 544 crore out of Rs 2,780 crore) during the entire 11th Plan period (2007–12).[69]

The results of this neglect are predictable. India's health system is in "crisis", warn the editors of *The Lancet*, one of the world's most respected medical journals.[70] Some alarming statistics:

- India has not succeeded in controlling many infectious diseases, including tuberculosis, malaria, kala azar, filariasis, dysentry, typhoid, hepatitis and Japanese encephalitis.* Malaria alone kills nearly 2 lakh people in India every year.[71]
- India is in the grip of a tuberculosis (TB) epidemic. WHO statistics for 2011 give an estimated incidence figure of 2.2 million cases of TB for India out of a global incidence of 8.7 million cases. WHO estimates that around 3 lakh people die of TB every year in the country, nearly 1000 a day.[72]
- According to the WHO (2008), of the total number of deaths due to disease in a sample of 192 countries across the world, India accounted for nearly one-fourth of the deaths due to diarrhoea, more than one-third of the deaths due to leprosy and more than half of the deaths due to Japanese encephalitis.[73]
- Children and women bear a particularly shocking and intolerable burden of death. Of the seven million children who died before the age of five in 2011 in the world, one-fourth of these child deaths (1·8 million) took place in India. The bulk of these deaths are preventable, with an appalling one-third of the deaths being due to pneumonia and diarrhoea alone. India also accounted for one-fifth (56,000) of the

* *Of course, not all these epidemics are solely due to the failure of the public health system. Many of these diseases, like for example tuberculosis, are due to factors like neglect of environmental issues and malnourishment. In that sense, the terrible health conditions in India, and the abysmal poverty levels, the dismal sanitation conditions, etc. are all closely interlinked.*

2,87,000 maternal deaths in the world in 2010, according to a UN report.[74]

- UNDP's *Human Development Report 2010* ranks India 143rd in infant mortality rate, 124th in maternal mortality rate, 132nd in life expectancy at birth, and 145th in under-five mortality rate. The indicators were below that of most South Asian countries and were just slightly above sub-Saharan Africa.[75]
- Even as India has failed to tackle these long standing health challenges, it is also faced with another epidemic, of chronic diseases (like cardiovascular diseases, mental health disorders, diabetes and cancer). More than 50% of the deaths in India occur due to chronic diseases, with cardiovascular diseases being a major contributor. As a *Lancet* study points out, it is possible to address this challenge too, many inexpensive strategies are available, but again their implementation would require strengthening the public health system.[76]

According to *The Lancet*, the underlying reason for this health crisis gripping India is that its health system is solely "focused on technologically advancing medical care for the urban elite population", and "lacks an adequately functional public health infrastructure that is essential for prevention of disease in all communities."[77]

India's public health care system is seriously sick, it is in ICU (intensive care unit). But the ruling classes are unconcerned. While slashing expenditures on public health to keep the fiscal deficit under control, the government is giving huge subsidies to corporate houses for setting up five star hospitals (see Box 14.4 for examples). The majority of the Indian population is too poor to afford treatment in these elite hospitals. And so they are busy providing healthcare services to the rich from across the world. (Another example of how globalisation is bringing the world closer!)

The government is in fact promoting this—it earns the country much needed foreign exchange. It has even been given a name—'medical tourism', and the Ministry of Tourism is organising road shows for this in the world's leading cities.[78] India has become one of the world's most favoured 'medical tourism' destinations, and the

Box 14.4: Government Subsidies to Corporate Hospitals

India's leading corporate houses have entered the health sector, and have set up five star multi-speciality hospitals. Many of them have registered themselves under the Public Trust Act, so that they can take advantage of generous government concessions. The list includes several of Mumbai's leading private hospitals—from Jaslok to Breach Candy, Leelavati, Hinduja, Nanavati and Ambani Hospitals. They have been given prime land at a fraction of the market value; several of them have in fact been given land on a token lease rent of Re 1 per annum. Other concessions include additional FSI, concessional rates for water and electricity, low-interest loans from public sector banks, customs duty exemptions on imported machinery, income tax exemption on more than 85% of their income, etc. In the case of Delhi's Indraprastha Apollo Hospital, the Delhi Government even invested $3.4 million in construction of the hospital and contributed $5.22 million as equity capital. In return for these concessions, these 'charitable hospitals' are supposed to provide free treatment to poor patients (from 10% to one-third of their in-patient capacity, and 25% to 40% of their out-patient capacity). However, many of them simply refuse to do so, and the government is unwilling to take action against them, or even withdraw their concessions.

[Source: Nikhila M. Vijay, "Medical Tourism—Subsidising Health Care for Developed Countries", Third World Resurgence, November/December 2007, http://www.twnside.org.sg; Ravi Duggal, "The Uncharitable Trust Hospitals", June 17, 2012, http://righttohealthcare.blogspot.in; Jyoti Shelar and Lata Mishra, "One-sided Deal: Hospitals Get But Don't Give Back", April 26, 2012, https://kractivist.wordpress.com.]

country's medical tourism industry is growing at the rate of 30% per annum. Four lakh foreigners flew down to India in 2012 for medical treatment—treatment costs for them in India are 60–90% lower than in their countries![79]

India is on its way to becoming a Medical Superpower too! Hip-hip-hurray!

Rollback of Food Subsidies

Measuring Poverty Levels in India

Some time ago, the Planning Commission, the Government of India's think-tank, announced that poverty in the country had fallen over the past decade, from 41.8% to 33.8% in rural India and from 25.7% to 20.9% in urban areas over 2004–05 to 2009–10. The overall percentage of population living below the poverty line had dipped by a huge 7.3 percentage points from 37.2% in 2004–05 to 29.8% in 2009–10.[80]

Chart 14.4: Per Head Calorie Intake[81]

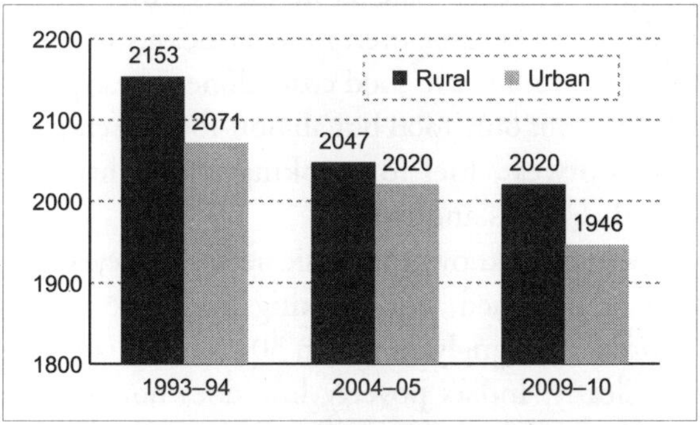

Chart 14.5: Per Head Protein Intake (*in grams*)[82]

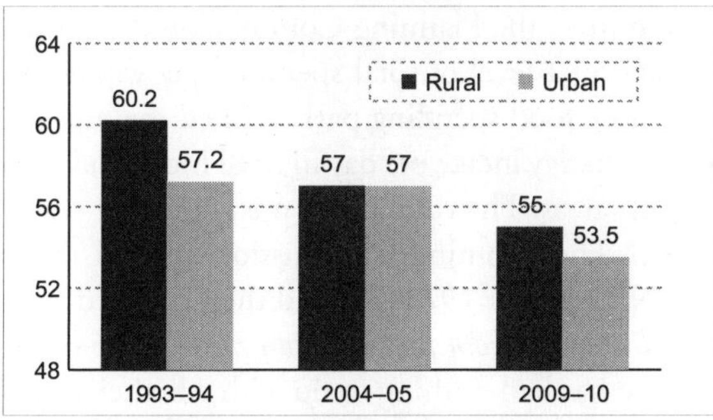

Strangely, this fall in poverty comes at a time when the same National Sample Survey (NSS) data from which the Planning

Commission drew the above conclusion shows that the average intake of calories per head had actually fallen over the same period. In fact, it has been falling continuously over the past two decades. And not just the average calorie intake, even the average protein intake per head had fallen (Charts 14.4 and 14.5).[83]

The discrepancy gets resolved when we examine the basis on which the Planning Commission has come to the conclusion that poverty in the country has fallen since 2004-05. According to the Commission, its figures are based on a monthly per-head poverty line of Rs 672.8 in rural and Rs 859.6 in urban areas, which works out to Rs 22.4 a day in rural areas and Rs 28.7 in urban areas.[84]

Clearly, the poverty line is absurdly low! The Planning Commission's figures become even more atrocious when it is kept in mind that they do not refer to food costs alone. These paltry sums are supposed to cover not only food but all non-food essentials, including clothing and footwear, fuel for cooking and lighting, transport, education, medical costs and rent![85]

Even a school child knows that basic necessities, even just adequate food, cannot be obtained, nor working health be maintained, by spending so little. Amazingly, however, 30 crore Indians subsist below these levels. Clearly, India's poverty line does not measure poverty anymore, it measures destitution.

The reason why India's poverty line is so abysmally low has an interesting history. In the 1970s, based on the recommendations of an expert committee, the Planning Commission defined the poverty line as that particular level of total spending per capita on all goods and services whose food spending part satisfied the nutrition level of 2,400 calories of energy intake per day in rural India, and 2,100 calories per day in urban areas. The rural norm was soon after scaled down to 2,200 calories.* The Planning Commission applied this definition only once, to NSS data of 1973–74, and then changed the definition in practice, *delinking it from the nutrition norm.* Ever since then, the new poverty line has had nothing to do with whether a person is able

---

* *Note that these are weighted averages. Recommended calorie allowance for adult males and females doing hard labour is much more than this.*

to access the minimum recommended calories. Thus, in 2009–10, while nutrition data from the NSS 66th Round showed that a person needed to spend Rs 1,100 in rural and Rs 2,120 in urban India a month to access 2,200 and 2,100 calories, respectively, the official monthly poverty lines for that year were only Rs 673 and Rs 860 respectively, at which only 1,870 calories could be accessed in rural areas and 1,720 calories in urban areas.

The noted economist Utsa Patnaik has estimated the number of people in India living below the poverty line based on the original poverty line of the 1970s that was based on nutrition norms wherein all people unable to access 2,200/2,100 calories per day in rural/urban areas are considered poor. The data from the National Sample Surveys of 2004–05 and 2009–10 then show that:

- In contrast to the claims of the Planning Commission, the number of people living below the poverty line has considerably gone up over this period.
- In 2004–05, the percentage of people in rural India unable to access 2,200 calories was 69.5%; this percentage had gone up to an appalling 75.5% in 2009–10!
- 64.5% of the urban population was unable to reach 2,100 calories energy intake in 2004–05; this too had gone up to 73% in 2009–10![86]

These figures are now in congruence with the data given in Charts 14.4 and 14.5 that indicate that calorie and protein intakes of Indian people had fallen over the period 2004–05 to 2009–10.

Under-Nutrition: A National Emergency

To most people fed on a daily diet of media propaganda that India is rapidly growing and is an emerging superpower, these figures that show three-fourths of the Indian people living in dire poverty would appear to be an exaggeration. But these appalling figures are borne out by other data too. According to the National Family Health Survey–3:

- more than 48% of children under the age of five are stunted (low height for age, indicating chronic malnutrition);
- 43% are underweight (low weight for age, indicating both

chronic and acute malnutrition);

- and about 20% have wasting (low weight for height, indicating acute malnutrition).[87]

Clearly, the poverty and mal/under-nutrition levels in India are nothing less than a national emergency. But the Shylocks are unconcerned, they must have their pound of flesh. As a part of globalisation conditionalities, the World Bank has asked for a reduction in food subsidies. Successive Indian governments have obsequiously been implementing its orders.

Targeted Public Distribution System

To reduce food subsidies, the Indian government came up with the argument that the majority of the food subsidy is being siphoned off by the middle classes, and so the benefits are not really reaching the poor. It proposed that the ration system should identify the 'really needy', and only they should be provided subsidised foodgrains. It then began manipulating the definition of 'really needy', that is, the poor, to reduce its food subsidy bill.

As a first step, the government replaced the Universal Public Distribution System by the Targeted Public Distribution System in 1996, wherein it introduced two kinds of ration cards, one for those above the poverty line (called APL cards), and one for those it considered poor (Below Poverty Line or BPL cards). On the one hand, it now gradually hiked the prices of foodgrains for APL households, bringing them closer to market prices, so that these households stopped buying grain from the public distribution shops—more popularly called the ration shops. And on the other, a majority of the poor were also pushed out of the public distribution system (PDS) by the simple stratagem of denying them BPL cards! This is admitted by NSS surveys, which show that 70.5% of rural households either possess no card or an APL card[88]—when three-quarters of the rural households do not earn enough to eat two full meals a day!

With a vast majority of the poor not buying foodgrains from the PDS, foodstocks with the Government of India have soared. In July 2013, foodgrain stocks with the State-owned Food Corporation of India (FCI) were more than 70 million tons, which is more than double the buffer stock and strategic reserve norm of 32 mt.[89]

What has the government been doing with these mounting stocks? Exporting them, to earn foreign exchange needed to finance the luxury goods imports of the rich! In 2012–13, India exported 9.5 million tons of wheat and 10 million tons of rice— making India the world's biggest rice exporter, in a country with the largest number of malnourished people in the world.[90]

National Food Security Act

The mounting foodgrain stocks on the one hand, and rising malnutrition levels and starvation deaths on the other, led to an uproar across the country. Activist groups and NGOs started mounting pressure on the government to expand the scope of the public distribution system. The Supreme Court too intervened, and passed a series of orders ensuring a multitude of food rights, such as providing 35 kg subsidised rations per family, heavily subsidised rations for poor families (the Antyodaya Anna Yojana), security to pregnant and lactating women, and so on.[91]

The government was in a quandary. The increasingly vociferous people's movement and Supreme Court orders were becoming a huge embarrassment. But the World Bank and foreign investors were also equally firm—that the government should do nothing to increase its expenditures on the poor. A way out of the dilemma was found by the government's sorcerous bureaucrats. They conjured up yet another bill—the National Food Security Bill—that ostensibly aimed to provide food security to all the poor, but in effect, subverted the whole issue. An exact parallel to the Right to Education Act discussed in the previous chapters, that in reality subverted the people's right to free and compulsory education.

Elections to the 16th Lok Sabha (2014) were approaching. To exhibit its hurry to provide 'Right to Food' to the people, the government first promulgated the National Food Security Ordinance on July 5, 2013, and then introduced the National Food Security Bill in the Lok Sabha on August 7, 2013 to replace the ordinance. The Parliament passed the Bill and it was signed into law on September 12, 2013.

Under the National Food Security Act (NFSA), 75% of the rural population and 50% of the urban population (on the whole, roughly 67% of the total population) will be entitled to five kilograms of grains (rice/wheat/millets) per person per month at the price of Rs 3/2/1 per kg. The Act also provides for children in the age group of 6 months to 6 years to be given an age-appropriate meal, free of charge, through the local anganwadi, and children in the age group of 6 to 14 to be given one free cooked mid-day meal every day (except on school holidays) in all government and government-aided schools. Another provision is that all pregnant women and lactating mothers would be entitled to maternity benefit of Rs 1,000 per month for six months.[92]

While the chairperson of the UPA Government, Sonia Gandhi, claimed that the food bill was a "historic step" to weed out hunger from the country,[93] the reality is that the NFSA is actually a disgrace for a country that claims to be an emerging economic superpower:

- Firstly, the Act provides the poor only starvation foodgrains. While the Indian Council for Medical Research recommends that an adult requires 14 kg of foodgrains per month and children 7 kg, the bill restricts the entitlement to only 5 kg per person per month!
- Secondly, the Act provides only for cereals, with no entitlements to other basic food necessities such as pulses and edible oil—whose prices have soared in recent years—required to combat malnutrition. The Empowered Group of Ministers, set up by the Central government to draw up the framework for the Act, was very clear about it. It proposed that the definition of food security should be "limited to the specific issue of foodgrains security (wheat and rice) and be delinked from the larger issue of nutrition security"—a stand which actually violates Article 47 of the Indian Constitution.[94] The aim of the Act is thus clear. People, including children, can remain hungry/ malnourished/anaemic, but shouldn't die of starvation because that makes bad publicity!
- Thirdly, the Act does not provide even this limited coverage

> **Box 14.5: Article 47 of the Indian Constitution**
>
> *"The State shall regard the raising of the level of nutrition and the standard of living of its people and the improvement of public health as among its primary duties."*
>
> By only providing for food security, and disregarding nutrition, the Food Security Act is clearly violative of the Constitution.

to all the poor—it expands the percentage of the population that would be provided subsidised foodgrains through the PDS to 67%, but as we have discussed above, 75% of the rural population and 73% of the urban population are unable to access the minimum recommended 2,200/2,100 calories.

- Even States like Tamil Nadu and Chhattisgarh have better food security acts.[95] Thus, for instance, Tamil Nadu has a universal public distribution system, wherein each and every family, whether below the poverty line or not, is entitled to 20 kg rice free of cost. The PDS in Tamil Nadu also supplies other essentials like wheat, sugar, kerosene and tur dal at subsidised rates.[96]

This explains why the National Food Security Act is actually more of a restructuring of the existing PDS than an expansion, as aggregate foodgrains to be distributed through the PDS do not go up significantly. In 2011–12, two years before the NFSA came into force, 44.5% of the population (of 1.21 billion) purchased 51.3 million tons of foodgrains from the PDS. This implies that per capita distribution of foodgrains from the PDS was 7.9 kg. The NFSA expands the percentage of the population that would now be provided subsidised foodgrains through the PDS to 67%, but reduces the per capita distribution to 5 kg. Therefore, as the schedule attached to the final version of the Bill that was signed into law mentions, the estimated foodgrain allocation under the NFSA is only 54.9 million tons, just a tad more than the 51.3 million tons distributed through the PDS in 2011–12. Other entitlements (such as midday meals) do not go beyond the rights that people already have under Supreme Court orders, with the main exception of maternity entitlements.[97]

And so, as some leading economists have shown, the additional cost of implementing the NFSA is just Rs 13,000 crore above the food subsidy that was being provided by the Government of India before the Act. They estimate that the total food subsidy bill of the Government of India will only go up to Rs 85,000 crore, from the Rs 72,000 crore in 2012–13.[98] The government too has admitted that the food subsidy bill is not going to increase significantly with the passage of the Act. Speaking in Parliament, Food Minister in the UPA Government, K.V. Thomas, stated that the additional financial burden after implementation of the National Food Security Ordinance is estimated at Rs 23,850 crore annually. He estimated the total food subsidy bill of the Government of India, after inclusion of all associated food-related welfare programs like mid-day meals, to go up to Rs 1,25,000 crore.[99] This sum is just one-fourth of the total tax concessions given to the rich in the 2013–14 budget.

Trust the Union Finance Ministers to be stingy about allocating even this niggardly sum. Chidambaram allocated only Rs 90,000 crore in the 2013–14 budget towards food security, and increased it to Rs 1,15,000 crore in his interim budget for 2014–15.[100] BJP leaders, during the debate in Parliament over the National Food Security Bill, had criticised the Bill as being very inadequate. Arun Jaitley had stated: "[A]re we substantially expanding the right over what existed prior to this Bill being brought in? Are we substantially increasing the outlay? The answer is 'no'..." Murli Manohar Joshi had even moved an amendment demanding that "every person ... shall be entitled to 10 kilograms of foodgrains, two and a half kilograms of pulses and nine hundred grams of cooking oil per person per month." The BJP election manifesto promised "Universal Food Security", saying that it is integral to national security. Yet, in the NDA Government's first budget after being voted to power, Finance Minister Arun Jaitley made a complete U-turn and kept the overall food subsidy allocation at the same level as Chidambaram's interim budget. Not only that, he also stated that the government would soon take steps "to overhaul the subsidy regime, including food and petroleum subsidies, and make it more targeted ..."[101] In World Bank diction, 'targeting' means that the government is soon going to reduce the food subsidy allocation.

BJP Government Racing Down the Same Road

Elections to the 16th Lok Sabha were held in April–May 2014. The BJP-led NDA coalition swept to power with a thumping majority. In his very first budget speech, the new Finance Minister Arun Jaitley declared that the government was planning to adhere to the fiscal deficit target set by his predecessor. Swaminathan S. Anklesaria Aiyar, the prominent journalist and consulting editor for the *Economic Times*, observed that Jaitley's budget speech was nothing "but a Chidambaram budget with saffron lipstick added"; the former Finance Minister P. Chidambaram commented that the "imprint of the UPA Government's policies" can be seen in the budget presented by Arun Jaitley; and even the former Prime Minister Manmohan Singh hailed the BJP Government's attempts to adhere to the fiscal deficit target set by his government for the current fiscal.[102]

Nay, the new BJP Government is not just seeking to go down the same path as the UPA, it is actually seeking to do so at an accelerated speed. As we have mentioned above, the budget documents reveal that in 2014–15, Jaitley gave away Rs 5.49 lakh crore in tax concessions to the country's richie rich. Because of these massive tax write-offs, Jaitley missed his gross tax revenue collection target of 10.6% of the GDP for 2014–15, and was only able to reach 9.9% of the GDP.[103] How then did he succeed in achieving the fiscal deficit target of 4.1% of the GDP? By slashing the Central government's social sector expenditures. The revised estimates for 2014–15 show that the government cut its budgetary spending on schemes for the most vulnerable and marginalised sections of the Indian society by as much as 14 to 37%, to meet its fiscal deficit target (Table 14.2)!

In his Budget for 2015–16, Jaitley has further reduced the government's already low social sector expenditures. As shown in Table 14.2, government spending on the disadvantaged sections—women, scheduled castes and tribes, and children—has been reduced by as much as 20–40% over the budget estimates for 2014–15.

More specifically, the various Ministries /Departments related to the social sectors have seen severe cuts in their budgetary allocations.

Table 14.2: India's Budget, 2014–15 and 2015–16: Reduction in Expenditures on Vulnerable Sections[104] (*in Rs crore*)

	2014-15 BE (1)	*2014-15 RE (2)*	*Reduction (1 – 2) (%)*	*2015-16 BE (3)*	*Reduction (1 – 3) (%)*
Scheduled Caste Sub-Plan	50,548	33,638	33	30,851	39
Tribal Sub-Plan	32,387	20,536	37	19,980	38
Schemes for Welfare of Children	81,075	69,888	14	57,919	29
Gender Budget	98,030	81,984	16	79,258	19

Table 14.3: India's Budget, 2015–16: Budget Allocations for Social Sectors[105] (*in Rs crore*)

	2014-15 BE	*2015-16 BE*	*Reduction (%)*
Ministry of Health and Family Welfare	37,965	32,068	15.5
Ministry of Drinking Water and Sanitation	15,267	6,244	59.1
Ministry of Rural Development	83,852	73,333	12.5
Ministry of Water Resources, River Development and Ganga Rejuvenation	13,837	4,232	69.4
Ministry of Panchayati Raj	7,001	95	98.6
Ministry of Housing and Urban Poverty Alleviation	6,009	5,634	6.2

The government is claiming that actual social sector expenditures are not going to fall as it has increased the states' share in Central taxes from 32% to 42%, and that would more than compensate for these cuts. However, simultaneously, the Centre has reduced its funding for Central Assistance for State and Union Territory Plans by a whopping 40%. Therefore, the net increase in spending capacity of the state governments is very modest, by just 5.9%.[106] On the other hand, the Centre has cut its social sector spending by as much as 20 to 40% in most sectors, with the cuts going up to as much as 50–70% for some Ministries and even 98% for the Ministry of Panchayati Raj. Therefore, the combined Central and state government spending on various social sectors is going to take a big hit in this financial year.

But when it comes to transferring funds from government coffers to the corporate houses, there is never any shortage of resources. In his budget 2014–15, the Finance Minister announced a host of new infrastructural projects, all involving huge transfers of government funds to the private sector via the PPP route. These include:[107]

- A slew of measures to fast-track PPP projects that have been held up for various reasons;
- Plans for new infrastructure projects such as port projects, airports in smaller cities, and expressways, all to be set up through the PPP route;
- Revival of Special Economic Zones;
- Setting up 100 smart cities;
- Setting up a National Industrial Corridor Authority to coordinate development of several new industrial corridors.

In Budget 2015–16, the Finance Minister announced an increase of Rs 70,000 crore in investment in infrastructure in 2015–16 over the current year. Since all government spending on infrastructure is today being done via the PPP route, this essentially means that Jaitley is proposing a huge increase in subsidies to corporate houses. Not only that, the Finance Minister called for a revamp of the Public–Private–Partnership or PPP model, stating that the private sector needs to be given yet more risk protection for its investments.[108] This essentially means that Jaitley is proposing yet higher levels of subsidy for corporate investors in the infrastructure sector!

To accelerate the acquisition of the thousands of hectares of land that will be needed for all these projects, the government has passed an ordinance to modify the Land Acquisition Act, omitting for a wide range of projects the requirements of a social impact assessment study, and also the informed consent of a large number of families affected by the acquisition of land, so as to make land acquisition easier.[109]

Keeping step, the new Environment Minister Prakash Javadekar, soon after taking charge, promised to ensure "fast clearances" for infrastructural projects.[110]

All this within just nine months! The corporates are delighted.

They had invested heavily in the BJP election campaign;[111] their investments are paying off ...

Secession of the Rich

There is little room for doubt.

India's Westoxicated elite has abandoned all concern for the tribal child dying of malnutrition in Melghat, the farmer in Andhra Pradesh committing suicide because of his inability to pay his medical bills, the old man dying of cold on the streets of Patna because of lack of social security, the village beauty sold off to pay her father's debts in Bundelkhand ... It has also abandoned the dream nurtured by the people of our country during their fight to free our country from colonial rule, and the vision of our nation's founding fathers embedded in the Directive Principles of our Constitution—to provide all our children free and compulsory education.

NOTES

1. See for instance: C.P. Chandrasekhar, "The Price of Reform", *Frontline*, March 24–April 6, 2012, http://www.frontline.in; "$75 Billion Subsidy Bill!", June 2008, http://www.nritoday.net.
2. "Budget 2012–13: Pranab Losing Sleep Over Rising Subsidy Bills", *BT Online Bureau*, February 8, 2012, http://businesstoday.intoday.in.
3. For quotations in Box 14.1: "More Effort Needed to Reduce Government Subsidies: C. Rangarajan", *PTI*, New Delhi, December 26, 2013, http://archive.indianexpress.com; "Government Will Meet its Fiscal Deficit Target: Raghuram Rajan", February 13, 2014, http://www.livemint.com; "India Could Revert to 8.5–9 Per Cent Growth in Two Years: Kaushik Basu", *PTI*, November 6, 2012, http://articles.economictimes. indiatimes.com.
4. "Fiscal Deficit Will be Contained at 4.8% of GDP: Chidambaram", January 15, 2014, http://zeenews.india.com.
5. "Jaitley Terms Chidambaram's Fiscal Deficit Target of 4.1% as 'Daunting'", *Business Standard*, July 10, 2014, http://www.business-standard.com.; figure for 2012–13 taken from Chart 14.1.
6. "Priorities Cut Out: Rajan Meets Jaitley, Talks Growth and Prices", *Hindustan Times*, May 28, 2014, http://www.hindustantimes.com.
7. "FM says FY15 fiscal deficit will be 4.1%", July 10, 2014, http://www.business-standard.com.

8. "Union Budget 2015–16: Fiscal deficit pegged at 3.9%; to reach 3% by FY'18", February 28, 2015, http://businesstoday.intoday.in.
9. *India – Macro-economic Summary: 1999–00 to 2013–14 (on August 2, 2014)*, http://planningcommission.nic.in; "Union Budget 2015–16: Fiscal Deficit Pegged at 3.9%; to Reach 3% by FY'18", February 28, 2015, http://businesstoday.intoday.in.
10. For more on this, see: Prabhat Patnaik, *The Humbug of Finance*, April 5, 2000, www.macroscan.org; *Keynes, Capitalism, and the Crisis: John Bellamy Foster Interviewed by Brian Ashley*, March 20, 2009, http://www.countercurrents.org.
11. Discussing this issue in detail is beyond the scope of this essay. It is discussed in detail in several articles published in the *Monthly Review*, the famed New York journal. See for example: John Bellamy Foster and Robert W. McChesney, "The Endless Crisis", *Monthly Review*, May 2012, http://monthlyreview.org.
12. Noam Chomsky, *Profit Over People*, Madhyam Books, Delhi, 1999, pp. 66–68; Walden Bello, *The Global Collapse: A Non-orthodox View*, 2009, http://mrzine.monthlyreview.org.
13. See Chapter 4 for more on this.
14. All this is well documented. See for instance: David Harvey, *A Brief History of Neoliberalism*, op. cit., pp. 7–8, 29, 64–66; Paulo Nakatani and Rémy Herrera, "The South Has Already Repaid its External Debt to the North: But the North Denies its Debt to the South", *Monthly Review*, June 2007, http://monthlyreview.org; Walden Bello and David Kinley, *An Analysis of the International Monetary Fund's Role in the Third World Debt Crisis, its Relation to Big Banks, and the Forces Influencing its decisions*, July 1983, http://multinationalmonitor.org; Walden Bello, *Structural Adjustment Programs: 'SUCCESS' for Whom?*, http://www.converge.org.nz; Harry Magdoff and Paul Sweezy, *Stagnation and Financial Explosion*, Monthly Review Press, New York and Aakar Books, Delhi, pp. 176–195.
15. For a brief discussion of these consequences, see Neeraj Jain, *Globalisation or Recolonisation*, Lokayat Publication, Pune, 2006, available on the Lokayat website at lokayat.org.in.
16. For a discussion on why the World Bank ordered India to replace budget deficit with fiscal deficit, see Neeraj Jain, *Globalisation or Recolonisation*, ibid., pp. 103–4.
17. "India: Trends, Issues and Options", World Bank, May 1990, p. 36, cited in *Aspects of India's Economy*, No. 2, Research Unit for Political Economy, Prabhadevi, Mumbai–25, p. 13.
18. "The 'Fiscal Deficit' Bogeyman and His Uses", *Aspects of India's Economy*,

May 2013, http://www.rupe-india.org.
19. Ibid.
20. *P. Sainath on Corporate Bailout #Rs. 36.5 trillion #Budget 2014*, July 13, 2014, http://www.indiaresists.com; GDP for 2013–14 estimated at Rs 113 lakh crore – see *Key Fiscal Indicators 2003–04 to 2014–15 BE (12/07/14)*, http://planningcommission.nic.in.
21. *Key Fiscal Indicators 2003–04 to 2014–15 BE (12/07/14)*, ibid.
22. *P. Sainath on Corporate Bailout #Rs. 36.5 trillion #Budget 2014*, op. cit.
23. P. Sainath, "The Feeding Frenzy of Kleptocracy", *The Hindu*, March 16, 2013, http://www.thehindu.com. Fiscal Deficit for 2013–14 was Rs 5.24 lakh crore – see *Key Fiscal Indicators 2003–04 to 2014–15 BE (12/07/14)*, op. cit.
24. *P. Sainath on Corporate Bailout #Rs. 36.5 Trillion #Budget 2014*, op. cit.; "The 'Fiscal Deficit' Bogeyman and His Uses", op. cit.; P. Sainath, "The Feeding Frenzy of Kleptocracy", ibid.
25. Original source: *IMF WEO Database*, www.imf.org; taken from: "The 'Fiscal Deficit' Bogeyman and His Uses", ibid.
26. Cited in: "The 'Fiscal Deficit' Bogeyman and His Uses", ibid.
27. "Budget 2015–16 in Eight Charts", March 3, 2015, http://www.thehindu.com; P. Sainath, "So Richie Rich? Have Another One On Us", March 23, 2015, http://www.outlookindia.com.
28. "Jaitley Gave Bonanza to Corporates: Chidambaram", *The Hindu Business Line*, March 1, 2015, http://www.thehindubusinessline.com.
29. Rahul Varman, *Cowboy Capitalism: The Curious Case of Reliance KG Basin Gas Business*, February 24, 2013, http://sanhati.com.
30. "A Modest Proposal Regarding Subsidies", *Aspects of India's Economy*, No. 51, August 2011, http://www.rupe-india.org.
31. Ibid.; Rahul Varman, *Cowboy Capitalism: The Curious Case of Reliance KG Basin Gas Business*, op. cit.
32. "A Modest Proposal Regarding Subsidies", ibid.
33. All facts given in this section taken from: *Iron and Steal: The POSCO–India Story*, Mining Zone Peoples' Solidarity Group, http://miningzone.org.
34. See, for instance: "A Modest Proposal Regarding Subsidies", op. cit.
35. G. Srinivasan, "Seeing a Sellout", *Frontline*, September 08–21, 2012, http://www.frontline.in.
36. "Doing Big Business in Modi's Gujarat", *Forbes*, March 12, 2014, http://www.forbes.com; "State Govt. Gifts Adani 5.78 cr sq mt of Land in Kutch for Peanuts", *DNA*, March 1, 2012, http://daily.bhaskar.com; "Thousands of Acres of Land Doled Out to Adani by Modi Govt. on Throwaway Prices", November 23, 2013, http://www.ummid.com.

37. "Foreign Investment and Land Acquisition: from Posco to Poena", *Aspects of India's Economy*, No. 51, August 2011, http://www.rupe-india.org; Sunil Jain, "7 Cities, 2,000 Sq Km, Rs 325,000 Crore", October 7, 2010, http://www.financialexpress.com.
38. All facts in this section summarised from: "Corporate Cronyism in 'Vibrant Gujarat'", July 10, 2012, http://www.hardnews media.com; Paranjoy Guha Thakurta, "India: Cheapest Car Rides on Govt. Subsidies", *Inter Press Service*, May 23, 2009, http://www.globalissues.org; "Rs. 30,000-Crore Sops for Nano Project: Document", *The Hindu*, November 12, 2008, http://www.hindu.com; "Modhwadia Blasts Modi Govt. Over Nano Sops to Tatas", March 5, 2011, http://archive.indianexpress.com.
39. "PM to Release Auto Mission Plan on 29th", *TNN*, January 26, 2007, http://articles.economictimes.indiatimes.com; "Private Corporate Sector-Led Growth and Exclusion", *Aspects of India's Economy*, Nos. 44–46, Apr 2008, http://www.rupe-india.org; "Auto Sector to Contribute $145 bln to GDP by 2016", January 29, 2007, http://news.oneindia.in.
40. Cited in: "Behind the Attack on 'Subsidies'", *Aspects of India's Economy*, No. 49, Aug 2010, http://www.rupe-india.org.
41. Ibid.; *FAQs – Public Private Partnership in India*, Ministry of Finance, Government of India, http://pppinindia.com.
42. *Draft Compendium of PPP Projects in Infrastructure, 2012*, Planning Commission, Government of India, January 2013, p. 14, www.infrastructure.gov.in.
43. "Yamuna Expressway to Become Operational This Month", *TNN*, April 7, 2012, http://articles.economictimes.indiatimes.com; Naazneen Karmali, "Road to Riches", April 12, 2010, http://www.forbes.com; Jyotika Sood, "Road to Disaster", June 15, 2011, http://www.downtoearth.org.in.
44. "Private Corporate Sector–Led Growth and Exclusion", op. cit.; "CPM Trains Divest Gun on Govt", *The Telegraph*, March 24, 2004, http://www.telegraphindia.com.
45. Praful Bidwai, "Of Sleazy, Criminalised Capitalism", *Frontline*, May 12–25, 2001, http://www.frontline.in; V. Sridhar, "Battle Over Balco", *Frontline*, March 17–30, 2001, http://www.frontline.in.
46. Purnima S. Tripathi, "A Familiar Ring", *Frontline*, February 26–March 11, 2011, http://www.frontline.in; Tapan Sen, "Now, 'Post-Closing' Fraud!", *People's Democracy*, February 16, 2003, http://pd.cpim.org.
47. "Why Do Credit Rating Agencies Press India to Reduce Government Spending?", *Aspects of India's Economy*, No. 53, May 2013, http://www.rupe-india.org.

48. K.C. Chakrabarty, "Two Decades of Credit Management in Banks", Bancon 2013, http://www.slideshare.net; Mayur Shetty, "Rs 1 Lakh Crore Bad Loans of Corporates Written Off: RBI", *TNN*, November 17, 2013, http://timesofindia.indiatimes.com.
49. "Corporate Debt Restructuring", *The Economic Times*, http://economictimes.indiatimes.com; "Corporate Debt Restructuring News", http://profit.ndtv.com; Samar Halarnkar, "Serve the Rich: Banks Go Easy on India's Big Loan Defaulters", November 28, 2013, http://www.hindustantimes.com.
50. "Need to Revamp Corporate Debt Restructuring Mechanism: Report", *PTI*, August 12, 2013, http://articles.economic times.indiatimes.com; *Report on Trend and Progress of Banking in India 2012–13*, Reserve Bank of India, 2013, p. 67, http://rbidocs.rbi.org.in.
51. Megha Bahree, "Top Indian Companies Burdened with Debt", August 19, 2013, http://www.forbes.com; Anand Adhikari, "India on Sale", October 13, 2013, http://businesstoday.intoday.in.
52. Sarita C. Singh, "Power Companies like Tata Power, Adani Power, Reliance Power and Others Breathe Easy as Government Plans Loan Recast", *ET Bureau*, December 2, 2013, http://articles.economic times.indiatimes.com.
53. *Report on Trend and Progress of Banking in India 2012–13*, op. cit., p. 65.
54. "A Modest Proposal Regarding Subsidies", op. cit.
55. "Modi Orders Inquiry into Nano MoU Note", *The Financial Express*, November 11, 2008, http://m.financialexpress.com.
56. "A Modest Proposal Regarding Subsidies", op. cit.; *Perspectives on Poverty in India : Stylised Facts from Survey Data*, World Bank, April 2011, https://openknowledge.worldbank.org.
57. "Crony Capitalism a Big Threat to Countries like India, RBI Chief Raghuram Rajan Says", *TNN*, August 12, 2014, http://timesofindia.indiatimes.com; Bharadwaj Sharma, "Crony Capitalism Leads to Decline in Economic Growth: Raghuram Rajan", August 12, 2014, http://www.ibtimes.co.in.
58. Noam Chomsky, *Neoliberalism and Global Order*, 1996, http://strategema.narod.ru.
59. For OECD: "Government Social Spending: Total Public Social Expenditure as a Percentage of GDP", OECD Library, December 20, 2013, http://www.oecd-ilibrary.org; For EU-27: "Chapter 3 – Social Protection Systems Confronting the Crisis" in *Employment and Social Developments in Europe 2012*, European Commission, Brussels, January 2013, www.europarl.europa.eu; For Latin America: *Sustainable Development in Latin America and the Caribbean: Regional Perspectives*

Towards the Post-2015 Development Agenda, United Nations ECLAC, July 2013, www.eclac.org.
60. *SAARC Development Goals: India Country Report 2013*, Ministry of Statistics and Programme Implementation, Government of India, p. 36.
61. Subrat Das, "Plan Spending on Social Sectors and a Paradox in Budgetary Policies, February 19, 2013, http://www.downtoearth.org.in.
62. *SAARC Development Goals: India Country Report 2013*, op. cit.
63. "The 'Fiscal Deficit' Bogeyman and His Uses", op. cit.; "India Ranks 135 in Human Development Index: UNDP", *TNN*, July 24, 2014, http://timesofindia.indiatimes.com.
64. David Coady et al. (ed.), *The Economics of Public Health Care Reform in Advanced and Emerging Economies*, International Monetary Fund, 2012, http://books.google.co.in.
65. Mita Choudhury, H.K. Amar Nath, "An Estimate of Public Expenditure on Health in India", National Institute of Public Finance and Policy, New Delhi, May 2012, http://www.nipfp.org.in; M. Govinda Rao and Mita Choudhury, "Health Care Financing Reforms in India", National Institute of Public Finance and Policy, March 2012, http://www.nipfp.org.in.
66. Nirmala M. Nagaraj, "India Ranks 171 out of 175 in Public Health Spending, says WHO Study", *TNN*, Aug 11, 2009, http://timesofindia.indiatimes.com.
67. *World Health Statistics 2013*, World Health Organisation, 2013, Switzerland.
68. P. Sainath, "Health as Someone Else's Wealth", *The Hindu*, July 1, 2005, http://www.hindu.com.
69. *Reclaiming Public Provisioning Priorities for the 12th Five Year Plan*, 2011, Centre for Budget and Governance Accountability, New Delhi, www.cbgaindia.org.
70. Richard Horton, Pam Das, "Indian Health: The Path from Crisis to Progress", *Lancet*, January 11, 2011, http://www.thelancet.com.
71. T.J. John, L. Dandona, V.P. Sharma, M. Kakkar, "Continuing Challenge of Infectious Diseases in India", *Lancet*, January 12, 2011, http://www.thelancet.com; N. Dhingra, P. Jha, V.P. Sharma, et al., "Adult and Child Malaria Mortality in India", *Lancet*, 2010, http://www.thelancet.com.
72. *Tuberculosis in India*, Wikipedia, http://en.wikipedia.org; *Global Tuberculosis Report 2012*, World Health Organisation, 2012, http://who.int.
73. David Coady et al. (ed.), *The Economics of Public Health Care Reform in Advanced and Emerging Economies*, op. cit., p. 288.

74. V.K. Paul, H.S. Sachdev, D. Mavalankar et al., "Reproductive Health, and Child Health and Nutrition in India: Meeting the Challenge", *Lancet*, January 12, 2011, http://www.thelancet.com; *UNICEF – Goal: Reduce Child Mortality*, www.unicef.org; "India Tops in Rate of Maternal Deaths Worldwide", *DNA*, May 16, 2012, http://www.dnaindia.com.
75. David Coady et al. (ed.), *The Economics of Public Health Care Reform in Advanced and Emerging Economies*, op. cit., p. 286.
76. V. Patel, S. Chatterji, D. Chisholm et al., "Chronic Diseases and Injuries in India", *Lancet*, January 12, 2011, http://www.thelancet.com.
77. T.J. John, L. Dandona, V. P. Sharma, M. Kakkar, "Continuing Challenge of Infectious Diseases in India", op. cit.
78. *Medical Tourism–Incredible India*, http://www.incredibleindia.org.
79. "International Medical Tourism Industry Pegged at $ 40 Billion a Year", *Bloomberg*, June 27, 2013, http://articles.economictimes.indiatimes.com; Vinay Grover, "India Seems to be the Most Promising Medical Tourism Destination", October 22, 2013, http://healthandcare.in.
80. "Poverty Dips to 29.8% in 2009–10: Planning Commission", March 19, 2012, http://www.dnaindia.com.
81. "Let Them Eat Fat", *Aspects of India's Economy*, No. 55, March 2014, http://www.rupe-india.org; C.P. Chandrasekhar, "Chronic Famishment", *The Hindu*, April 15, 2012, http://www.thehindu.com.
82. "Let Them Eat Fat", ibid.; C.P. Chandrasekhar, ibid.
83. "Let Them Eat Fat", ibid.; C.P. Chandrasekhar, ibid.
84. Utsa Patnaik, "Poverty Trends in India 2004–05 to 2009–10: Updating Poverty Estimates and Comparing Official Figures", *Economic and Political Weekly*, October 5, 2013, http://www.epw.in.
85. Utsa Patnaik, "Number Games: India's Declining Poverty Figures Based on Flawed Estimation Method; Accurate Figures Show 75 Percent in Poverty", *World Poverty*, August 25, 2012, http://academicsstand.org.
86. Ibid.; Utsa Patnaik, "Poverty Trends in India 2004–05 to 2009–10: Updating Poverty Estimates and Comparing Official Figures", op. cit.
87. *Children in India 2012: A Statistical Appraisal*, Ministry of Statistics and Programme Implementation, op. cit.; "India–Nutrition", www.unicef.org.
88. Madura Swaminathan, "Public Distribution System and Social Exclusion", *The Hindu*, May 7, 2008, http://www.thehindu.com.
89. "Foodgrain Stocks Fall Below 70 mt, Exceed Reserve Norms by a Margin", August 9, 2013, http://www.financialexpress.com.
90. "India's Food Crisis: Rotting Food-grains, Hungry People", April 1, 2013, http://www.rediff.com.

91. Sachin Kumar Jain, *India's National Food Security Act: Entitlement of Hunger*, Asian Human Rights Commission, April 2010, http://www.humanrights.asia.
92. *National Food Security Act, 2013*, Wikipedia, http://en.wikipedia.org; "Summary of the National Food Security Bill 2013", *Tehelka Bureau*, March 22, 2013, http://www.tehelka.com.
93. "Parliament Approves Food Security Bill with Amendments", *IANS*, Sept 3, 2013, http://indiatoday.intoday.in.
94. Ravi S. Jha, "India's Food Security Bill: An Inadequate Remedy?" *Guardian Professional*, July 15, 2013, http://www.theguardian.com; Sachin Kumar Jain, *India's National Food Security Act: Entitlement of Hunger*, op. cit.
95. Jean Dreze, *The Food Security Debate in India*, July 9, 2013, http://india.blogs.nytimes.com.
96. *Ration Card Types and Commodity Entitlements*, Civil Supplies and Consumer Protection Department, http://www.consumer.tn.gov.in; S. Vydhianathan, R.K. Radhakrishnan, "Behind the Success Story of Universal PDS in Tamil Nadu", August 11, 2010, http://www.thehindu.com.
97. Bharat Ramaswami, Milind Murugkar and Ashok Kotwal, "Correct Costs of the Food Security Bill", 28 Aug 2013, http://ideasforindia.in; Jean Dreze, "Why the Food Bill is Sound Economics", April 13, 2013, http://www.tehelka.com.
98. Bharat Ramaswami, Milind Murugkar and Ashok Kotwal, ibid.
99. "Digestion Pangs", September 29, 2013, http://businesstoday.in today.in; Sreenivasan Jain, "All About the Food Security Bill Myth", September 4, 2013, http://www.rediff.com; "Centre Releases Rs 46,000 Crore as Food Subsidy so far: K.V. Thomas", *PTI*, August 23, 2013, http://articles.economictimes.indiatimes.com; *Brief of the Points Made by Shri Arun Jaitley, Leader of Opposition, Rajya Sabha, While Speaking on the Ordinance and the Bill Relating to Food Security*, http://www.bjp.org.
100. "Major Cut in Fuel, Food, Fertiliser Subsidies", February 28, 2013, http://www.thehindu.com; "Centre Releases Rs 46,000 Crore as Food Subsidy So Far: K.V. Thomas", ibid.; "Interim Budget 2014: Subsidy Bill Pegged Marginally Higher at Rs 2.5 Lakh Crore", *PTI*, February 17, 2014, http://profit.ndtv.com.
101. Sanjeeb Mukherjee, "Outlay Shows States May Go Slow on Food Security Plan", July 12, 2014, http://www.business-standard.com; *Right to Food Campaign on Budget 14*, July 12, 2014, http://www.india resists.com.

102. "Budget 2014 Lacks in Specifics, Says Manmohan Singh", July 10, 2014, http://profit.ndtv.com; Swaminathan S. Anklesaria Aiyar, "Arun Jaitley's Maiden Budget is Like Chidambaram's with a Saffron Lipstick", *ET Bureau*, July 11, 2014, http://articles.economictimes.india times.com; "Chidambaram Says Jaitley's Budget Has UPA Imprint", July 10, 2014, http://www.livemint.com.
103. *The Medium Term Fiscal Policy Statement – Union Budget*, http://www.indiabudget.nic.in.
104. Union Budget 2015–16 documents, available at: *Union Budget 2015–2016*, http://indiabudget.nic.in.
105. Ibid.
106. "Of Bold Strokes and Fine Prints: Analysis of Union Budget 2015–16", CBGA, March 2015, p. 9, http://www.cbgaindia.org; Union Budget 2015-16 documents, op. cit.
107. "PPP is New Mantra for Infra in Jaitley's Maiden Budget", July 10, 2014, http://zeenews.india.com; "Budget 2014-15: PPP is the New Mantra for Infrastructure", July 10, 2014, http://www.outlookindia.com; *Institution for Mainstreaming PPPs Will be Set-Up: Shipping, Inland Navigation, Airports and Roads Sector Given Priority*, Press Information Bureau, Government of India, Ministry of Finance, July 10, 2014, http://pib.nic.in; "Big-ticket Infrastructure Projects in Sight, All Roads Lead to PPPs", July 11, 2014, http://www.indiantollways.com; M. Rajendran, "Revival of SEZs on the Cards", *Hindustan Times*, July 11, 2014, http://www.hindustantimes.com.
108. "Budget 2015: Infrastructure Investment to be Raised by Rs70,000 crore", February 28, 2015, http://www.livemint.com.
109. There are several articles on this available on the internet. See for instance: "Hasty Changes in Land Law", January 2, 2015, http://www.the hindu.com; "Change in Land Act Will Lead to Forcible Acquisition: Jairam Ramesh", *Express News Service*, Dec 31, 2014, http://www.financial express.com.
110. "Prakash Javadekar Promises Fast Clearances to Infrastructure Projects", PTI, May 29, 2014, http://articles.economictimes.indiatimes.com.
111. "Black Money Power", May 4, 2014, http://www.economist.com; Siddharth Varadarajan, "The Cult of Cronyism", *Seminar*, April 2014, http://svaradarajan.com; "Corporate Sector Lauds Narendra Modi Government's Maiden Union Budget", July 10, 2014, http://www.newswala.com; "Budget 2014–15: Scores High on Infra and Highways Building", July 11, 2014, http://www.nbmcw.com.

15

EDUCATE! ORGANISE! FIGHT!

If we don't fight
If we don't continue the fight
Then the enemy bayonets
Will finish us off
And later
Pointing towards our bones
They'll say:
They are bones of slaves
Of slaves!

Unbridled Plunder

Ever since 1991, when the government began the globalisation of the Indian economy and opened it up to foreign corporations, successive Indian governments have been running the economy solely for the profit maximisation of giant foreign corporations—also known as Multinational Corporations (MNCs)—and India's big business houses.

The MNCs and their Indian collaborators are on a no-holds barred looting spree. With the naked connivance of the politicians, police and the bureaucracy, they are seizing control of the lands, forests, rivers, mountains, coastal zones. So that they can commandeer the resources—bauxite, iron ore, coal, water ... Or set up special economic zones, infrastructural projects ... Or build resorts, golf courses, residential projects for the rich, etc. Overnight, the people living on these lands and forests since times immemorial have become encroachers, and are being told to shoo off.

These big corporate houses are seizing control of public sector corporations, created through the sweat and toil of the common people, at throwaway prices. Worse, over the last two decades, the government has been attempting to gradually privatise the financial sector too, including the public sector banks, insurance companies, workers' provident fund corpus and pension funds. Once it succeeds in doing so, that would mean control of lakhs of crores of rupees of domestic savings will pass into the hands of foreign "crooks, scoundrels and fast operators"—epithets used by a sub-committee of the US Congress to describe US insurance companies.[1] These corporations are obviously not going to invest these funds in infrastructural and socially oriented sectors, and instead will plunder these hard-earned savings of the Indian people, like they have done all over the globe.

Foreign and Indian corporations are wanting to take over Indian agriculture too—and so the government is deliberately implementing policies that is pushing the agricultural sector into deeper and deeper crisis. It has led to a massive increase in indebtedness of the peasantry. Seventy-five lakh farmers have abandoned agriculture over the last decade. Even more bone-chilling is that it has spurred the worst-ever recorded wave of suicides in the country's history—since 1995, more than 2.5 lakh Indian farmers have killed themselves.[2]

In its feverish desire to promote investment, the government is relaxing environmental laws, allowing corporations to cut down entire forests, over-exploit groundwater, indulge in indiscriminate mining, destroy coastal lands in the name of aquaculture, pollute our seas–rivers–soil–groundwater–air, damage the health of not just the living but also of those yet to be born ...

Consequences: Obscene Inequality

This barbarous assault on the people is transforming the country into a 'first world–fourth world' society.

On the one hand, the rich have never had it so good! "Its raining billionaires in India"—to quote one newsreport.[3] India now boasts of 56 billionaires with a collective net worth of $191.5 billion, as per the latest global ranking of the super-rich by *Forbes* magazine. That amounts to Rs 11.7 lakh crore, or one-tenth of India's GDP for 2013–14.[4] India now has the sixth largest number of billionaires in the world, and is ahead of the UK, Japan and Canada.[5]

Last year (2013), the number of Ultra High Net Worth individuals in India, defined as those having net assets (meaning company shares, real estate, art, cars, planes, yachts, etc.) of above $30 million (Rs 200 crore or so), increased by 120 to reach 7850, and their total wealth grew to $935 billion. To give an idea of what this means, this amount is just a tad above 50% of India's GDP.[6]

On the other hand, crores of ordinary people have been pushed down to fourth world immiseration. They have never had it so bad! We have given some statistics in the previous chapters. To recap:

- 75.5% of the rural and 73% of the urban population were unable to access the minimum recommended 2,200/2,100 calories in 2009–10.
- 50% of the children under the age of five suffer from malnourishment. According to UNICEF, malnutrition is more common in India than in sub-Saharan Africa. One in every three malnourished children in the world lives in India.[7]
- 42% of the children in India drop out of school without completing basic schooling (elementary education).
- One-fourth of all the child deaths in the world take place in India—in actual numbers, a whopping 1.8 million children; the bulk of these take place due to preventable diseases, such as diarrhoea and pneumonia.
- India accounts for one-fifth of all maternal deaths in the world.
- India is in the grip of a tuberculosis epidemic, with 3 lakh people dying due to the disease every year.
- 62.6 crore people do not have access to toilets and are forced to defecate in the open—60% of the global total.[8]
- More than 44% of the households in the country still have no access to electricity, more than six decades after independence.[9]

In the Clutches of Foreign Brigands

As discussed in Chapter 4, India began globalisation because it was entrapped in an external accounts and foreign exchange crisis. Two decades later, because of the very consequences of opening up the economy to unrestricted inflows of foreign capital and goods, India's external accounts are in a far worse state as compared to 1991.[10] Some statistics:

- Our trade deficit has gone up to $191 billion as on March 31, 2013, a rise of 60 times over our trade deficit of $2.8 billion in 1991–92.[11]
- Consequently, our current account deficit (CAD) zoomed to $87.8 billion in 2012–13, from $2.8 billion in 1991–92. India's CAD to GDP ratio was 4.8% in 2012–13, the highest ever, even more than its value in 1991–92 when it was 3%.[12] (It is true that since then, the trade deficit and CAD has declined, but that was primarily because of restrictions imposed by the government on gold imports. With the government bowing to pressure from the gold import lobby and removing gold import controls in November 2014, both the trade deficit and the CAD should rise further in the coming months.[13])
- And our external debt has gone through the roof! It stood at an astronomical $400 billion as on March 31, 2013, up by nearly five times from $83.8 billion in end-March 1991. By end-March 2014, it had further gone up to $440 billion.[14]

This spiralling whirlpool of trade deficit/current account deficit/ foreign debt has made the country more and more dependent on foreign capital inflows (both FDI and foreign speculative capital) to prevent the economy from once again plunging into foreign exchange bankruptcy. And so the foreign corporate armies and their concubine governments and international financial institutions are able to impudently trample upon our honour and dignity, yankee-kick us into implementing more and more economic reforms, devastating the lives and livelihoods of yet more people ...

A funeral hymn for Swaraj in just 60 years is too treacherous, yet true. What a fall, O fellow citizens! Possibly it was concern for just such a situation that prompted Dr. Ambedkar to speak thus to the Constituent Assembly in his final address:

On January 26, 1950, India will be an independent country. What

> *would happen to her independence? Will she maintain it or will she lose it again?*
>
> *The point is that she once lost the independence she had. Will she lose it a second time? It is this thought which makes me most anxious for the future. What perturbs me greatly is the fact that not only has India once before lost her independence, but she lost it by the infidelity and treachery of some of her own people.*

Unfortunately, the apprehension of the father of the Indian Constitution is proving to be prophetic!

Conspiracy of Silence

While we were writing this book, India was in the midst of elections to the 16th Lok Sabha. Unfortunately, none of the many critical issues facing the country and raised by us in this book became a subject of debate in the elections. None of the major political parties, neither the ruling coalition (UPA), nor the leading "pretender to the throne" (NDA), and neither the other major opposition parties, raised any of these issues—India's astronomical external debt and the growing dependence of the economy on foreign capital, terrible poverty levels, half the children suffering from malnutrition, 40% of the children unable to complete basic schooling and 85% of the children unable to cross Class XII, millions dying of preventable diseases, half the population forced to defecate in the open ...

The reason for this conspiracy of silence—all of them are representatives of India's corporatocracy and are in agreement with the globalisation policies that have pushed our economy into this crisis.

BJP: Accelerating Globalisation

Taken in by the massive propaganda campaign of the BJP promising better days ahead—a campaign that was liberally funded by the corporate–financial oligarchy that dominates the country's economy—the people voted the BJP-led NDA to power in the 2014 Lok Sabha elections.

The BJP is however a 'neoliberal twin' of the Congress, albeit with a 'saffron lipstick' (to quote Swaminathan Anklesaria Aiyar once again). The country's biggest business houses had backed Modi as Prime Minister in the hope that he would be even more 'decisive' than the Congress in implementing neoliberal policies. Modi is indeed living up to the trust bestowed on him by the 'Adanis and Ambanis'—the BJP Government is implementing globalisation at an even greater speed than the UPA Government.

The 'Swadeshi' government is pulling out all stops to woo foreign investors to invest in the country. Prime Minister Modi is leading from the front—in just his first six months in office, he has made more foreign trips than any other Prime Minister in the history of independent India.[15] In early August (2014), just two months after assuming power, the Union Cabinet approved the opening up of the defence sector and railways to foreign direct investment. Jagdish Bhagwati, Professor of Economics at Columbia University, USA and a well-known Modi sycophant, publicly stated in New Delhi in January this year that Modi is not opposed to FDI in multi-brand retail and would open up this sector to FDI within a year.[16] The government is bending over backwards to meet US objections to India's nuclear liability law, so that giant US corporations can set up nuclear power plants in India without having to worry about paying indemnities in case of design defects causing a nuclear accident—this basically means they are being encouraged to supply risky equipment, which is nothing but an invitation to disaster![17] The BJP has also got the Insurance Laws Amendment Bill passed by Parliament to increase FDI inflows into the insurance sector, yet another step towards eventually handing over control of India's insurance sector to foreign insurance corporations. It has further loosened controls on inflows of foreign speculative capital. The more the foreign capital inflows, the more the profit outflows; which means that all these measures are only going to further worsen our external accounts situation, and push us closer to foreign exchange bankruptcy.

Domestically, the BJP is implementing the most retrograde pro-corporate and anti-poor economic policies with even more enthusiasm and eagerness than the previous UPA Government. It has been in power for less than a year, and within this short time, it has already doled out sops to corporate houses to the tune of lakhs of crores of rupees, and mercilessly chopped government expenditures on schemes meant for the most marginalised sections of Indian society, including the Dalits, adivasis, women and children, by as much as 20 to 40 to even 50%.

Unite and Fight ... for the Future of Our Children!

In the dark times,
Will there also be singing?
Yes, there will also be singing,
About the dark times.

– *Bertolt Brecht*

Yes, these are difficult times, but there is no reason to despair. Like flowers spring up in every nook and corner with the onset of spring, people are beginning to organise in small-small groups all over the country.

The Struggle for a Genuine Right to Education

Teacher and student organisations, parents and ordinary citizens have been organising and fighting all over the country against the neoliberal assault on the education system. A few glimpses of some recent struggles:[18]

- In Tamil Nadu, where students have been segregated into four boards, student and teacher organisations together with educationists and other people's organisations have fought long and hard demanding the integration of these boards into a single board. Their struggle achieved a major breakthrough when the state government finally passed a law for a common syllabus for all the boards, known as the Tamil Nadu Uniform System of School Education Act 2010.[19]
- Thousands of students from 18 states across the country organised under the banner of All India Students Association marched to Parliament on August 9, 2012, the anniversary of the Quit India movement, demanding equitable education and dignified employment as fundamental rights.
- In Chhattisgarh, nearly 2 lakh contract teachers, known as Shikshan Karmis, went on strike in December 2012

demanding regularisation of their jobs.

- In February 2013, nearly 2.25 lakh contract teachers in Madhya Pradesh began an agitation demanding 'equal pay for equal work'.
- More than 2.5 lakh teachers have been agitating in Bihar since 2012, demanding regularisation of jobs and pay parity with government teachers. On March 5, 2013, the police brutally assaulted a peaceful demonstration of the teachers in Patna; in protest, the entire state of Bihar shut down on March 7.
- In September 2013, school and college teachers across Meghalaya went on a three-day strike demanding regular payment of salaries to teachers.
- Delhi University students and teachers waged a sustained struggle against attempts by the university authorities to introduce a Four Year Undergraduate Programme as a part of neoliberal educational reforms, eventually forcing the government to intervene and push Delhi University to scrap the Programme.

All India Forum for Right to Education

In an exhilarating development, several student and teacher organisations, people's organisations and many eminent educationists from all over the country have come together under the banner of 'All India Forum for Right to Education' (AIFRTE) to wage a united fight against the neoliberal assault on education and for a genuine Right to Education Act to establish a fully public funded common school system based on the concept of neighbourhood schools managed in decentralised, democratic and participatory mode.

AIFRTE was established at a seminar on 'Right to Education and Common School System' organised at the Osmania University campus in Hyderabad on June 21–22, 2009. The government had recently introduced 'The Right of Children to Free and Compulsory Education Bill, 2009', in Parliament. The educationists from all over the country who had come together for the seminar decided to constitute the AIFRTE with the aim of building a nationwide campaign to resist the RTE Bill and mobilise people to fight for an alternative genuine Right to Education Bill.

The Parliament passed the RTE Bill on August 4, 2009. Three days later, the AIFRTE, together with some progressive students organisations of Delhi, organised a rally on Parliament Street and burnt copies of the Bill. This was followed by an all-India Parliament March on February 24, 2010 during the budget session of the Parliament. About 5,000 people representing 26 member-organisations of AIFRTE from 11 states and several other associated grassroots organisations joined the Protest March.

Since then, several student and teacher organisations from all over the country have joined the AIFRTE. The AIFRTE and its member organisations have taken innumerable initiatives to organise awareness campaigns regarding the inequities of the present education system and the neoliberal assault on the education system under World Bank and imperialist pressures, and mobilise people to fight for an alternative, publicly funded, equitable common school system, and an affordable higher education system accessible to all those wanting to pursue higher education. A few examples:

- The Andhra Pradesh Save Education Committee, a joint platform of several student and teacher organisations of Andhra Pradesh, has organised several struggles against the ongoing commercialisation of education. It has demanded that the government take steps to improve government schools by recruiting more teachers, abolishing para-teachers, filling up all teaching vacancies in schools and colleges, abolishing self-financing courses and instead providing adequate grants to all higher educational institutions, etc.
- The All Manipur Students Union has organised numerous workshops, seminars and campaigns to create awareness regarding the inequities of the present education system and building a movement for a common school system.
- In Karnataka, students and intellectuals organised under the banner of Karnataka Jan Shakti have organised street plays, poster exhibitions and seminars against commercialisation of education demanding a common and equitable school

Box 15.1: Global Student Movement

The Welfare State is being rolled back all across the developed and 'developing' world. And so education too is under attack. In all the developed countries—from the USA and Canada to Europe, and also in all the underdeveloped countries of Asia, Africa and Latin America (except in countries like Cuba and Venezuela where revolutionary governments are in power), cuts are being made in government spending on education, fees are being hiked, education is being privatised ...

The students and teachers are fighting back. It has led to some of the biggest student movements in the world since the Second World War. Here is a brief sampling of some of the recent protests:

- Students have been agitating in Australia for the past few months (in 2014) against cuts in government funding for education, which will lead to a huge rise in college fees. In Albania too, students have been agitating against neo-liberal reforms, which include cuts in government funding for public universities, and increased government subsidies for private universities. On June 25, 2014, students and teachers organised protest actions across Germany against the chronically underfunded public education system. The same month also saw widespread student protests across the Netherlands against a government plan to introduce a loan system for college students, replacing State funding for higher education. In Bangladesh, in January 2014, tens of thousands of students at Rajshahi University organised rallies to protest government moves to hike tuition fees.
- College students all across Italy went on a strike in November 2013 against proposed education spending cuts in the 2014 budget. The same month saw college protests in Sweden too, with students protesting against government moves to give more autonomy to Universities by allowing private foundations to manage them—a clear step towards their eventual privatisation.
- In Britain, in 2013, student protests have taken place in several universities across the country against the growing marketisation of education.
- University and high schools students in Chile organised a heroic struggle that continued for more than 3 years, demanding increased

State funding for education and free education at all levels of education. Lakhs of students joined the protests, with students repeatedly occupying high schools and universities. The struggle ended victoriously in 2013, after Michelle Bachelet won the 2013 presidential elections, one of her campaign promises being to establish a system of universal and free access to higher education within a time frame of six years.

- In April 2013, polytechnic and university teachers went on an indefinite strike in Nigeria demanding increased government funding for education.
- Over the last decade, the dismantling of the Welfare State and privatisation of public services, including education, has led to powerful student movements all across the Balkans, from Croatia and Slovenia and Bulgaria to Serbia, Kosovo and Albania. In several countries, including Slovenia, Serbia and, especially in Croatia, the student movement has extensively experimented with occupations and direct democracy.
- "Black Protests" were observed in several public and private colleges and universities across the Philippines between March 18 and 22, 2013, to commemorate the death of Kristel Tejada who committed suicide on March 13, because she couldn't pay for tuition fees in time. Tens of thousands of students joined the protests.
- In 2012, university students in the province of Quebec (Canada) organised the largest student strike in the country's history; their 6-month long struggle, including a 300,000–person demonstration, forced the government to withdraw the proposed tuition hikes.
- For nine days in September 2012, Chicago belonged to teachers, students, their parents and community supporters. They picketed at schools across the city, marched through neighborhood streets, and brought downtown Chicago to a standstill with mass rallies of thousands, day after day. They were protesting the attempt by the Mayor of the city to break teachers' unions and dismantle public education.

[Source: Ben Kohler, "Students Fight Back Against Education Cuts", August 15, 2014, https://www.greenleft.org.au; "Students Protest Over Austerity Cuts in Italy", November 15, 2013, http://www.bbc.com; Eric (Rico) Gutstein and Pauline Lipman, "The Rebirth of the Chicago Teachers Union and

Possibilities for a Counter-Hegemonic Education Movement", Monthly Review, June 2013, http://monthlyreview.org; "2012 Quebec Student Protests", http://en.wikipedia.org; "International Student Movement", http://ism-global.net; "Student Protest Has Been Quietly Sweeping the Nation. Now, it's Getting Louder", December 14, 2013, http://www.newstatesman.com; Igor Štiks and Sreæko Horvat, "The New Balkan Revolts: From Protests to Plenums, and Beyond", http://www.citsee.eu; "2011–13 Chilean Student Protests", http://en.wikipedia.org.]

system.

- In Maharashtra, several students, teachers and people's organisations have come together under the banner of Mumbai Shikshan Companikaran Virodhi Abhiyan to fight the decision of the BMC to hand over all its 1,200 schools to NGOs and corporates in the name of public–private partnership.
- Teacher and student organisations all over the country, from Karnataka to Jammu and Manipur to Rajasthan, have organised innumerable awareness campaigns, seminars and protests in their respective states against the higher education bills introduced in Parliament by the UPA Government.
- On June 30 and July 1, 2012, a historic "All India Conference for Abolishing Commercialisation of Education and Building a Common School System" was organised in Chennai at the initiative of the State Platform for Common School System (SPCSS), Tamil Nadu. More than 2000 delegates from all over the country attended the conference. The gathering included jurists, social scientists, scientists, educationists, doctors, engineers, lawyers, administrators, writers, artists, journalists, researchers and other intellectuals/professionals drawn from 20 states/UTs of India.
- As we give the finishing touches to this book, in a new and inspiring initiative, the AIFRTE has galvanised its 45-member organisations and 100 fraternal organisations to organise an All India Shiksha Sangharsh Yatra-2014 (AISSY-2014). The AISSY-2014 commenced on November 2, 2014 [in solidarity with Irom Sharmila's struggle against the AFSPA] from five

different points in North-East, South, West, East and North of India. Crossing through diverse cultural, historical, linguistic, political, social and geographical mass of our country, the Yatra will culminate on December 4, 2014 in Bhopal [in solidarity with the 30th year of the struggle of Bhopal Gas Disaster victims observed on December 3 against imperialist capital's profit-driven cruelty, ruthlessness and hegemony].

Joining Hands

In another exciting experiment, people's organisations, trade unions and NGOs from all over the State of Maharashtra have joined hands to form the Jaganyachya Hakkachya Andolan (Movement for Dignified Right to Life). These organisations were earlier fighting separately against privatisation or for improved delivery of this or that social service, like health/education/food/pensions, etc. At a convention in Pune held in August 2013, they decided to forge a joint front to demand that all essential social services—education, health care, food security, domestic water and sanitation, pension, employment security and transport—be recognised as people's basic rights by the government. They further raised the following important demands:

- The government (state + Centre) should substantially increase its spending on social services to at least 15% of the GDP;
- Privatisation of social services must be stopped, and public systems for delivery of social services must be strengthened;
- Quality of social services must be improved, and people must be involved in monitoring the delivery of social services;
- Targeting of social services must end, and they should be universalised.

People are Beginning to Stir All Over the Country ...

As the country's economy becomes more and more crisis-ridden, the country's foreign creditors—multinational corporations—international institutions—domestic business houses are demanding more and faster economic reforms. A necessary consequence of these reforms is more and more brutal assault on the lives and livelihoods of people all over the country.

People are obviously going to fight back, and they are doing so, in innumerable small–big struggles being waged all over the country. We have given several examples above of people's struggles demanding Right to Education–Health–Food–Water–Pensions. Apart from these struggles for better social services, people have also been organising across the country on various other aspects of globalisation. To give a few examples:

- farmers have staged militant protests against seed patents, genetically modified crop varieties, entry of Western agri-business corporations into the country's farming sector, and slashing of agricultural subsidies;
- insurance and bank employees have repeatedly gone on walk-outs and strikes against financial sector reforms;
- women have organised protests against the increasing commodification of women;
- unorganised workers are getting organised in various parts of the country—recent examples being the heroic struggle of half a lakh anganwadi workers across Andhra Pradesh and 2 lakh anganwadi workers in Maharashtra, and the struggle waged by 26 lakh mid-day meal workers across the country that they be recognised as workers, paid minimum wages and given social security benefits;
- despite severe repression:
    - the entire leadership (147 workers) has been jailed and has been repeatedly denied bail in a complete travesty of justice
    - 2,346 workers (regular and contract both) have been thrown out of their jobs while the legal cases go on endlessly

  the Maruti Suzuki workers in Manesar have refused to cow down and continue to fight heroically;
- government employees in Haryana recently went on a 72-hour strike demanding that the government stop privatisation and contractualisation, and regularise all contract workers;

- lakhs of fishermen have organised militant struggles against new policies affecting their livelihood;
- braving heavy police repression and even firings in which many people were martyred, tribals in Odisha are valiantly fighting giant corporations like the Tatas, Vedanta and POSCO who are seeking to take over their lands and destroy their livelihoods and the environment of the entire region;
- the Jharkhandis and Chhattisgarhis are similarly fighting fierce battles to prevent their regions from being ravaged by giant mining corporations;
- traders across the country have organised dharnas–rallies–strikes protesting the government nod to FDI in Retail;
- people in rural areas all over the country have been fighting tooth and nail to prevent governments from forcibly acquiring their lands to set up Special Economic Zones.

But a Lot More Needs to Be Done ...

All these struggles have however not prevented the ruling classes from going ahead with their sordid agenda. At the most, these struggles have slowed the pace of globalisation of the Indian economy.

Clearly, a lot more needs to be done. We need to involve more people in our struggles. We need to widen the scope of our struggles, broaden our demands. Most important, we need to unite our different struggles, and advance our struggles from opposing this or that aspect of globalisation to challenging the entire project of capitalist globalisation being implemented by the ruling classes of the country at the behest of the imperialists.

Apart from the large number of people who are fighting against one or the other aspect of globalisation, there are an even larger number of people who are passive spectators to what is happening. Quite a many of them support this or that aspect of globalisation—they have been taken in by the propaganda that foreign cars, expressways, shopping malls and luxury consumer goods are indicators of the development of our country. We will need to have a dialogue with them, explain to them that they should stop looking at the world through the eyes of the rich, and instead examine their own life realities as to whether globalisation is actually benefiting them or not.

Then, there are also quite a few people who, instead of fighting the real enemy, are fighting amongst themselves. The ruling class parties today have nothing to give to the ordinary people—no jobs, welfare benefits, programme for rejuvenation of agriculture, etc. On the contrary, they are gradually withdrawing all the welfare benefits given to the ordinary people in the past. So, the only slogans they have when they go to the people for votes are that they are the representatives and saviours of their religion, caste, region. They are deliberately dividing people, instilling fear in their minds that they are under threat from the 'other'. With the result that instead of coming together to fight the real and common enemy, people are torching each other's houses, shops, religious places, beating–raping–killing each other. Meanwhile, the giant corporations are laughing all the way to the bank. The biggest communal leaders have become the poster-boys of the big business houses.

The largest number of people are those who have given up all hope, who have stopped believing that people can come together and change the world, who have become cynics. We will need to inspire them, remind them that history—including the history of our country—has always advanced through people's struggles, that history has its ups and downs, and that while the atmosphere around us may not be very encouraging, the global people's movement against globalisation has taken tremendous strides. The most exhilarating developments are taking place in Latin America, where in several countries, people's movements have been elected to power and are challenging capitalist–imperialist globalisation and implementing alternate pro-people policies. If they can do it, so can we ...

Dear friends, fellow citizens, the ruling classes are telling us—there is no alternative to globalisation. For their interests of profit maximisation, "There Is No Alternative (TINA)" indeed! And so they have proclaimed, that capitalist globalisation is a historical endpoint.

It is time we stopped believing the propaganda of the intellectuals of the ruling classes, and buckle down to fighting for building a new society that will promote selflessness and co-operation, where production will be oriented not for the profit maximisation of a few, but for fulfilling the basic needs of all human beings—healthy food, best possible health care, invigorating education, decent shelter, security in old age, clean pollution-free environment.

This is not utopia. After all, it is we, the working men and women of India, who have created all the wealth of our country. We have all the necessary skills. Our country has enormous resources. Our collective strength, if we create the conditions to properly harness it, can build heaven on earth. Of course, it is going to be a long and arduous struggle, but it can be won.

Yes, it is possible to build a new world! Every end needs a beginning, only if there is a beginning will there be an end. The innumerable people's struggles building up all over the country are showing the way. Let us support their struggles, and build our own small initiatives.

NOTES

1. *In Defence of Nationalised LIC and GIC, Part I*, All India Insurance Employees Association pamphlet, 1994, pp. 45–46.
2. P. Sainath, "FDI in Retail—UPA 'Retired Hurt'", *The Hindu*, December 12, 2011, http://www.thehindu.com; P. Sainath, "In 16 years, Farm Suicides Cross a Quarter Million", *The Hindu*, May 27, 2012, http://www.thehindu.com.
3. "India's Top 10 Billionaires", April 13, 2010, http://www.rediff.com.
4. India's GDP for 2013–14 is estimated at Rs 113 lakh crore – see *Key Fiscal Indicators 2003–04 to 2014–15 BE (12/07/14)*, http://planningcommission.nic.in.
5. "Billionaires Wealth Compared to GDP", March 19, 2014, http://stats.areppim.co; "List of Countries by the Number of US Dollar Billionaires", http://en.wikipedia.org, accessed on May 2, 2014.
6. Saritha Rai, "Amid Economic Distress, India Gains the Most Uber-Wealthy Among BRICS", September 11, 2013, http://www.forbes.com.
7. *UNICEF India – The Children – Nutrition*, http://www.unicef.org.
8. R. Prasad, "India is Drowning in its Own Excreta", June 15, 2012, http://www.thehindu.com.
9. I*ntegrated Energy Policy, 2006*, p. 2, http://planningcommission.nic.in.
10. Discussing the conditions and their impact on our external accounts is beyond the scope of this book. For more on this, see: Neeraj Jain,

Globalisation or Recolonisation?, published by Lokayat, Pune, 2006, available on Lokayat website: lokayat.org.in.

11. *India's Foreign Trade: 2013–14*, August 11, 2014, http://rbi.org.in; *Balance of Payments*, http://indiabudget.nic.in/es98-99/chap62.pdf.
12. "The External Crisis", *Aspects of India's Economy*, No. 54, June 2013, http://www.rupe-india.org; "Current Account Deficit Widens to Record 4.8%", June 27, 2013, http://timesofindia.indiatimes.com; indiabudget.nic.in/es1992-93/5%20Balance%20of%20Payments.pdf.
13. "Current Account Gap Falls Further on Lower Gold Imports", *PTI*, May 26, 2014, http://articles.economictimes.indiatimes.com; "Gold Import Surge Widens India's CAD to 2.1% of GDP in Sep Quarter", December 9, 2014, http://www.business-standard.com; Avantika Chilkoti, "Could India Curb Gold Imports Again?", January 6, 2015, http://blogs.ft.com; "What the Fall in the Current Account Deficit Reveals", *Aspects of India's Economy*, No. 55, March 2014, http://www.rupe-india.org.
14. *India's External Debt: A Status Report*, Ministry of Finance, Government of India, June 2003, http://finmin.nic.in; *India's External Debt: A Status Report 2013–14 Released*, August 29, 2014, http://pib.nic.in; *Databook for Use of Deputy Chairman, Planning Commission*, March 10, 2014, Planning Commission, Government of India, p. 1, http://planningcommission.nic.in.
15. Archis Mohan, "PM's Foreign Visits May be a Record of Sorts", November 7, 2014, http://www.business-standard.com.
16. "PM to Back Multi-brand FDI: Bhagwati", *TNN*, January 14, 2015, http://timesofindia.indiatimes.com.
17. Suvrat Raju, M.V. Ramana, "Nuclear Deal No Cause for Celebration", January 31, 2015, http://www.thehindu.com; Suhasini Haidar, "N-deal Logjam Cleared: Modi, Obama Agree Not to Dilute Liability Law", January 26, 2015, http://www.thehindu.com. On the terrible effects of nuclear accidents, see: Neeraj Jain, *Nuclear Energy: Technology from Hell*, Aakar Books, New Delhi, 2012.
18. For more information on these struggles, see the website of AIFRTE, http://www.aifrte.in.
19. S. Dorairaj, "Uniform and Equitable", *Frontline*, August 27–September 9, 2011, http://www.frontline.in.

Appendix

WHAT AMERICANS KEEP IGNORING ABOUT FINLAND'S SCHOOL SUCCESS*

– Anu Partanen, December 29, 2011,
http://www.theatlantic.com

The small Nordic country of Finland used to be known—if it was known for anything at all—as the home of Nokia, the mobile phone giant. But lately Finland has been attracting attention on global surveys of quality of life—*Newsweek* ranked it number one last year. Finland's national education system has been receiving particular praise, because in recent years Finnish students have been turning in some of the highest test scores in the world.

Finland's schools owe their newfound fame primarily to one study: the PISA survey, conducted every three years by the Organisation for Economic Cooperation and Development (OECD). The survey compares 15-year-olds in different countries in reading, maths and science. Finland has ranked at or near the top in all three competencies on every survey since 2000, neck and neck with super-achievers such as South Korea and Singapore. In the most recent survey in 2009 Finland slipped slightly, with students in Shanghai, China, taking the best scores, but the Finns are still near the very top.

Compared with the stereotype of the East Asian model—long hours of exhaustive cramming and rote memorisation—Finland's success is especially intriguing because Finnish schools assign less homework and engage children in more creative play. All this has led to a continuous stream of foreign delegations making the pilgrimage to Finland to visit schools and talk with the nation's education experts,

---

* *Edited. For the full article, see the original article available on the internet.*

and constant coverage in the worldwide media marveling at the Finnish miracle.

* * *

So when one of the leading Finnish authorities on education reform, Pasi Sahlberg, director of the Finnish Ministry of Education's Centre for International Mobility and author of the new book *Finnish Lessons: What Can the World Learn from Educational Change in Finland?* visited the USA recently, his visit received wide media coverage. Sahlberg spoke at a gathering of educators and students at the Dwight School in New York City.

However, one of the most significant things Sahlberg said while in New York passed practically unnoticed. "Oh," he mentioned at one point, "and there are no private schools in Finland."

This notion may seem difficult for an American to digest, but it's true. Only a small number of independent schools exist in Finland, and even they are all publicly financed. None is allowed to charge tuition fees. There are no private universities, either. This means that practically every person in Finland attends public school, whether for pre-K or a PhD ...

Sahlberg knows what Americans like to talk about when it comes to education ... Americans are consistently obsessed with certain questions: How can you keep track of students' performance if you don't test them constantly? How can you improve teaching if you have no accountability for bad teachers or merit pay for good teachers? How do you foster competition and engage the private sector? How do you provide school choice?

The answers Finland provides seem to run counter to just about everything America's school reformers are trying to do.

For starters, Finland has no standardised tests. The only exception is what's called the National Matriculation Exam, which everyone takes at the end of a voluntary upper-secondary school, roughly the equivalent of American high school.

Instead, the public school system's teachers are trained to assess children in classrooms using independent tests they create themselves. All children receive a report card at the end of each semester, but these reports are based on individualised grading by each teacher.

Periodically, the Ministry of Education tracks national progress by testing a few sample groups across a range of different schools.

As for accountability of teachers and administrators, Sahlberg shrugs. "There's no word for accountability in Finnish," he later told an audience at the Teachers College of Columbia University. "Accountability is something that is left when responsibility has been subtracted."

For Sahlberg what matters is that in Finland all teachers and administrators are given prestige, decent pay, and a lot of responsibility. A master's degree is required to enter the profession, and teacher training programs are among the most selective professional schools in the country. If a teacher is bad, it is the principal's responsibility to notice and deal with it.

And while Americans love to talk about competition, Sahlberg points out that nothing makes Finns more uncomfortable. In his book Sahlberg quotes a line from Finnish writer named Samuli Paronen: "Real winners do not compete." It is hard to think of a more un-American idea, but when it comes to education, Finland's success shows that the Finnish attitude might have merits. There are no lists of best schools or teachers in Finland. The main driver of education policy is not competition between teachers and between schools, but cooperation.

Finally, in Finland, school choice is noticeably not a priority. "Here in America," Sahlberg said at the Teachers College, "parents can choose to take their kids to private schools. It's the same idea of a marketplace that applies to, say, shops. Schools are a shop and parents can buy what ever they want. In Finland parents can also choose. But the options are all the same."

Herein lay the real shocker. As Sahlberg continued, his core message emerged, whether or not anyone in his American audience heard it.

Decades ago, when the Finnish school system was badly in need of reform, the goal of the program that Finland instituted, resulting in so much success today, was never excellence. It was equity.

* * *

Since the 1980s, the main driver of Finnish education policy has been the idea that every child should have exactly the same opportunity to learn, regardless of family background, income, or geographic location. Education has been seen first and foremost not as a way to produce star performers, but as an instrument to even out social inequality.

In the Finnish view, as Sahlberg describes it, this means that schools should be healthy, safe environments for children. This starts with the basics. Finland offers all pupils free school meals, easy access to health care, psychological counseling, and individualised student guidance.

In fact, since academic excellence wasn't a particular priority on the Finnish to-do list, when Finland's students scored so high on the first PISA survey in 2001, many Finns thought the results must be a mistake. But subsequent PISA tests confirmed that Finland—unlike, say, very similar countries such as Norway—was producing academic excellence through its particular policy focus on equity.

* * *

Finland is a relatively homogeneous country—as of 2010, just 4.6% of Finnish residents had been born in another country, compared with 12.7% in the United States. But the number of foreign-born residents in Finland doubled during the decade leading up to 2010. Immigrants tended to concentrate in certain areas, causing some schools to become much more mixed than others. Yet, the country didn't lose its edge in education, and there has not been much change in the remarkable lack of variation between Finnish schools in the PISA surveys across the same period.

Samuel Abrams, a visiting scholar at Columbia University's Teachers College, has addressed the effects of size and homogeneity on a nation's education performance by comparing Finland with another Nordic country: Norway. Like Finland, Norway is small and not especially diverse overall, but unlike Finland it has taken an approach to education that is more American than Finnish. The result? Mediocre performance in the PISA survey. Educational policy, Abrams suggests, is probably more important to the success of a country's school system than the nation's size or ethnic makeup.

Despite their many differences, Finland and the US have an educational goal in common. When Finnish policymakers decided to reform the country's education system in the 1970s, they did so because they realised that to be competitive, Finland couldn't rely on manufacturing or its scant natural resources and instead had to invest in a knowledge-based economy.

With America's manufacturing industries now in decline, the goal of educational policy in the US is to preserve American competitiveness by doing the same thing. Finland's experience suggests that to win at that game, a country has to prepare not just some of its population well, but all of its population well, for the new economy. To possess some of the best schools in the world might still not be good enough if there are children being left behind.

Is that an impossible goal? Sahlberg says that while his book isn't meant to be a how-to manual, it is meant to be a "pamphlet of hope."

"When President Kennedy was making his appeal for advancing American science and technology by putting a man on the moon by the end of the 1960s, many said it couldn't be done," Sahlberg said during his visit to New York. "But he had a dream. Just like Martin Luther King a few years later had a dream. Those dreams came true. Finland's dream was that we want to have a good public education for every child regardless of where they go to school or what kind of families they come from, and many even in Finland said it couldn't be done."

Clearly, many were wrong. It is possible to create equality. And perhaps even more important—as a challenge to the American way of thinking about education reform—Finland's experience shows that it is possible to achieve excellence by focusing not on competition, but on cooperation, and not on choice, but on equity.

About Us: Lokayat

The Directive Principles of the Constitution direct the Indian State to orient its policy towards:

- building an egalitarian society and a social order in which justice, social, economic and political, shall inform all the institutions of the national life [Article 38 (1)];
- minimising inequalities in income and ensuring that there is no concentration of wealth [Articles 38 (2) and 39 (c)];
- ensuring that all citizens have the right to an adequate means of livelihood [Article 39 (a)];
- ensuring that children are given opportunities and facilities to develop in a healthy manner and in conditions of freedom and dignity [Article 39 (f)];
- regard raising the standard of living of the people, improvement of public health and making effective provision of education for all children as among the primary duties of the State [Articles 41 and 47].

Unfortunately, the major political parties that dominate the Indian Parliament have decided to abandon this vision of the founding fathers of the nation, and secede from the people of the country. Ever since they decided in 1991 to globalise the Indian economy and open it up to foreign multinational corporations, they have been running the economy solely for the profit maximisation of giant foreign and Indian business houses:

- Giant corporations have launched a ferocious assault to dispossess the poor of their lands, forests, water and resources—in order to set up SEZs, huge infrastructural projects, golf courses, residential complexes for the rich, etc.
- Public sector corporations, including banks and insurance companies, are being privatised at throwaway prices.
- Indian agriculture is being deliberately strangulated—so that it can be taken over by giant agribusiness corporations. The consequence: more than 2.5 lakh farmers have committed suicide since the 'reforms' began.
- Tens of thousands of small businesses have downed their shutters.
- Welfare services are being privatised and transformed into instruments of naked profiteering:
    - government hospitals and municipal schools are being privatised; medicine prices have zoomed; college fees have gone through the roof; electricity prices are rising; bus fares are rising; the ration system designed to make available foodgrains and other essential items to the poor at affordable rates is being eliminated.
- There are simply no decent jobs for the youth; probably nearly half the population is unemployed or underemployed.
- The country is heading towards an ecological catastrophe: corporations are being allowed to cut down entire forests, destroy coastal lands in the name of aquaculture, over-exploit groundwater, pollute our seas–rivers–soil–groundwater–air, damage the health of not just the living but also of those yet to be born ...

These policies have produced the most obscene inequalities, that are becoming worse by the day:

- While on the one hand, the rich are becoming extremely rich—the wealth of India's 56 billionaires equals 10% of the country's GDP, and the wealth of India's richest 7800 people equals 50% of the country's GDP;

- On the other hand, the poor are becoming even more poor. According to the government's own statistics:
  - 75.5% of the rural and 73% of the urban population are not able to eat two full meals a day;
  - 50% children below the age of 5 are malnourished;
  - 42% children drop out of school without completing basic schooling;
  - Lakhs of children die every year due to entirely preventable diseases; ...

As the economic system becomes more and more sick, the social and political system is also becoming more and more degenerate. All-pervasive corruption; an educational system that makes us think we are incompetent fools; continuation of the age-old caste-based social system because of which atrocities on Dalits take place almost daily, and which is exploited by politicians to make the upper caste youth believe that the reservation system is responsible for lack of jobs; a communal political system that divides people in the name of religion and fills them with hatred against each other; a value system that promotes crass selfishness and unconcern and apathy for others; a society where cynicism and moral bankruptcy permeate every nook and cranny—this is the reality of today.

The common people have not been silent spectators to this betrayal of the Indian Constitution. Like flowers spring up in every nook and corner with the onset of spring, people are coming together all over the country, getting organised, forming groups and raising their voices in protest. Though these struggles are presently small, scattered and without resources, the future lies in these magnificent struggles. As more and more people join them, they will strengthen, join hands and become a powerful force which will transform society.

We must stop being sceptics, dream of a better future, believe that it is possible to change the world. *Yes, Another World is Possible!* But to make it a reality, we must start our own small struggles. These will ultimately unite, like the small rivulets hurtling down the Himalayas which ultimately form the mighty Ganges, to build a new society in accordance with the dreams of our freedom struggle that are embedded in the Directive Principles of the Indian Constitution. And so, we have started this forum, *Lokayat.*

We organise a wide range of activities/programs in Pune colleges, schools, city and slums, including:

- We organise seminars, talks, film screenings, song concerts, street campaigns, street plays, poster exhibitions, rallies–dharnas and even solidarity hunger fasts, on various issues of deep concern to common people, such as: rising inflation; privatisation of essential services; destruction of the environment and livelihoods of common people in the name of development; the dangers of GM foods; the horrifying consequences of nuclear power plants on human health and environment; the impact of Coca-Cola and Pepsi on our health and environment; the deepening crisis of global warming; Pune's transportation problems; etc.
- We have also staged numerous protests on the growing atrocities on Dalits, on the genocide of Muslims in Gujarat and Christians in Odisha, and against the targeting of minorities in the name of fighting terrorism.
- Lokayat's women's wing, named Abhivyakti, actively campaigns and organises programs on various aspects of gender inequality and the social roots of violence against women.
- Lokayat has a very active cultural wing which makes use of a wide variety of cultural forms—including songs, rock concerts, street plays, dramas, dance and traditional folk art—to reach out to people, raise their cultural consciousness, stimulate them to question the present decadent social–cultural order and its decadent values, and motivate them to come together to act for social change.

Recently, after the coming to power of the BJP-NDA Government at the Centre, and with the fascist forces launching an offensive that is threatening the very conception of India as a sovereign, socialist, secular, democratic republic, Lokayat has decided to align with the Socialist Party (India). We strongly feel that all progressive forces who share the values of the Indian Constitution need to join hands, and so this decision.

Dear friends, if you would like to know more about us, or participate in our activities, you may contact us at any of the addresses given below.

Contact Phones:

Neeraj Jain 94222 20311
Abhijit A.M. 94223 08125

Website and E-mail:

www.lokayat.org.in
lokayat.india@gmail.com

Contact Address:

Lokayat, Opp. Syndicate Bank, Law College Road,
Near Nal Stop, Pune 411 004.

INDEX